# THE EUROPEAN UNION AND INDUSTRIAL RELATIONS



MANCHESTER
1824
Manchester University Press

# EUROPE IN CHANGE

*SERIES EDITORS THOMAS CHRISTIANSEN AND EMIL KIRCHNER*

**The formation of Croatian national identity** ALEX J. BELLAMY

**The European Union and the accommodation of Basque difference in Spain** ANGELA K. BOURNE

**Theory and reform in the European Union, 2nd edition** DIMITRIS N. CHRYSSOCHOOU, MICHAEL J. TSINISIZELIS, STELIOS STAVRIDIS AND KOSTAS IFANTIS

**From integration to integrity: administrative ethics and reform in the European Commission** MICHELLE CINI

**The transatlantic divide** OSVALDO CROCI AND AMY VERDUN

**Germany, pacifism and peace enforcement** ANJA DALGAARD-NIELSEN

**The changing European Commission** DIONYSSIS DIMITRAKOPOULOS (ED.)

**Supranational citizenship** LYNN DOBSON

**Reshaping Economic and Monetary Union** SHAWN DONNELLY

**The time of European governance** MAGNUS EKENGREN

**Adapting to European integration? Kaliningrad, Russia and the European Union** STEFAN GÄNZLE, GUIDO MÜNTEL AND EVGENY VINOKUROV (EDS)

**An introduction to post-Communist Bulgaria** EMIL GIATZIDIS

**Non-state actors in international relations: the case of Germany** ANNE-MARIE LE GLOANNEC

**Globalisation, integration and the future of European welfare states** THEODORA ISMENE-GIZELIS

**Habermas and European Integration: social and cultural modernity beyond the nation-state** SHIVDEEP GREWAL

**Mothering the Union** ROBERTA GUERRINA

**European internal security: towards supranational governance in the area of freedom, security and justice** CHRISTIAN KAUNERT

**A political sociology of the European Union: reassessing constructivism** MICHEL MANGENOT AND JAY ROWELL (EDS)

**Turkey: facing a new millennium** AMIKAM NACHMANI

**Europolis: constitutional patriotism beyond the nation state** PATRIZIA NANZ

**The changing faces of federalism** SERGIO ORTINO, MITJA ŽAGAR AND VOJTECH MASTNY (EDS)

**The road to the European Union**
- **Volume 1 The Czech and Slovak Republics** JACQUES RUPNIK AND JAN ZIELONKA (EDS)
- **Volume 2 Estonia, Latvia and Lithuania** VELLO PETTAI AND JAN ZIELONKA (EDS)

**A political sociology of the European Union: reassessing constructivism** MICHEL MANGENOT AND JAY ROWELL (EDS)

**The activation of citizenship in Europe** THOMAS PFISTER

**Democratising capitalism? The political economy of post-Communist transformations in Romania, 1989–2001** LILIANA POP

**Europe and civil society: movement coalitions and European governance** CARLO RUZZA

**Constructing the path to eastern enlargement** ULRICH SEDELMEIER

**Governing Europe's new neighbourhood: Partners or periphery?** MICHAEL SMITH, KATJA WEBER AND MICHAEL BAUN (EDS)

**Two tiers or two speeds? The European security order and the enlargement of the European Union and NATO** JAMES SPERLING (ED.)

**Recasting the European order** JAMES SPERLING AND EMIL KIRCHNER

**The Europeanisation of conflicts: Integration and conflict resolution from the 1950s to the twenty-first century** BOYKA STEFANOVA

**Political symbolism and European integration** TOBIAS THEILER

**Rethinking European Union foreign policy** BEN TONRA AND THOMAS CHRISTIANSEN (EDS)

**The Europeanisation of the western Balkans: EU justice and home affairs in Croatia and Macedonia ...** FLORIAN TRAUNER

**The European Union in the wake of Eastern enlargement** AMY VERDUN AND OSVALDO CROCI (EDS)

**Democratic citizenship and the European Union** ALBERT WEALE

**Inclusion, exclusion and the governance of European security** MARK WEBBER

EDITED BY STIJN SMISMANS

# THE EUROPEAN UNION AND INDUSTRIAL RELATIONS

New procedures, new context



MANCHESTER UNIVERSITY PRESS
Manchester and New York

*distributed in the United States exclusively by Palgrave Macmillan*

*Published by* Manchester University Press
Oxford Road, Manchester M13 9NR, UK
*and* Room 400, 175 Fifth Avenue, New York, NY 10010, USA
www.manchesteruniversitypress.co.uk

*Distributed in the United States exclusively by*
Palgrave Macmillan, 175 Fifth Avenue, New York,
NY 10010, USA

*Distributed in Canada exclusively by*
UBC Press, University of British Columbia, 2029 West Mall,
Vancouver, BC, Canada V6T 1Z2

*British Library Cataloguing-in-Publication Data*
A catalogue record for this book is available from the British Library

*Library of Congress Cataloging-in-Publication Data applied for*

ISBN 978 0 7190 8672 4 *hardback*

First published 2012



Edited and typeset
by Frances Hackeson Freelance Publishing Services, Brinscall, Lancs
Printed in Great Britain
by TJ International Ltd, Padstow

# Contents

# *List of tables*

# *List of figures*

## *List of contributors*

**Roland Erne** has been Lecturer in international and comparative employment relations at University College Dublin since 2003. He is also Adjunct Professor at the Department of International and Comparative Labor, ILR School, Cornell University and was Marie Curie Fellow at the Centre for the Study of Social Justice, University of Oxford. He is a graduate of the FU Berlin and Sciences Po (Paris) and obtained his Ph.D. in political sciences at the European University Institute in Florence. His work centres on EU governance and its social and political implications. He is interested in how interest associations and social movements – particularly unions – respond to processes of regional integration and globalisation. In his most important book *European Unions: Labor's Quest for a Transnational Democracy* (2008) Erne describes the emergence of a European trade union movement that crosses national boundaries and challenges the assertion that no realistic prospect exists for remedying the EU's democratic deficit.

**Janine Goetschy** is both a political scientist and sociologist. She is Senior Research Fellow at CNRS (France) and is also part-time Professor at the Institute for European Studies at the University of Brussels. She is a member of several EU-level networks (Capright, Garnet, doctoral Erasmus Mundus). She has been working on comparative industrial relations and EU-level social, economic and institutional issues, and is the author of around 100 publications. She sits on various editorial boards of EU journals.

**Michael Kaeding** is Senior Lecturer at the European Institute of Public Administration (EIPA). He was a Ph.D. fellow at the Department of Public Administration and a post-doc fellow at the Department of Tax Law and Economics of Leiden University. His work experience includes the Delegation of the European Commission to the US, and the Secretariat General of the Council of the European Union. His publications include articles for *European Union Politics*, *Journal of Public Policy*, *Journal of European Public Policy*, *Journal of Common Market Studies*, *Comparative European Politics*, *French Politics*, *Journal of European Integration*, *European Law Journal*, *Journal of Legislative Studies* and *International Political Science Review*. His fields of specialisation include EU decision making, comitology, European social dialogue, Europeanisation and the transposition of EC law.

**Nicole Kerschen** is a Senior Researcher at the French National Centre for Scientific Research (CNRS). She teaches social policy at the University of Paris West Nanterre La Défense. Her research field includes the European Employment Strategy, the Open Method of Coordination, and Social Dialogue. Recent publications include: 'The Welfare System of Luxembourg: from past dependency to European approach' in K. Schubert, S. Hegelich and U. Bazant (eds), *The Handbook of the European Welfare Systems* (2009); (with Roussel-Verret), 'Stratégie européenne pour l'emploi et dialogue social. Vers la construction d'un modèle européen de relations professionnelles', *Le lien social et Politiques* 56 (2006); 'The Social Partners in European Employment Strategy. Specific

Guidelines and National Action Plans for Employment', in O. De Schutter and S. Deakin (eds), *Social Rights and Market Forces: Is the Open Coordination of Employment and Social Policies the Future of Social Europe?* (2005).

**Maarten Keune** is Professor at the University of Amsterdam and holds the Chair in Social Security and Labour Relations. He is associated to the Amsterdam Institute for Advanced Labour Studies and the Hugo Sinzheimer Instituut. He holds a Ph.D. in Political and Social Sciences from the European University Institute in Florence. He has widely published on industrial relations, labour market and welfare state developments and European integration.

**Norbert Kluge** holds a Ph.D. in sociology from the University of Kassel and is Coordinator and Adviser to the European Works Council of ThyssenKrupp, Essen, and member of the GOODCORP expert network of ETUI. He has previously been Project Manager of Hans Böckler Foundation, Düsseldorf, in the field of industrial relations and co-determination (1988–2002), and Senior Researcher and Expert Adviser on European co-determination and corporate governance at the European Trade Union Institute (ETUI) until September 2010.

**Evelyne Léonard** is Professor at the Université catholique de Louvain, Belgium. She teaches human resource management and industrial relations. She has widely published on industrial relations in the European Union and has held several research projects for the European Foundation for the Improvement of Living and Working Conditions. Her recent research activities include studies on the European sectoral social dialogue and on relationships between transnational company agreements and the European social dialogue. She has also co-edited a recent book on industrial relations in Belgium.

**Tobias Müllensiefen** is an official working for the European Commission. He studied German and French law in Cologne and Paris (Panthéon-Sorbonne), graduating with a bilingual law degree (LL.M.). He also holds a Master's degree in European Political and Administrative Sciences from the College of Europe in Bruges (Belgium). Having worked in a private consulting firm for two years, he joined the European Commission, DG Employment, Social Affairs and Equal Opportunities, in 2004. After four years in the social dialogue unit, he is now based in the unit dealing with legal questions in relation to equal opportunities and anti-discrimination. This article is written in his personal capacity and does not necessarily reflect the views of the European Commission.

**Lukas Obholzer** is a Ph.D. student at the London School of Economics.

**Nick Parsons** is Reader at the School of European Studies, Cardiff University. He has published extensively on British, French and EU social and employment policy and industrial relations. His recent books include *French Industrial Relations in the New World Economy* (2005) and (co-edited with Yuan Zhigang) *Economic Globalization and Employment Policy* (2005).

**Nieves Pérez-Solórzano Borragán** is Senior Lecturer in European Politics in the Department of Politics at the University of Bristol. She has written on civil society and the politics of participation in the European Union and the Europeanisation of interest politics in Central and Eastern Europe. Her latest research project analyses the link between lobbying regulation, transparency and ethics. Her work has been published in the *Journal of Common Market Studies, Perspectives on European Politics and Society* and the *Journal of Civil Society*. She is co-editor of *European Union Politics* (2009) and co-author of *Constitutional Politics in the European Union* (2007). Nieves holds a Ph.D. from the University of Exeter and an MA from the College of Europe. She has previously worked at the University of East Anglia and at the University of Exeter, and provided expert advice to the King Baudouin Foundation (Belgium) and to the Electoral Commission. She has also served as Honorary Secretary of the University Association for Contemporary European Studies (2005–08).

**Emmanuelle Perin** is Research Assistant and a Ph.D. student at the Institute for Labour Studies (IST) and in the Department of Political Science of the Université catholique de Louvain. She also acts as Belgian correspondent for the European Foundation for the Improvement of Living and Working Conditions *(Eurofound)* and has contributed to reports for both Eurofound and Cedefop.

**Philippe Pochet** is General Director of the European Trade Union Institute (ETUI) and Visiting Lecturer at the Université catholique de Louvain (UCL). Prior to becoming Director of ETUI in 2008, he was Director of the Observatoire social européen (OSE) for sixteen years. During this time, other temporary positions included Adjunct Professor and Visiting Scholar at the Griffith University (Brisbane), Associate Researcher at the Interuniversity Research Centre on Globalization and Work (CRIMT), Montréal University, Visiting Scholar at the Max-Planck-Institut für Gesellschaftsforschung (Cologne), EU Fulbright-in-Residence Scholar at the University of Wisconsin-Madison (USA) and Visiting Scholar at Center for European Studies, Harvard University, Cambridge (USA).

**Valeria Pulignano** is Professor in Labour Sociology and Industrial Relations at the Center voor Sociologisch Onderzoek (CESO) at the Katholieke Universiteit Leuven (Belgium). She is Associate Fellow at the IRRU at Warwick University and core researcher at the Interuniversity Research Centre on Globalization and Work (CRIMT) (Canada). She has widely published in comparative industrial relations nationally and internationally. Her research interests include employment relations and restructuring in multinational companies, systems of employee representations at both the European and national level, trade unions and the labour market. In 2008, she co-edited a book entitled *Flexibility at Work: Critical Developments in the International Automobile Industry.*

**Stijn Smismans** is Professor and Jean Monnet Chair in EU Law and Governance at the Law School of Cardiff University. He obtained his Ph.D. at the European University Institute (EUI), and has held fellowships at the EUI and the Institut d'Etudes Politiques in Paris. Before joining Cardiff University, he was a Lecturer at the Faculty of Sociology of the University of Trento, teaching industrial relations and EU law. He has undertaken projects for the European Commission, the European Foundation for the Improvement of Living and Working Conditions, and the European Economic and Social Committee. He has widely published on European institutional questions and European social policy including *Law, Legitimacy and European Governance: Functional participation in Social Regulation* (2004), and edited *Civil Society and Legitimate European Governance* (2006), and articles in *West European Politics, Journal of Public Policy, Journal of European Public Policy, Journal of Common Market Studies, European Law Journal, European Law Review, Columbia Journal of European Law, European Public Law*, and *International Journal for Comparative Labour Law and Industrial Relations.*

**André Sobczak** is a Professor at Audencia Nantes School of Management, and Founding Director of Audencia's Center for Global Responsibility. He received his doctorate in

Comparative and Community Social Law from the European University Institute of Florence and a DEA in Social Law from the University of Nantes. His research interests include global responsibility, corporate organisational transformations, regulation/governance and French, German, Italian and EC employment law.

**Peter Turnbull** is Professor of Human Resource Management and Labour Relations at Cardiff University, and Head of the Business School's Human Resource Management Section. He has published widely on labour relations in the port transport industry around the world. His current research focuses on transport policy and industrial relations in the European Union. He has recently undertaken two projects for the European Transport Workers' Federation, on professional training standards for dockworkers and the employment of women in European ports, and he recently led a technical cooperation project between the European Commission and the International Labour Organisation to strengthen social dialogue in the ports and road transport industries of Bulgaria, Croatia and Romania.

# *Preface*

This book finds its origin in a workshop on 'The European Union and Industrial Relations' organised at the Centre for European Law and Governance of Cardiff University, which was made possible by the financial support provided by the European Commission through its Jean Monnet Programme. I would like to thank all the participants at the workshop and the contributors to this book in particular. Special thanks are due to Deborah Hann for excellent language assistance. Finally I would like to thank Manchester University Press for publishing this volume.

As the work on the book progressed, the European Union and industrial relations have gone through turbulent times. We have paid particular attention to ensuring that the book kept up with the latest developments, in particular in relation to changing European economic governance, until delivery of the final manuscript of this book in January 2012.

Stijn Smismans
Cardiff

# *List of abbreviations*

| | |
|---|---|
| ACAS | Advisory, Conciliation and Arbitration Service |
| BNP | British National Party |
| CEEP | European Centre of Employers and Enterprises providing Public services |
| CEMR | Council of European Municipalities and Regions |
| CESI | Confédération européenne des syndicats indépendants/European Confederation of Independent Trade Unions |
| CFDT | Confédération française démocratique du travail (French Democratic Confederation of Labour) |
| CGT | Confédération générale du travail (General Confederation of Labour) |
| CTP | Common Transport Policy |
| DG | Directorate General |
| DG ADMIN | European Commission Directorate-General Personnel and Administration (now Human Resources and Security) |
| DG EMPL | European Commission Directorate-General Employment, Social Affairs and Equal Opportunities (now Employment, Social Affairs and Inclusion) |
| DG TREN | Directorate-General for Energy and Transport |
| EC Treaty | Treaty establishing the European Community |
| ECIA | Engineering Construction Industry Association |
| ECJ | European Court of Justice |
| ECSA | European Community Shipowners' Association |
| EMCEF | European Mine, Chemical and Energy Workers' Federation |
| EMF | European Metalworkers' Federation |
| EPSU | European Public Sector Union |
| ESC | European Shippers' Council |
| ESPO | European Sea Ports Organisation |
| ETF | European Transport Workers' Federation |
| ETUC | European Trade Union Confederation |
| EUPAE | European Union Public Administration Employers |
| EUPAN | European Union Public Administration Network |
| EWC | European Works Council |
| FEPORT | Federation of European Private Port Operators |
| MEP | Member of the European Parliament |
| MNC | Multinational Company |
| NACE | Statistical Classification of Economic Activities in the European Community (Nomenclature statistique des activités économiques dans la Communauté européenne) |
| NPM | New Public Management |
| OMC | Open Method of Coordination |

| | |
|---|---|
| PP1 | Ports Package 1 |
| PP2 | Ports Package 2 |
| PWD | Posting of Workers Directive |
| TAW Directive | Temporary Agency Work Directive |
| TEC | Treaty Establishing the European Communities |
| TFEU | Treaty on the Functioning of the European Union |
| TRUST | Trade Union vision on Sustainable Transport |
| TUNED | Trade Union National and European Delegation |
| UKIP | United Kingdom Independence Party |
| UNI | Union Network International |

*Stijn Smismans*

# 1

# The European Union: institution-builder, arena and policy context for industrial relations

## Industrial relations and European studies

There is currently a clear gap between the field of Industrial Relations (IR) and the field of European Studies. On the one hand, the discipline of European studies has developed into an interdisciplinary research field taking the European Union (EU) and European integration as central focus of analysis. It is inspired particularly by political science, but also by law, history and economics, and more recently sociology (Favell and Guiraudon 2009, Saurugger 2009). While interacting with 'the mainstream' of these disciplines, EU studies has been at the origins of new theories, in particular those explaining the nature of the European integration process (such as neo-functionalism and intergovernmentalism) and conceptual and analytical frameworks to study the complex European polity, such as 'multi-level governance', or 'Europeanisation'. However, IR as a discipline has largely remained off the radar of EU studies. Even the social reality of IR and the role of management and labour in governance arrangements in the European polity have been given relatively little attention by EU studies. Most EU scholars consider the place of management and labour in the European integration process through the lenses of Haas's neofunctionalist theory: the sector-by-sector approach to European integration and the 'Monnet method' (Featherstone 1994) was based on the involvement of the economic elites, including organised labour, from the particular sector within which integration should be realised (Milward 1992). The way to European integration was to engage key economic elites in building transnational coalitions in support of European policies (Wallace 1993). The empirical testing of this theory contributed to an extensive literature on how business, but also labour, lobby the EU institutions (Kirchner 1977, Mazey and Richardson 1993, Greenwood 2003, Coen and Richardson 2009). However, the place of IR and collective bargaining as an autonomous system and its interaction with the governance of the European polity remains out of the scope of most EU scholars' work.

On the other hand, the field of IR has developed as a separate discipline from political science and sociology, with its own publications and disciplinary associations. A similar gap exists in the relation of IR towards the field of European studies. For a long time, the EU received hardly any attention in the field of IR, which tended to focus on (comparative) national studies. Still today, insights and conceptual frameworks of EU studies have only found their way to IR in a modest way.

Certainly, during the first few decades of the European integration process, it was difficult to imagine how the European Economic Community (EEC) could have any impact on IR, other than being a potential focus for lobbying by management and labour in relation to the functionally defined (socio-) economic competences the EEC had been given. The EEC had been given hardly any social competences, and the core issues concerning employment, labour and wages that constitute the object of IR remained clearly at the level of national competence. Despite neo-functionalist predictions, nobody could really foresee the spill-over effects the creation of a common market would have. Although the EEC created tripartite advisory committees (composed of representatives from national social partners and administrations) and encouraged the establishment of bipartite joint committees in some policy sectors as early as the 1960s, these committees functioned at best as a forum to express opinions on European policy initiatives, and never as a structure for collective bargaining. It was only with the encouragement by Jacques Delors for the European cross-sectoral Val Duchesse dialogue in the mid-1980s, and in particular with the institutionalisation of the European social dialogue procedure by the Maastricht Treaty, that the role of management and labour in European governance and the relation between the EU and IR started to attract serious scholarly attention. Labour lawyers and EU scholars were particularly intrigued by this new institutional mechanism, while IR scholars also dealt with the internal dynamics of the European social partners organisations. The adoption of the European Works Council Directive in 1994 constituted another source of research and discussion for IR scholars as it provided a European dimension to IR at company level. Thus, to begin with, the literature on the EU and IR predominantly had an institutional perspective, focusing on the development of a European level infrastructure of IR. Gradually more attention also emerged as to how the broader policy setting of the EU affects existing IR systems at the national level. Particular attention has been paid to the consequences of monetary union (EMU) on IR. The concept of a European social model, which triggered a more interdisciplinary approach to IR, political economy, employment and social policy analysis (see Chapter 11), framed the debate to address the question of whether European integration would lead to the convergence of IR systems or not.

However, our picture of the relationship between the EU and IR remains patchy. The EU's institutional framework for IR has developed over the last two decades and the way in which different levels of social dialogue interact and how the European institutional framework affects institutional settings at national level needs further clarification. Moreover, the way in which the EU as a larger policy framework affects IR remains understudied. Beyond the way in which EMU would affect IR, and in particular wage bargaining, much remains to be said on how the basic institutional set-up of the internal market in terms of free competition and free movement affects IR, and on how more recent policy developments such as the European employment strategy and the broad ideational framework of the (post-) Lisbon Strategy relate to IR.

The aim of this book, therefore, is to place the EU central focus and to provide an overview of the many ways in which it relates to developments in IR. The next section will set out a framework to identify the many ways in which the EU affects IR. While not all these elements can be dealt with in detail in a single book, the chapters of the book cover the most important recent developments both in relation to the EU's role as an institutional and as a policy framework affecting IR.

## The EU and industrial relations, a broad concept of 'Europeanisation'

The way in which the EU relates to IR can be described in terms of 'Europeanisation'. However, this requires a broad conceptualisation of the term. 'Europeanisation' entered the EU literature at the end of the 1990s and constituted a 'turn' in EU studies by paying increased attention to the impact of EU membership on member states (Hix and Goetz 2001). EU scholars have certainly long acknowledged the multi-level nature of the European polity but EU studies had extensively focused on the institutional dynamics in Brussels while much less attention had been paid to what happens at the national level. Regulatory fatigue and implementation gaps after the extension of EU competences in the 1990s strengthened the need for such analysis. Initially, the Europeanisation concept inspired EU scholars to pay particular attention to analysing to what extent and why EU Directives and European policies were implemented or not (Knill 1998, Boerzel 2001), but it gradually also provided a European analytical lens for scholars of domestic politics, analysing how, for instance, the EU affected national party systems (Mair 2000). The initial top-down focus, as exemplified in the 'goodness of fit' argument, was gradually complemented with a bottom-up dimension (Graziano and Vink 2012). Europeanisation is not only about downloading but also about uploading. European policies have first to be defined with the participation of national actors, and inspired by national solutions, before they can subsequently be implemented at the national level. Claudio Radaelli (2004: 3) thus provides a very broad definition of Europeanisation:

> Europeanisation consists of processes of a) construction, b) diffusion and c) institutionalisation of formal and informal rules, procedures, policy paradigms, styles, 'ways of doing things' and shared beliefs and norms which are first defined and consolidated in the EU policy process and then incorporated in the logic of domestic (national and subnational) discourse, political structures and public policies.

It is this broad definition of Europeanisation that we will apply to the field of IR. In fact, the concept is not entirely new in this field. On the one hand, the emergence of the concept in IR runs parallel to developments in EU studies. As in the latter, Europeanisation started to be used in the field of IR at the end of the 1990s and early 2000s to focus the attention on the effects of the EU on national IR systems after the initial attention had been on the development of a European level institutional framework for IR. Falkner, Treib, Hartlapp *et al.* (2005), for instance, study the Europeanisation of national IR patterns related to the negotiation and transposition of EU Social Policy Directives, while Leisink, Steijn and Veersma (2007) suggest analysing the effect of the EU on national IR by applying the three types of Europeanisation mechanisms distinguished by Knill and Lehmkuhl (2002); namely, Europeanisation by i) prescriptive norm-setting, ii) changing domestic opportunity structures, and iii) framing domestic beliefs. On the other hand, when IR refers to Europeanisation it tends to start, ironically enough, from the opposite perspective to EU studies. For EU studies, Europeanisation has been a way to shift the focus of attention from the EU institutional set-up to the EU's impact at the national level. However, for IR, the core business has always been the national level. 'Europeanisation' then rather becomes a concept to identify whether there is anything 'European' to IR at all, and, if so, to what extent. Keller and Platzer (2003: 2), for instance, refer not only to patterns of reaction and adaptation of national systems to the EU, but use the concept of Europeanisation, in particular, to refer to an EU-level dimension of IR, either by the establishment of an institutional setting for IR at EU level (at cross-sectoral, sectoral and company level), or by the development of transnational horizontal coordination initiatives between social partners. Moreover, when IR scholars have looked at the impact of the EU on national IR it has often been on the assumption that, or at least on the question whether, adjustment to the EU implies convergence between the national systems, in particular with reference to the notion of the European social model (Vos 2007). The concept of Europeanisation in IR thus tends to equal the concept of European integration, or at least implies a tendency to some common European solutions and processes. When Marginson and Sisson (2004: 8) analyse the impact of EMU on IR as a process of multi-level governance in which convergence and divergence co-exist, 'Europeanisation' is defined as 'a tendency or trend in which there is discernible movement with common policies leading to common outcomes achieved by common processes', as opposed to 're-nationalisation' and 'Americanisation', and to be placed in a context of wider globalisation.

In this volume we want to distinguish the concept of Europeanisation from that of European integration. With Europeanisation we do not imply any idea of convergence, nor a particular form of furthering European integration. The aim of this book is to provide an overview of the multiple ways the EU affects IR (see Table 1.1). All these dimensions together can be described as a process of 'Europeanisation', in the broad definition of Radaelli as given above. We want in particular to distinguish between two main ways in which the EU affects IR. On the one hand, the EU provides a new institutional framework for IR. On the other hand, it provides a policy framework, namely a set of substantive policies,

**Table 1.1 The EU and IR: forms of Europeanisation**

| | *Top down* | *Bottom up* | *Horizontal* |
|---|---|---|---|
| *EU as institutional framework* | EU as institution-builder: 1) EU-level institutional framework for IR: • cross-sectoral • sectoral • EWCs 2) Driver of institutional change at national level: • impact on IR framework of MS • national company level • enlargement conditionality | institutional arena: political opportunity structure to influence European policy making, and new arena for bipartite action | • coordination of national members in European social partner organisations in context of European social dialogue • horizontal learning, exchange of best practice between national social partners • institutional twinning between national social partners (with support of, or via European social partners) |
| *EU as policy framework* | • prescriptive social acquis • the EU's economic constitution (four freedoms, competition) (as interpreted by the ECJ) • EMU • the Lisbon Strategy and Agenda 2020 • policy paradigms, policy solutions, best practices | • influencing the policy framework via institutional structure and/or lobbying • organised protest • national pacts, and national wage bargaining in European context • European social partners' working programme placed in context of Lisbon Strategy | • cross-border wage coordination |

which have an effect on IR. These two effects are obviously interrelated, but do not entirely overlap.

In a similar, but not identical, manner to the Europeanisation literature, which refers to 'downloading' European policies to the national level and 'uploading' national solutions to European common policies, in this book we also want to distinguish between a top-down and a bottom-up perspective on the EU's effect on IR. On the one hand, the EU has played a top-down role as an institution-builder by providing a new institutional framework for IR at the European level, and imposing certain institutional requirements for IR at the national level. On the other hand, this European institutional framework for IR constitutes a new arena for bottom-up action by the social partners. Similarly, the EU's policy framework can be addressed top-down as conditioning IR, but can equally be addressed from a bottom-up perspective, as the social partners try to influence this framework or take autonomous action in the context of that policy framework. Finally, in addition to these top-down and bottom-up processes of Europeanisation, we can identify processes of horizontal Europeanisation (Vink and Graziano 2007: 10) based on cross-border exchange of information, mutual learning and coordinated action between social partners in different Member States.

## The EU as institutional framework (1): institutional change in the European social dialogue

The emergence of the European institutional framework for IR, at cross-sectoral, sectoral and European company level, is well documented and does not need repetition here.[1] Two developments characterise the last decade, namely strengthening of the autonomous action of the European social partners (Branch 2005, Smismans 2008), and increased activity at the sectoral level (Pochet 2005, Léonard 2008, European Commission 2010, Degryse and Pochet 2011, Keller and Weber 2011).

In Chapter 2, Tobias Müllensiefen, who has been working until recently in the European Commission's Directorate General of Employment and Social Affairs, provides an insider's view on the development of the European cross-sectoral dialogue. The first few years of the new millennium saw a shift from social dialogue as a regulatory technique (via collective agreements implemented by Council Directive) towards a more autonomous social dialogue with the first multi-annual working programmes of the European social partners, and the first autonomous agreements and frameworks of action. Although there remains concern regarding the different implementation levels of autonomous instruments in the different Member States, and the extent to which autonomous dialogue can really develop out of the shadow of hierarchy of EU action (Smismans 2008), Müllensiefen points to a gradually increasing esteem for such autonomous instruments amongst key actors, illustrated in particular by the willingness of many Member States to become involved in the implementation of autonomous agreements by amending or introducing legislation or by *erga omnes* extension of collective agreements. Moreover, the European social partners have recently adopted their first cross-sectoral agreement that can be considered entirely autonomous, namely on inclusive labour markets: it is both introduced at their initiative (and not following Commission consultation) and implemented by their own means. At the same time, Müllensiefen notes that in the second half of the 2000s the social partners again became increasingly involved in European legislation, which he argues is due, in particular, to the stronger role of the European Parliament and its capacity to pressure the second Barroso Commission to come up with new legislative proposals in the social field. However, while parliamentary pressure led to a stronger politicisation of symbolic topics such as working time, posting of workers, and European works councils, the final legislative outcome has been more modest; with the adoption of a revised European Works Council (EWC) Directive, a revised parental leave agreement implemented by Directive, and a temporary agency Directive. The revision of the posted workers Directive, on the other hand, failed to progress due to highly contrasting opinions amongst social partners and political actors, whereas the Commission has even withdrawn its amended working time Directive which Council and European Parliament failed to agree on. Hence, while the cross-sectoral dialogue may be better off than the bleak picture at the start of the decade characterised by legislative inaction and doubts on the viability of autonomous dialogue, the current output remains modest.

In Chapters 3 and 4, we focus our attention on the European sectoral social dialogue. There is no need to provide an overview of all sectoral activities here, which can be found elsewhere (Pochet 2005, Degryse and Pochet 2011, European Commission 2010). We focus on two aspects, namely the driving role of the European Commission in sectoral social dialogue, and the extent to which such dialogue leads to horizontal Europeanisation as a coordination tool across Europe. In Chapter 3, Michael Kaeding and Lukas Obholzer study the influence of the European Commission on sectoral social dialogue by way of a case study on the central public administration sector, a sector that merits particular attention in times of economic crisis as it is both a central pillar for social cohesion and particularly at risk under austerity plans. While the social partners are the central actors of the dialogue, so that much will depend on their willingness and organisational strength, the contribution of the European Commission to successful sectoral dialogue cannot be underestimated. The Commission supported sectoral dialogue as early as the 1960s, and provided a formal structure for sectoral social dialogue committees in 1998, which triggered further activity in many sectors (although substantive outcomes are often modest in nature, with less than 2 per cent of the texts adopted being agreements with binding effect). In the sector of public administration the formalisation of the European sectoral social dialogue was only set on track very recently, with an initial two-year test phase in 2007. Analysing this process, Kaeding and Obholzer explain why sectoral social dialogue committees are formalised. They identify different aspects of the Commission's role in sectoral social dialogue, namely as agenda-setter and initiator (for instance via consultation on the future of social dialogue), as mobiliser (for instance via providing translation services and financial support for sectoral dialogue activities), and as mediator (based on its experience in other sectors). Their analysis also shows that the Commission's role does not end with the setting up of a sectoral committee, but that it can still play a role in supporting the social partners once the institutional framework has been set on track.

In Chapter 4, Philippe Pochet, Emmanuelle Perin and Evélyne Léonard analyse the extent to which the European sectoral social dialogue acts as a networking platform and whether it plays a role in the coordination among its national member organisations across the Member States. Such coordination has an upstream dimension when the European social partners try to integrate a diversity of interests among their own national members, and a downstream dimension when a given text has to be implemented in each national context. The authors address this question by means of four dimensions of (potential) coordination: the representation of heterogeneous members; the various degrees of national players' commitment in the European committees, which ranges from active involvement to simple absence; the definition of a common agenda among members; and finally the implementation of the European texts in the member states. Despite the immense challenge posed by the diversity of cultures, languages and organisational capacities of the national members, the European umbrella organisations have managed to successfully coordinate upstream allowing the discussion of joint texts. Downstream they have provided different types of follow-up procedures, but the implementation depends in the end on the initiative of the national organisations. Yet, the authors conclude that, while the texts are mainly soft in nature and implementation varies, the European sectoral dialogue provides opportunities to actors to learn from each other, contributing to the constitution of a new collective identity transcending national boundaries.

In Chapter 5, Evélyne Léonard and André Sobczak take the analysis of transnational IR to another level, namely that of transnational companies. More particularly, they place the traditional IR question regarding the interaction between different levels of social dialogue, usually addressed at the national level, within a transnational context. Part of that context is created by the institutional framework of the EU, with the European cross-sectoral, sectoral dialogue, and EWCs. However, transnational social dialogue also exists at a more global level. The status of transnational company agreements (TCAs) and their place in a multi-level IR system needs still much clarification. TCAs, for instance, are generally characterised by an asymmetry with a single employer on the one side, and a sector-level trade union on the other side. One can see TCAs as the transnational expression of a general trend towards decentralisation of IR towards the company level, at the expense of cross-sectoral and sectoral dialogue, and developing independent of them. However, analysing TCAs in relation to their territorial scope, actors involved and topics covered, Léonard and Sobczak show the partial overlap between such agreements and the European social dialogue, and the sectoral social dialogue in particular. Some TCAs, for instance, are signed by the EWCs, others by the European sectoral trade union federations, which obviously also play a key role in the European sectoral social dialogue. The subject matter of that dialogue and of TCAs also partially overlap, although sectoral dialogue is more framed by European policies while TCAs deal mainly with fundamental rights and International Labour Organisation standards. The authors conclude that TCAs and European social dialogue are not automatically in competition but can be complementary, due to involvement of many of the same players, although the relationship between European (sectoral) social dialogue and TCAs, and the status of the latter, need further clarification.

## The EU as institutional framework (2): the EU as driver of institutional change at national level

Although the EU has, according to Article 153 TFEU, the competence to regulate in the field of 'representation and collective defence of the interests of workers and employers, including co-determination', it has never been the objective of the EU to set out an entire framework for IR in a binding manner at the national level. European regulation regarding the right of association, the right to strike or the right to impose lock-outs is explicitly excluded by the Treaty (Article 153(5) TFEU). Regulatory action on 'representation and collective defence of interests' is only possible via a Directive and requires unanimity in the Council, and would in any case need to respect the principle of subsidiarity. Even when the Treaty requires the EU to promote the role of the social partners at the European level, this should be done while 'taking into account the diversity of national systems' (art 152 TFEU).

Nevertheless, in several ways, the EU has been a driver of institutional change of IR at the national level. First of all, it has directly regulated some aspects of IR at company level, particularly with binding measures regarding the information and consultation of workers, which can be adopted by a qualified majority. In addition to regulating worker involvement at transnational company level (EWCs, European Company Statute, and cross-border mergers), the EU played an important role in relation to worker participation and information at national company level (with directives on information and consultation; collective redundancies, and transfer of undertakings) (see Marginson, Hall, Hoffmann *et al.* 2004, Pulignano and Kluge 2007, Carley and Hall 2009, Ribarova 2011, Stollt and Kluge 2011). In Chapter 6, Valeria Pulignano and Norbert Kluge provide an overview of the EU's regulatory framework for employee involvement at company level and analyse the practices and experiences through which local actors inhabit that framework and contribute to the Europeanisation of employee involvement from the bottom up.

Secondly, the EU has not only intervened with binding provisions on company level involvement, but has developed wider activities to promote social dialogue more broadly at national level, since a vibrant social dialogue at the national level is considered a precondition for a functioning social dialogue at EU level. Such action has been particularly explicit in the context of enlargement. In Chapter 7, Nieves Pérez-Solórzano and Stijn Smismans analyse how the EU has aimed to steer and support institutional change in industrial relations in the context of enlargement. The weak IR infrastructure of the new Member States contrasted with IR traditions in most old Member States and could constitute a problem both for the functioning of the European social dialogue and for the implementation of European policies at national level. The EU, and in particular the Commission, therefore, tried to frame social dialogue as part of the acquis communautaire which the new Member States would have to adjust to. However, besides some provisions regarding mainly workers' involvement at company level, there is no real legally binding acquis that would impose a particular IR infrastructure, despite Commission discourse and persuasive attempts to sell this as part of a wider 'administrative' or 'institutional acquis'. There is also no single model of IR which the EU could promote as a template, and the establishment of the social reality of IR does not simply happen by legal decree. Hence the EU has engaged in encouraging and funding horizontal twinning and exchange of best practice initiatives between social partners in the old and new Member States, and via the European social partners.

Finally, besides prescriptive rules, and persuasive and supporting activities geared at strengthening and changing national IR structures, such change may also emerge through bottom-up developments. National social partners and social dialogue obviously adjust to functioning in the context of the European social dialogue (as analysed in Part I), but the latter may also be used by the national social partners as a model and leverage for change at the national level. Nicole Kerschen provides an example of that by analysing in chapter 8 the EU's impact on the institutional framework for IR in one of the old Member States, namely France. France is an interesting case, since it has been traditionally more etatist than other Member States, leaving hardly any scope for autonomous IR action. However, the institutional framework for IR in France has undergone several important changes over the last decade in the light of European integration. Although the EU does not impose a particular IR structure on its Member States (besides some of the legal acquis affecting the company level), and it has not geared its attention to institutional change at national level in the old Member States with the intensity it has done for candidate and new Member States, it may nevertheless serve as the basis for institutional change in a more indirect way. Kerschen's analysis shows how the French social partners strengthened their position in socio-economic policy making through the requirements of the European Employment Strategy (EES). Moreover, their strengthened role led to a broader national debate on how the relationship between legislation and social partners' action should be organised, leading to a final institutional solution that was clearly inspired by the European social dialogue mechanism.

## The EU as policy context for IR

The third part of this volume analyses how the EU provides a policy framework that affects IR.

The EU's policy framework is constituted of different sectoral policies, but above all also of the economic constitutional principles of market integration set out in the Treaties, centred on the four freedoms of movement (goods, persons, services, capital) and free competition. This policy framework can affect IR by way of prescriptive norms (the Treaties, Regulations, Directives, Decisions), but equally by soft norms, providing policy solutions, policy paradigms, best practice, and shared beliefs.

The most direct way in which the EU's policy framework relates to the social partners is via their involvement in both the drafting and the implementation of policies directly affecting them, in particular in the area of social policy via the European social dialogue. Thus one has analysed how the (European) social partners can influence the drafting of European social legislation (also where negotiation fails) (Falkner *et al.* 2005), and how such legislation is implemented within national IR settings[2] at either cross-sectoral, sectoral or company level.[3]

The literature has also paid attention to how the constitutionally enshrined framework of EMU set out at Maastricht has affected IR at the national level and in particular wage bargaining (Kauppinen 1998, Marginson and Sisson 2004, Johnston and Hancké 2009). However, much remains to be said on the effects on IR of many other aspects of the EU's policy framework.

In Chapter 9, Peter Turnbull turns our attention to the socio-economic constitutional basics of the European construction. The core of European integration has always been a market-building project, with free competition and the liberalisation of the market at the heart of the process. Such liberalisation may undermine acquired rights and positions of (some) workers, but equally create losers as well as winners amongst employers, in particular in relation to public service provision. From this perspective, the European social dialogue – which has attracted most scholarly attention – appears as a rather cosy (European level) process within the relatively small area of social policy provision, whereas the wider economic fundamentals of the EU may well create profound resistance and outright protest by IR actors, in particular at the national level. The European policy framework is not only one for (cosy) co-decision making, but can also be fiercely contested.

Scholars have long since pointed to the collective action problems of organising protest at a European level. First of all, national and local actors need to be aware of the impact of European integration and policy on their situation. Even if they are, the fact that IR structures are ingrained in the nation states and the lack or weak sense of cross-border solidarity make concerted European action difficult. However, as Turnbull's analysis shows, for labour, such a concerted action against European liberalisation initiatives is not impossible. Turnbull focuses on the EU's liberalisation attempts in the sector of port services. The initial approach of labour was one of contentious politics, creating rank-and-file awareness about the European impact on their interests, and combining local action with the first pan-European dock strikes, and mass demonstrations in several European cities. This contentious action was successful enough to win over the European Parliament to their cause. However, as the European Commission reloaded the gun with a second liberalisation Directive, labour opted to combine the 'argument of force' with the 'force of argument'. While the port sector had been characterised by an absence of structured dialogue, lacking, for instance, a sectoral social dialogue committee, the unions decided now to engage with the EU's 'deliberative institutions', such as setting up a sectoral dialogue committee, and participating in Commission consultations and policy workshops. They made successful use of the European opportunity structures by forming alliances with national port service providers against transnational capital and the Commission. While this meant on the one hand partially moderating their contentious action to keep their alliance alive, it was also thanks to their contentious action that the force of argument was taken more seriously. Turnbull concludes that the example of port services may serve as a lesson for trade unions which, in their engagement with the EU, have too often abdicated contentious politics (Hyman 2005: 35). By expanding the (industrial and political) range of issues and (geographically) extending the site of contention, trade unions can influence the European policy framework to ensure the defence of social policy at the national and local levels (see equally Erne 2008).

Contentious IR politics in relation to the European policy framework is in fact clearly on the rise. Not only has the European socio-economic governance structure become ever more encompassing, in times of economic crisis its potential negative effects are also felt much more strongly. In Chapter 10, Nick Parsons provides another recent example of contentious European IR, namely in relation to posted workers, i.e. a worker who, for a limited period of time, carries out his or her work in a Member State other than the State in which he or she normally works. Posted workers lie at the heart of a strong tension between the EU's Treaty enshrined principle of free movement of services allowing employers to temporarily provide a service in another Member State by 'importing' their own workers rather than relying on local workforce, and the risk of social dumping this can entail through undermining local labour conditions. The 1996 Posted Worker Directive, to which the European social partners contributed through the opportunity structure of the social dialogue, aimed to address this tension. However, the balance struck in the Directive, in particular as interpreted by the European Court of Justice in a series of highly discussed cases (Laval, Viking, Ruffert) concerning the balance between on the one hand free movement of services and freedom of establishment, and on the other hand individual and collective labour rights, has been a source of serious concern for labour, in particular in the context of enlargement of the European Union, and more recently of economic crisis. Posted workers, for instance, are guaranteed a minimum standard of employment conditions set out in the legislation of the host country, but not necessarily the extra conditions agreed in collective agreements. Moreover, the ECJ's case law has also put national IR structures at risk by opening the door for employers to immediately take IR disputes to national courts for judgment on the justified nature of industrial action. Hence while the EU's institutional framework encourages strong IR structures at national level too, its policy framework may at the same time put at risk some of these structures.

In his analysis, Parsons focuses in detail on three disputes that emerged around posted workers in the context of the European Court's decisions, namely the Swedish Laval case, and the disputes around the Lindsey Oil Refinery and the South Hook natural gas terminal in the UK. Posted workers conflicts create a difficult tension for labour. The defence of local working conditions and critique on the European rules leads to easy accusations of nationalistic and xenophobic behaviour, in particular by employers' organisations, while populist political actors may try to influence their rank-and-file with exactly such behaviour. The Lindsey dispute, in particular, which led to sympathy actions hitting more than twenty sites around the country, got also strongly politicised with populist actors, such as the UK Independence Party, arguing for 'British jobs for British workers'. The trade unions tried to avoid that trap by arguing for an improvement of the European policy framework, and a revision of the Posted Workers Directive in particular, which would ensure both the EU's free movement principles and local working conditions. Although the Commission has promised to propose a revision of the Directive and has made preparatory studies in this regard over the last few years, such proposal has not yet been made. The local protest actions themselves, however, have not been entirely unsuccessful. Although much of the labour action, in particular in the UK, could easily have been ruled in court as illegal, employers have rather given in to some of the demands, by providing some guarantees to also employ local workers, rather than further escalating the conflict that may damage them both economically and in PR terms.

While Turnbull and Parsons deal with the IR consequences of the hard economic principles of the European integration process as set out in Treaties and European legislation, in Chapter 11 Janine Goetschy turns our attention to the more muddied waters of the Lisbon and 'Europe 2020' Strategies. The EU's policy framework is indeed not limited to the constitutionalised principles of the internal market (four freedoms, competition), and the binding provisions of the acquis communautaire. Policy frames, concepts and ideas have always been developed in both hard law provisions and soft law persuasive policy tools. However, the latter are taking an increasingly important role in the policy mix the EU is relying on, in particular since the emergence of the Open Method of Coordination (OMC) in the 1990s and its use as central tool in the Lisbon Strategy. The Lisbon Strategy has been said to be perhaps the most high-profile initiative of the EU in the first decade of the 2000s (Begg 2007, Rodrigues 2003) and has been described as a 'governance architecture' composed of both ideational and institutional components providing a specific frame of reference that is supposed to make sense of a complex world of cross-cutting policy problems (Borràs and Radaelli 2011: 470). Soon after the Maastricht Treaty defined EMU, the Commission acted as a norm entrepreneur in developing a framework to discuss employment policy in the European context (De la Porte 2011: 492). In the absence of binding EU competence, the solution was for a process of guidelines and exchange of best practice between the Member States, but with a central role for European assessment and potential European impact on framing core concepts and approaches of national employment policies. The 2000 Lisbon Strategy extended this OMC method to other policy areas and aimed at providing an overall encompassing European framework for socio-economic governance, in particular by linking different policy areas. Janine Goetschy describes how the political economy design of the Lisbon Strategy was largely inspired by the intellectual debate around the concept of the European social model that stressed the interdependence of employment, social, macro-economic and welfare reform policies. The increased European involvement in these areas, even if not in a binding way, affects IR in multiple ways. This broad 'governance architecture' has affected IR both at the institutional and at the ideational level.

Hence, the social partners have been given a role in the Lisbon Strategy's institutional framework, for instance, via the Treaty obligation for the Employment Committee to consult the European social partners on the European Employment Strategy, or via the institutionalisation of the tripartite summit preceding the spring socio-economic European Council summit. Social partners are also expected to play a role in the implementation of the OMCs at the national level, by implementing particular guidelines and participation in the national action plans. This has been discussed extensively in the literature (Foden 1999, Léonard 2001, Smismans 2004, Homs, Kruse, Lafoucrière *et al.* 2007, Natali and de la Porte 2009), concluding that social partner participation differs strongly according to the country, often in line with national IR traditions, and happens mainly at a technocratic level. One can conclude that the Lisbon strategy and the OMC have not been sufficiently 'appropriated' by the social partners, except for the European-level elite dealing with these aspects (Léonard, Erne, Marginson *et al.* 2007:70)

However, in Chapter 11, Goetschy also points to the fact the Lisbon Strategy and 'Europe 2020' has not only led to more technocratic governance, but has also been characterised by increasing politicisation since the European Council has been institutionalised as core player in the design of the Strategy. Moreover, the ongoing economic crisis management and revision of Europe's economic governance is pushing such politicisation even further. For the social partners it remains to be seen how they can really weigh on this new governance structure (beyond their consultation in the tripartite summit), and how they organise their own actions in this wider policy framework.

Since the mid-2000s, the European social partners have already placed their multi-annual action programmes, and thus also their autonomous action, in the context of the Lisbon Strategy. The Lisbon Strategy and Europe 2020 do indeed not only provide a new institutional setting but provide a wider ideational framework that steers the initiatives of IR actors at multiple levels. In Chapter 12, Maarten Keune analyses how one of the core ideational frames of the Lisbon Strategy has affected IR, namely the idea of flexicurity. Flexicurity was 'uploaded' from some national debates, in particular in the Netherlands and Denmark, but the Commission became a very strong promoter of the idea in the early 2000s in the context of the wider Lisbon Strategy. The assumed 'win-win' solution of flexicurity, combining labour market flexibility with ensuring the security of workers and their families, appeared particularly attractive for European policy-making, which inherently attempts to overcome the contradictions between very diverging interests. Moreover, its added value of inspiring broad agreements that interconnect measures dealing with a broad range of labour market and welfare issues fitted well with the approach of the Lisbon Strategy, which stresses such interconnections. The flexicurity discourse also supposes close links between flexicurity and social dialogue; on the one hand, social dialogue is argued to be a precondition for comprehensive flexicurity strategies; on the other hand, it is expected to offer new impulses to social dialogue as it would provide a win-win solution to the opposed interests of management and labour. However, Keune's analysis shows that while management and labour agree on the importance of flexicurity, they profoundly disagree on the interpretation of the concept. Although the European flexicurity debate may have influenced national policy solutions, the concept has not been able to foster consensus amongst the social partners and trigger collective agreements and joint solutions that would not have been adopted if the concept did not exist.

## The EU and industrial relations in times of economic crisis

In a special issue of the *Journal of European Public Policy* on the tenth anniversary of EMU, Henrik Enderlein and Amy Verdun (2009) look back at the initial academic literature on EMU to conclude that most of the often pessimistic predictions on the viability and consequences of EMU, for instance on retrenchment of the welfare state (Bolukbasi 2009), had not come true. However, the rather positive assessment of the Euro at its tenth anniversary was followed by the caveat that it remained uncertain how EMU would develop in times of economic crisis. The then banking crisis has meanwhile turned into an even more profound sovereign debt crisis putting the survival of the Euro itself at risk. Assessing the evolution of IR in this context is a difficult task, and if there is one thing we should learn from Enderlein and Verdun's analysis it is that predicting the future is as difficult for academic scholars as it is for the politicians taking the decisions.

The initial effects of the economic crisis on IR at the national level show important differences among the EU Member States. It has been argued that social dialogue has contributed to social acceptance when governments were forced to take unpopular steps in order to tackle recession, and that social partners have been vital for Europe's employment, by enabling companies to cope with financial downturn without necessarily resorting to redundancies (Eurofound 2009: 24). The initial reaction to the financial crisis was based, on the one hand, on rescue packages for the banks and, on the other hand, attempts to stimulate macroeconomic demand showing some signs of a Keynesian policy agenda (Dølvik, Lind and Waddington 2011). This resulted in tripartite action at the national level and crisis-specific collective bargaining (in particular at company level), on issues such as short-time working (often co-funded by the State), measures to prevent or mitigate job losses, wage moderation and support for redundant workers. Such crisis-led social dialogue was clearly dependent on the role of the State in cushioning employment effects. One can therefore notice a clear divide in Europe between countries with a strong tradition of coordinated governance, where social dialogue has indeed contributed to cushioning the effects of the crisis, and countries with more liberal market economies, such as Ireland, the UK and most new Member States, with far less evidence of negotiated responses to the crisis, with in particular in Central and Eastern Europe firms imposing large-scale redundancies (Hyman 2010: 10).[4]

As the bank crisis turned into a sovereign debt crisis and policy turned to austerity rather than stimulus, social dialogue appeared to have increasingly less space for manoeuvre, showing particular difficulties in those countries worst hit, with for instance a real collapse of social dialogue in Ireland, and risks of serious deadlock in Spain and Portugal (Hyman 2010: 7). Overall the economic crisis also confirmed the trend to further decentralisation of IR (European Commission 2011, Glassner, Keune and Marginson 2011).

The EU's role in these developments is at the same time modest (in terms of social dialogue and social policy capacity) and having a huge impact (in terms of the economic governance context affecting IR). European social policy went ahead at its usual modest pace, but with several measures particularly relevant for coping with the economic crisis, such as the Directive on temporary agency and the adoption and reform of the European Globalisation Fund and the European Social Fund. The cross-industry social dialogue contributed in particular with the autonomous agreement on inclusive labour markets.

At the same time, a number of sectoral social dialogue committees have agreed on joint statements addressing the crisis, including those for the chemical industry, construction, road transport, commerce, live performance, regional and local government, woodworking and furniture sectors (European Commission 2011: 174). Skills and training in particular continued to be a core area of European sectoral social dialogue with committees in sixteen sectors being active in this area.

It can be argued that, so far, the social partners have largely resisted the temptation to call for protectionist national responses and shown a degree of coordination and solidarity across Europe (European Commission 2011). However, there are also profound differences of opinion that make common action difficult. Above all, as some Member States have been far more profoundly hit by the crisis than others, the social partners did not always agree on the added value of common European action. Moreover, management and labour held very different opinions on how to address the crisis. Despite intensive efforts, in March 2009 the cross-industry social dialogue committee failed to agree on a joint declaration on actions to address the crisis. Within the context of the more medium-term Europe 2020 strategy, however, the social partners achieved consensus around a joint statement in June 2010. As Janine Goetschy's analysis here shows, compared to the Lisbon Strategy, Europe 2020 places more stress on the issues of social inclusion and training and skills and gives new attention to the objective of a low carbon economy. However, as Goetschy also notes, how can these objectives of the mainly soft-law based Europe 2020 strategy be reconciled with the ever demanding requirements of European economic governance that have been formulated in an attempt to save the Euro – and with it, the banks and the global economy?

In the last chapter of this volume, Roland Erne sets out the new contours of European economic governance, as based on the 'six-pack' of five regulations and one directive adopted on 4 October 2011. While European decision-makers are permanently running after the speculation of the financial markets and the 'six-pack' of economic governance is already up for a promised adjustment following the European Council's summit decision of 26 October 2011 to strengthen European economic governance and budgetary control with a Treaty reform by March 2012; the main features of the package are clear, namely austerity measures and European level technocratic governance. It would be too easy just to blame the European Union for this approach. In the end, the current crisis is only partially due to the inherent limits of the EMU, namely lack of European competence to accompany monetary policy with economic and fiscal policy. The lack of regulation of the speculation and governance of the banks is a global problem, as is the policy paradigm to revert its costs on the tax payer and citizens by technocratic imposed austerity measures. It is ironic enough that the UK sets the example for this approach, while pressuring the Eurozone countries to get their act together to do the same, meanwhile telling the British electorate that transfer of competence to the EU level is an inherently bad thing.

However, while the policy paradigm to tackle the crisis may not differ whether it is dealt with at European or national level, the EU is more likely to get the blame, not only in case where the Euro still fails but also if the EU sticks to the approach now taken for economic governance. The crisis raises profound questions about solidarity within the EU, while Member States may end up too easily passing the blame for austerity measures to the EU.

Industrial action has strongly increased due to the economic crisis (Eurofound 2009: 17–18, Hyman 2010: 4–5), but in 2010 Richard Hyman still argued that although one has seen more radical forms of action it did not necessarily imply similar radicalism of objectives. Actions appeared often as gestures of defiance, aimed at limiting the number of dismissals or improving redundancy packages, without little belief that job losses could be prevented, and were, for that reason, relatively easy to resolve (Hyman 2010: 5). However, as the crisis deepens, protest becomes more systemic with industrial action that may put into question the legitimacy of economic governance and political decision making more broadly. Yet, while populist and protectionist pressures may find in the EU construction the easiest scapegoat, the more underlying problems of global market design may remain unresolved. The question is whether management and labour will be able to resist the potential rise of protectionist and populist pressures as the crisis profoundly hits an increasing part of the population, and whether the EU will be able to offer something other than imposing austerity to help survive the Euro and the global markets rather than its social model.

## Notes

1 For a more legal take on the topic, see also Franssen (2002) and Welz (2008).
2 Article 153(3)TFEU allows Member States to implement European social Directives by way of collective agreements.
3 See, for instance, on the social partners' role on the implementation of the Working Time

Directive in all Member States: 'Commission Staff Working Paper. Detailed report on the implementation by Member States of Directive *2003/88/EC concerning certain aspects of the organisation of working time*', SEC(2010) 1611 final, Brussels, 21.12.2010, pp. 164–5. For a critical assessment of the implementation of this Directive in the UK's decentralised IR system, see Barnard, Deakin and Hobbs (2005).

4 Although in countries less hit by the crisis, such as Poland, a considerable degree of policy consensus was able to emerge among the social partners (European Commission 2011).

## References


Barnard, C., Deakin, S. and Hobbs, R. (2005), 'Reflexive Law, Corporate Social Responsibility and the Evolution of Labour Standards: The Case of Working Time', pp. 205–44 in De Schutter, O. and Deakin, S. (eds), *Social Rights and Market Forces*, Brussels: Bruylant.

Begg, I. (2007), 'Lisbon II: Two Years On: An Assessment of the Partnership for Growth and Jobs', *CEPS Special Reports*.

Boerzel, T. (2001), 'Non-compliance in the European Union: Pathology or Statistical Artefact?' *Journal of European Public Policy* 8(5), 803–24.

Bolukbasi, H.T. (2009), 'On Consensus, Constraint and Choice: Economic and Monetary Integration and Europe's Welfare States', *Journal of European Public Policy* 16(4), 527–44.

Borràs, S. and Radaelli, C. (2011), 'The Politics of Governance Architectures: Creation, Change and Effects of the EU Lisbon Strategy', *Journal of European Public Policy* 18(4), 463–84.

Branch, A. (2005), 'The Evolution of the European Social Dialogue Towards Greater Autonomy: Challenges and Potential Benefits', *International Journal of Comparative Labour Law and Industrial Relations*, 21(2), 321–46.

Carley, M. and Hall, M. (2009), *The Impact of the Information and Consultation Directive on Industrial Relations*, European Industrial Relations Observatory, www.eurofound.europa.eu/eiro/studies/tn0710029s/tn0710029s.htm, accessed 5 May 2011.

Coen, D. and Richardson, J. (2009), *Lobbying the European Union: Institutions, Actors, and Issues*, Oxford: Oxford University Press.

De la Porte, C. (2011), 'Principal-agent Theory and the Open Method of Co-ordination: The Case of the European Employment Strategy', *Journal of European Public Policy* 18(4), 485–503.

Degryse, C. and Pochet, P. (2011), 'Has European Sectoral Social Dialogue Improved since the Establishment of SSDCs in 1998?', *Transfer* 17(2), 145–57.

Dølvik, J.E., Lind, J. and Waddington, J. (2011), Editorial, *Transfer* 17(3), 291–302.

Enderlein, H. and Verdun, A. (2009), 'EMU's Teenage Challenge: What Have we Learnt and Can We Predict from Political Science?', *Journal of European Public Policy* 16(4), 490–507.

Erne, R. (2008), *European Unions: Labor's Quest for Transnational Democracy*, Ithaca, NY: Cornell University Press.

Eurofound, European Foundation for the Improvement of Living and Working Conditions (2009), *Social Dialogue and the Recession*, Dublin: Eurofound.

European Commission (2010), Commission staff working document on the functioning and potential of European sectoral social dialogue, Brussels, 22 July, SEC(2010) 964 final.
European Commission (2011), *Industrial Relations in Europe 2010*, Social Europe, Luxembourg: Publications Office of the European Union.
Falkner, G., Treib, O., Hartlapp, M. and Leiber, S. (2005), *Complying with Europe: EU Harmonisation and Soft Law in the Member States*, Cambridge: Cambridge University Press.
Favell, A. and Guiraudon, V. (2009), 'The Sociology of the European Union: An Agenda', *European Union Politics* 10(4), 427–55.
Featherstone, K. (1994), 'Jean Monnet and the "Democratic Deficit" in the European Union', *Journal of Common Market Studies* 32, 149–70.
Foden, D. (1999), 'The Role of Social Partners in the European Employment Strategy', *Transfer* 5(4), 215.
Franssen, E. (2002), *Legal Aspects of the European Social Dialogue*, Antwerp: Intersentia.
Glassner, V., Keune, M. and Marginson, P. (2011), 'Collective Bargaining in a Time of Crisis: Developments in the Private Sector in Europe', *Transfer* 17(3), 303–21.
Goetschy, J. (2001), 'The European Employment Strategy from Amsterdam to Stockholm: Has it Reached its Cruising Speed Yet?', *Industrial Relations Journal* 32, 410
Graziano, P. and Vink, M. (forthcoming), 'Europeanization', in Bulmer, S. and Lequesne, C. (eds), *The Member States and the European Union* (2nd edn), Oxford: Oxford University Press.
Greenwood, J. (2003), *Interest Representation in the European Union*, London: Palgrave.
Hix, S. and Goetz, K. (eds) (2001), *Europeanised Politics? European Integration and National Political Systems*, London: Frank Cass.
Homs, O., Kruse, W., Lafoucrière, C. and Tilly, P. (2007), *European Employment Strategy and the Integrated Guidelines for Growth and Jobs*, European Trade Union Confederation.
Hyman, R. (2005), 'Trade Unions and the Politics of the European Social Model', *Economic & Industrial Democracy* 26(1), 9–40.
Hyman, R. (2010), *Social Dialogue and Industrial Relations during the Economic Crisis: Innovative Practices or Business as Usual?*, Working Paper no. 11, Geneva: International Labour Office.
Imig, D. and Tarrow, S. (eds) (2001), *Contentious Europeans: Protest and Politics in an Emerging Polity*, Lanham, MD: Rowman and Littlefield.
Johnston, A. and Hancké, B. (2009), 'Wage Inflation and Labour Unions in EMU', *Journal of European Public Policy*, 16(4), 601–22.
Kauppinen, T. (ed.) (1998), *The Impact of EMU on Industrial Relations in European Union*, no. 9. Helsinki: Finnish Industrial Relations Association.
Keller, B. and Platzer, H.-W. (eds) (2003), *Industrial Relations and European Integration: Trans- and Supranational Developments and Prospects*, Aldershot: Ashgate.
Keller, B. and Weber, S. (2011), 'Sectoral Dialogue at EU Level: Problems and Prospects of Implementation', *European Journal of Industrial Relations* 17, 227–43.
Kirchner, E. (1977), *Trade Unions as a Pressure Group in the European Community*, Westmead: Saxon House.

Knill, C. (1998), 'European Policies: The Impact of National Administrative Traditions', *Journal of Public Policy* 18(1), 1–28.

Knill, C. and Lehmkuhl, D. (2002), 'The National Impact of European Union Regulatory Policy: Three Europeanization Mechanisms', *European Journal of Political Research* 41, 255–80.

Leisink, P., Steijn, B. and Veersma, U. (eds) (2007), *Industrial Relations in the New Europe. Enlargement, Integration and Reform*, Cheltenham: Elgar.

Léonard, E. (2001) 'Industrial Relations and the Regulation of Employment in Europe', *European Journal of Industrial Relations* 7 (2001), 32.

Léonard, E. (2008), 'European Sectoral Social Dialogue: An Analytical Framework', *European Journal of Industrial Relations*, 14(4), 401–19.

Léonard, E., Erne, R., Marginson, P. and Smismans, S. (2007), *New Structures, Forms and Processes of Governance in European Industrial Relations*, European Foundation for Living and Working Conditions.

Mair, P. (2000), 'The Limited Impact of Europe on National Party Systems', *West European Politics* 23(4), 27–51.

Marginson, P. and Sisson, K. (2004), *European Integration and Industrial Relations: Multi-level Governance in the Making*, Basingstoke: Palgrave.

Marginson, P., Hall, M.J., Hoffmann, A. and Muller, T. (2004), 'The Impact of European Works Councils on Management Decision-making in UK- and US-based Multinationals: A Case Study comparison', *British Journal of Industrial Relations* 42: 209–33.

Mazey, S. and Richardson, J. (eds) (1993), *Lobbying in the European Community*, Oxford: Oxford University Press.

Milward, A. (1992), *The European Rescue of the Nation-State*, London: Routledge.

Natali, D. and de La Porte, C. (2009), 'Participation through the Lisbon Strategy: Comparing the European Employment Strategy and Pensions OMC', *Transfer* 15(1), 71–91

Pochet, P. (2005), 'Sectoral Social Dialogue? A Quantitative Analysis', *Transfer* 11(3), 313–32.

Pulignano, V. and Kluge, N. (2007), 'Employee Involvement in Restructuring: Are we able to Determine the Price?, *Transfer* 13(2), 225–40.

Radaelli, C. (2004), 'Europeanisation: solution or problem?', *European Integration Online Papers* (EIoP) 8(16), http://eiop.or.at/eiop/texte/2004–016a.htm, accessed 14 July 2011.

Ribarova, E. (2011), 'Information and Consultation Arrangements: Results from a Transnational Study', *Transfer* 17(2), 229–37.

Rodrigues, M.J. (ed.) (2003), *European Policies for a Knowledge Economy*, Cheltenham: Edward Elgar.

Saurugger, S. (2009), 'Sociological Approaches in EU Studies', *Journal of European Public Policy* 16(6), 935–49.

Smismans, S. (2004), 'EU Employment Policy: decentralisation or centralisation through the Open Method of Coordination?, Working Paper European University Institute, LAW 2004/01, http://cadmus.iue.it/dspace/bitstream/1814/1881/1/law01–1.pdf, accessed 15 March 2011.

Smismans, S. (2008), 'The European Social Dialogue in the Shadow of Hierarchy', *Journal of Public Policy*, 28(1), 161–80.

Stollt, M. and Kluge, N. (2011), 'The Potential of Employee Involvement in the SE to Foster Europeanization of Labour Relations', *Transfer* 17(2), 181–91.

Vink, M.P. and Graziano, P. (2007), 'Challenges of a New Research Agenda', pp. 3–20 in Graziano, P. and Vink, M.P. (eds), *Europeanization: New Research Agendas*, Basingstoke: Palgrave.

Vos, K. (2007), 'European Convergence and the EU Social Model', pp. 23–40 in Leisink, P., Stejn, B. and Veersma, U. (eds) (2007), *Industrial Relations in the New Europe. Enlargement, Integration and Reform*, Cheltenham: Elgar.

Wallace, H. (1993), 'European Governance in Turbulent Times', *Journal of Common Market Studies* 31(3), 293–304.

Welz, C. (2008), *The European Social Dialogue Under Articles 138 and 139 of the EC Treaty*, Alphen aan den Rijn: Kluwer Law International.

# PART I

## The EU and institutional change in the European social dialogue

*Tobias Müllensiefen*[1]

# 2

# The European cross-sectoral social dialogue between autonomous action and regulatory involvement

## Introduction

Since the early 2000s, European social dialogue at cross-sectoral level has taken a turn towards more autonomy. Social partners do not want to remain dependent on the activity of the European Union's (EU) institutions, but determine their own bargaining agenda. But while the national agenda is dominated by the fight over wages, there is no such natural topic for the European dialogue. Nevertheless, the European social partners have managed to work out an agenda which keeps them busy on issues of greater consensus and maybe secondary importance.

While this autonomous dialogue is not meaningless, it has not attracted huge attention and has exposed the social partners to criticism of watering down their co-legislative dialogue, including in their own ranks. By the late 2000s, the European social partners have become more involved again in the regulatory work in European labour law. This is, of course, also due to the slight increase of legislative activity in the second half of the first Barroso Commission's mandate after several years of relative inertia in the social field. This renewed activism may seem to be a result of the Commission's political decisions, but can at least partly be attributed to the European Parliament's growing awareness that the lack of social rights in Europe is difficult to sell to European citizens.

## More autonomy for European social dialogue

The call for more autonomy in European social dialogue dates from 2001. Until then, European social dialogue, launched in 1985 under the auspices of Jacques Delors, had been characterised by two phases: a first 'exploratory' phase, where social partners learnt to communicate with each other at European level, resulting in 'joint opinions' which were neither binding nor followed by any concrete actions at national level; and a second 'legislative' phase where social partners experimented with the new powers granted by the Social Protocol annexed to the Maastricht Treaty (now enshrined in Articles 154 and 155 of the Treaty on the Functioning of the EU (TFEU)).[2] They negotiated agreements on parental leave, part-time work and fixed-term work which were then given legal effect by Council Directive. Both phases were marked by strong influence of the European Commission, since the social partners' power to co-legislate is in fact dependent on a formal consultation by the Commission.

For probably different reasons, both employers and trade unions wanted their dialogue to be more independent from the Commission. Under the Belgian Presidency in 2001, the European social partners put this demand in writing in a joint declaration. In the following year, they started to put this ambition into practice through three different instruments.

First, their first joint multi-annual work programme, in which they listed the activities they wanted to implement during 2003–05. Forward-planning and structuring of European social dialogue has become common practice and the social partners are currently working on the basis of their third work programme, which started in 2009.

Second, their first framework of action of 2002 was on the lifelong development of qualifications and competences, i.e. social partner initiatives to promote lifelong learning. This was a new method of encouraging members at national level to engage in various activities in a field considered crucial by European actors, without taking any legal commitment. Nevertheless an annual reporting mechanism is foreseen to ensure that results of the process are documented and shared at EU level.

Third, the social partners negotiated their first autonomous agreement on the issue of telework. An autonomous agreement is an agreement which is to be implemented using the first possibility provided by Article 155(2) TFEU, i.e. 'in accordance with the procedures and practices specific to management and labour and the Member States'. In practical terms it means that national social partners have to ensure that the agreement is applied in each Member State through the normal channels of collective bargaining or social partner relations. Four autonomous agreements have been concluded since 2002.[3]

These three main elements of the autonomous dialogue were further developed and improved in the years that followed. Social partners pursued and structured their work and, increasingly aware that the growing complexity of their instruments and processes required explanations, also carried out activities to disseminate knowledge about their work and to train their members on what was expected from them.

To illustrate how the autonomous dialogue has further evolved over the years, this chapter will briefly review some important developments in the three fields identified in recent years.

***A 'transitional' work programme***

In early 2009, the European social partners published their most recent work programme (ETUC *et al.* 2009). Contrary to the previous work programmes which both covered three-year periods (2003–05, 2006–08), this new agenda was only for 2009 and 2010.[4] Two reasons have been put forward for this shorter time span: first, social partners expected the new Commission to come forward with a new post-Lisbon strategy in 2010[5] and wished to adapt their plan to this new policy agenda. Second, major initiatives foreseen in the 2006–08 programme (which experienced a considerable delay due to difficult discussions between the social partners over labour market issues) had not yet been finalised or even launched. The aim of this 'transitional' programme was therefore also to treat those items before engaging in new initiatives.

One of these 'leftovers' was the negotiation of the social partners' fourth autonomous agreement, the 'framework agreement on inclusive labour markets' which was finally adopted in March 2010. Its novelty is that it is the first agreement to be truly autonomous. The previous agreements have all been negotiated following a formal Article 154 consultation and have been inspired by the Commission's ideas and suggestions. In this case the social partners have for the first time defined the topic of their negotiations themselves. On the other hand, the level of commitment is rather low so that the question arises whether this 'agreement' should not rather be classified as a 'framework of action' (see definition in next section).

Interestingly, the European social partners also plan a lot of introspection in order to review the workings of their autonomous dialogue as well as the results it yields. So next to 'monitoring, assessing and evaluating the implementation of EU social dialogue framework agreements and frameworks of action', they want to 'develop their common understanding of the various instruments resulting from their negotiations' and 'determine their impact on the various levels of social dialogue' (ETUC *et al.* 2009). This agenda item shows that there seems to be some need to closer define the responsibilities resulting from the adoption of social dialogue instruments, but also that there is a willingness to address these issues.

Finally, and this will be developed further below, social partners do not give up on their legislative role, as they declare that 'this work programme does not constitute an exhaustive list' and that, in addition, they 'will continue to take actions … in reaction to European Commission proposals and initiatives' (*ibid.*).

***Frameworks of action: the social partners' own 'open method of coordination'***

Next to autonomous agreements, in which social partners take commitments, they have developed another non-binding instrument: so-called frameworks of action. In this method, the European social partners define priorities in a specific policy area on the basis of previously presented best practice and give examples for possible action. The text calls on national social partners to carry out activities within these priority areas. An annual report is compiled on the basis of contributions from national social partners. After a number of years, an evaluation of the process is carried out. Although this instrument does not set targets or benchmarks, it is clearly inspired by the Open Method of Coordination (OMC).

After a first experience with the framework of action on lifelong learning, social partners decided to test the method in another policy area: gender equality. A framework of action was negotiated in 2005 setting out four priorities and possible actions to their members at national level (gender roles, women in decision-making, work-life balance, gender pay gap). In their work programme, social partners have planned to negotiate a third framework of action in the area of employment, although it is not yet clear what exactly it will cover.

Judging from the experience with two frameworks of actions,[6] there is clearly room for some criticism of this method, both in terms of process and of results. There is little incentive for national social partners to take any action since no sanctions are foreseen. This had led to a situation where often only slightly more than half of Member States' social partners have reported on their activities. Those who have not reported are often those where action would be most needed. And for Member States where national reports have been provided, these often cover ongoing activities often not related to the EU level. In any case, it is difficult to assess which of the reported activities have indeed been triggered by the follow-up process and which would have taken place anyway without it.

On the other hand, the process also has merits. Frameworks of action spell out the most urgent priorities where social partners should concentrate their efforts at national level. They help to raise the visibility of the role and experience that social partners have in addressing specific concerns. The reporting process allows for an exchange among trade union and employer experts at national level and the documentation of experiences. It also provides the opportunity to meet and discuss at European level and learn from each other. The results of this process, similarly to the OMC, are obviously very difficult to assess.

#### *The implementation test for autonomous agreements*

Experience has also been made with the implementation of autonomous agreements since 2002. Social partners have presented their first implementation report (on the telework agreement) in 2006 and the Commission has carried out subsequently its own analysis and published a report in 2008 (European Commission 2008a). This report considered the implementation process to be a success even though it highlighted a number of shortcomings: a complete lack of implementation in a small number of Member States and uneven results across Member States, ranging from binding legislation or collective agreements to simple recommendations by the social partners. Nevertheless the results were better than predicted by a number of observers.

While the telework case was certainly the litmus test for autonomous agreements, it will be necessary to follow closely the implementation process of the later texts. For the stress and harassment/violence agreements are very different in nature from the telework one.[7]

The social partners have recognised the difference between their agreements in the implementation report (ETUC *et al.* 2008a) of the stress agreement which was published in 2008. While the telework agreement defined rules applicable to this new form of work organisation, the stress agreement only provides an 'action-oriented framework' to identify, prevent or manage stress problems. Indeed the content of the stress agreement seems rather weak in comparison with telework. Moreover, the telework agreement was innovative since telework had not yet been regulated in most Member States, whereas the stress agreement had to be implemented in an already existing framework of occupational health and safety laws and policies.

The social partners' report observes that these dissimilarities have practical implications for implementation. In terms of outcome, the stress agreement sparked relatively little new regulation in the form of law or collective agreements. Many instruments already existed at national level, and if at all, the stress agreements allowed social partners to 'fine-tune' this regulatory framework. According to the report, the legal or conventional framework in place in several countries (e.g. Belgium, Denmark, Norway) already covered the content of the stress agreement, therefore the social partners saw no need for further implementation.

Instead of new rules, the national social partners developed a lot of 'soft' tools and complementary activities, focused on awareness-raising (brochures, studies, campaigns), training or development of practical tools, e.g. for assessment of stress levels. The level of intervention was often not the national one, but closer to the workplace.

Nevertheless several similarities with the telework implementation can be observed. In many Member States (e.g. Spain, United Kingdom, Italy, France, Iceland, Finland, Sweden, Latvia, Netherlands) social partners used exactly the same procedures, instruments and/or bodies to implement the stress agreement as they did for telework. In some cases (France, Italy), last-minute negotiations had to be conducted again in order to be ready in time for the social partners' implementation report. It could therefore be argued that the precedent of telework is gradually evolving into established implementation practices depending on the system in each Member State.

The wide range of very diverse implementing measures makes it even more difficult to assess the impact of the stress agreement, and in particular the extent to which the individual implementing measures have been sparked or influenced by the European text (which was easier to define in the case of telework). The soft wording of the stress agreement – its aim is to 'increase awareness and understanding' (ETUC *et al.* 2004) – and its rather best-practice than rights-based approach[8] gave much more leeway to social partners in terms of possible implementation outcomes. Critics could therefore argue a softening of autonomous agreements, but the more solid content of the third agreement on harassment and violence might prove the contrary, as national trade unions can be expected to insist that the key principles of the agreement are reflected in the implementation outcome.

***Higher esteem for autonomous agreements among key actors***

Five broader developments seem to confirm that autonomous agreements are increasingly being taken seriously both by social partners and public authorities as an alternative tool to agreements implemented by Directives – depending on the aim of the initiative concerned.

Firstly, there seems to be a widening consensus regarding the existence of an obligation on social partners to implement autonomous agreements. This position was first stated by the Commission with reference to Article 155(2) TFEU which stipulates that EU-level agreements '*shall* be implemented' (emphasis added) (European Commission 2004). This convergence of views is confirmed by the social partners' decision to abandon the misleading term of 'voluntary agreement' in favour of 'autonomous agreement' in their latest agreement on harassment and violence. The view that autonomous agreement may not be legally but 'contractually binding' seems to be gaining important ground.

Secondly, the social partners have put in place an institutionalised system of regular monitoring and reporting on their autonomous agreements. Every year, national member federations are requested to report jointly about the progress made with implementation in each Member State and about difficulties encountered, before a final implementation report is presented in the fourth year. The Commission went so far as to say that the signatory parties had the duty to 'exercise influence on their members in order to implement the European agreement' (*ibid.*). To facilitate the implementation process, the European organisations are also providing support facilities for their members (e.g. translation fund, possibilities for exchange and mutual learning, European Trade Union Confederation (ETUC) interpretation guide).

Thirdly, as stated above, European social partners agreed in their joint work programme to 'further develop their common understanding of [social dialogue] instruments and how they can have a positive impact at the various levels of social dialogue' (*ibid.*). The aim of this exercise is to further define the status of autonomous agreements (and other instruments), the obligations deriving from them as well as questions regarding interpretation, dispute settlement and similar issues.

Fourthly, the Commission has become more involved in recent years in the follow-up of autonomous agreements. It presented its vision with regard to autonomous agreements in 2004, stating that it had 'a particular role to play if the agreement was the result of an Article 154 consultation, inter alia because the social partners' decision to negotiate an agreement temporarily suspends the legislative process at Community level initiated by the Commission in this domain' (*ibid.*). The Commission committed itself to publish autonomous agreements and to inform the European Parliament and the Council following an *ex-ante* check of the content and *ex-post* analysis of the implementation. The agreement on harassment and violence was thus officially communicated to the other institutions (European Commission 2007).

Finally Member States have become more involved in the process as would have been expected, through amending existing or introducing new legislation to implement or adjust to the agreement, through *erga omnes* extension of collective agreements, or other forms of cooperation with social partners.

***A situation of permanent dialogue***

Even though there is clearly room for improvement in the implementation on the ground and the follow-up process, these examples nevertheless show that social partners have successfully structured their dialogue and given meaning to the new instruments they have developed. In defining the role and the scope of their instruments, the social partners have broadly followed the 'typology' of social dialogue outcomes proposed by the Commission in its 2004 Communication. Processes have not only become more autonomous, but also more automatic and institutionalised. Once a new agreement or framework of action is adopted, the machinery of implementation and reporting processes is starting to work. European social partners now also provide assistance to their members in the form of translations, interpretation guides and training in order to facilitate the implementation process.

Thus the trade unions have successfully pushed the employers into a situation of permanent dialogue, negotiation and, not least, monitoring of results. Employers decided that it was in their interest to play the game. They always argued that labour market issues should not be regulated by public authorities, but should be left for the key players in the labour market to decide upon. Their own credibility was thus at stake and they had to prove that social dialogue works and leads to results. Any discontinuation of the dialogue would be immediately understood as a failure and would be extremely difficult to justify.

***Remaining involved in legislating social Europe***

This move towards more autonomous social dialogue at European level was viewed with scepticism both within the trade union movement and among external observers. To some this meant that social partners were turning away from their role in the legislative process in European social affairs, embracing an approach of exclusively soft-law norms.

This may have been true for the beginning of the 2000s and the beginning of the Barroso Commission's mandate. Indeed social partners were not in a very ambitious mood after the failure of their latest attempt to reach an agreement to be implemented by Directive on the issue of temporary agency work. Negotiations broke down in 2001 and the Commission had to present a proposal for a Directive which encountered similar difficulties in Council negotiations. (A deal was eventually struck within Council and with Parliament in 2008.)

Another reason for the loss of momentum in normative social dialogue was the relative absence of Commission initiatives in the social field. Apart from a number of consultations on rather technical health and safety issues, such as musculoskeletal disorders, carcinogens and needlestick injuries, few real social policy topics were proposed for possible legislation in 2004–06, where social partners could have engaged in serious negotiations.

This changed slightly from mid-2007 when some new impetus was given to EU social policy. The Commission decided to move ahead with several initiatives which also spurred again the activity of the social partners in the legislative field.

***A new deal on parental leave***

The first area where things got moving again was the area of work-life balance, which is very much linked to gender equality, as better possibilities for reconciling work and family life can help particularly mothers to (re)enter the labour market. In its five-year gender equality strategy for 2006–10, called the 'roadmap', the Commission already announced it would review the existing legislation in that area 'with a view to updating, modernising and recasting where necessary' (European Commission 2006). The most important pieces of EU legislation concerning work-life balance are two Directives on maternity protection (1992) and parental leave (1996), the latter giving legal effect to the first ever European social partner agreement concluded in 1995 (Council Directive 96/34/EC).

The first consultation round on 'reconciliation of professional, private and family life' that the Commission started in October 2006 under Article 154 of the Treaty made the case for further action at EU level. Two main arguments were brought forward: enabling parents to have as many children as they would like and thereby contributing to the fight against Europe's demographic decline; and promoting an equal sharing of caring responsibilities and thereby raising the labour market participation rate of women. Social partners broadly shared this view, but differed on the means to reach these objectives.

The Commission then launched the second-stage consultation in May 2007, where it put the following legislative items on the agenda: reforming maternity protection, revising parental leave and introducing new forms of leave, asking the social partners for their views and whether they wanted to take the opportunity to negotiate (instead of the Commission submitting a proposal). The subject of parental leave was a particularly delicate one, as social partners claimed ownership of their 1995 agreement. Now the Commission seemed to put pressure on them, threatening to propose itself a revision of this text, if social partners did not enter into negotiations. Social partners even contested the competence of the Commission to propose itself a revision of the Directive, as there is a review clause in the agreement which gives that power to the social partners.[9]

Realising that social partners were at best hesitant to be pushed into negotiations to review and update their agreement, the Commission granted them more time than the usual six weeks to respond to its consultation. It invited them to assess the provisions of their framework agreement on parental leave with a view to its review and to report on progress by March 2008. Social partners did not seem very eager to negotiate, even though the trade unions also recognised the opportunity to relaunch their legislative dialogue. In July 2007, both sides wrote to the Commission, accepting the extra time to assess the implementation of the old agreement and to explore whether negotiations could be successful.

The social partners set up an ad hoc working group with their members to assess parental leave arrangements at national level in the wider context of other reconciliation policies (flexible working, childcare). These internal consultations with members dragged on into mid-2008. At the March deadline, in a progress report, they could only agree in vague terms to 'undertake joint action to better achieve the aims of the Parental Leave Directive as part of wider work on reconciliation' (ETUC *et al.* 2008b). During the summer the employers finally agreed to reopen the dossier, and negotiations started in September.

After six months and seven rounds of negotiations, both sides came to an agreement on a text in March 2009. After internal approval by the respective decision-making bodies, the revised framework agreement on parental leave was signed on 18 June 2009. The main novelty in the agreement is the extension of the individual right to parental leave from three to four months, of which one is strictly non-transferable. This means that this month cannot be transferred from one parent to the other, thus encouraging fathers to avail of their own leave. The agreement also brings better protection against discrimination for applying for or taking parental leave, better protection of fixed-term and other atypical workers as well as the right for working parents returning from parental leave to request flexible working – a request which the employer must seriously consider and respond to.

While the final outcome of the negotiations does not represent a revolution in reconciliation policy, the new agreement will certainly mean some progress for working parents to better balance family and work, in particular in Member States where this has not been high on the agenda in recent years. The Commission presented its proposal for a Directive on the basis of the revised social partner agreement in July 2009. As expected, the Directive was adopted rather quickly in March 2010 (Council Directive 2010/18/EU), thanks to the relatively limited scope of the agreement, the impossibility for Council to amend its wording and qualified majority voting. It is the first revision ever of a Directive on the basis of an agreement by social partners.

### *Quasi-negotiations on European works councils*

The second area where new activism on the European Commission's side pushed the social partners into legislative dialogue is the revision of the European Works Council Directive. The purpose of European Works Councils (EWCs) is to ensure better information and consultation of employees in transnational companies. The Directive adopted in 1994 spurred the development of more than 820 EWCs in large European undertakings operating in several Member States.

A revision of this Directive had been on the agenda for a long time due to shortcomings in the text of the Directive. In April 2004 the Commission had already launched a first-stage consultation of social partners on a possible revision of the Directive. As in 1994 when they were not able to enter into negotiations despite pressure from the Commission, both sides could not agree on opening talks, because employers were fundamentally opposed to a revision, fearing higher consultation standards. They did, however, agree to examining specific cases of EWC in order to assess their functioning and also managed to draw some shared conclusions, including on the usefulness of the instrument as such.

Moving towards the end of its mandate and under increased pressure to show achievements in the social field, the Commission took the consultation procedure up again in February 2008 and launched formally the second stage on the revision of the EWC Directive (European Commission 2008b). The possible content of a EU action was described in detail, covering measures to strengthen the effectiveness of consultation and information, to solve problems in the application and to correct legal gaps as well as those designed to ensure coherence with other EU acts, and social partners were asked to give their view or inform the Commission of their wish to enter into negotiations.

Trade unions and employers haggled over whether they should enter into negotiations. The trade union side demanded a sort of pre-negotiation to ensure there was sufficient common ground on substance and asked for guarantees for the timing of the negotiation, so that the result of such a negotiation could still be endorsed and adopted as a legislative proposal before the end of the Commission's mandate in 2009.

The employers (BUSINESSEUROPE, CEEP and UEAPME) declared to be ready to negotiate but rejected the trade unions' conditions, so that the ETUC declined the offer, feeling such negotiations were unrealistic and 'not practical'. In a letter to the Commission on 11 April 2008 the ETUC declared that 'unfortunately it was not possible to agree with BUSINESSEUROPE on a concluding date for any talks, nor reach a robust understanding on substantial amendments to the Directive' (ETUC 2008) and urged the Commission to quickly come forward with a proposal. This was a difficult decision to take for the trade union movement which usually stresses the pre-eminent role of social dialogue. The employer side protested against this refusal, underlining the seriousness of their offer, including in terms of opening negotiations within a short timeframe.

The Commission reacted to the deadlock by making its proposal for a recast Directive in early July 2008, which tried to propose an approach balancing the views of both sides of industry (European Commission 2008c). The French Council Presidency, which started at that time, aimed for a quick success on this file in the form of a first-reading agreement with the European Parliament, to demonstrate its commitment to Social Europe. Some days later the French Minister asked the social partners at the informal Council meeting in Chantilly whether they were able to agree on the broad lines of the Commission's proposal, in order to facilitate a political deal between the European institutions.

Even if this appeal did not trigger formal negotiations, talks were taken up over summer between the Secretaries General and Brussels secretariats of the relevant organisations. These talks resulted in a 'joint advice' in the form of a letter sent on 29 August 2008 by all four organisations to the French Minister, in which they declared to 'accept the Commission proposal … as the basis for the revision' of the Directive. Furthermore they listed in an annexe a 'restricted number of issues on which either side particularly considers that changes to that proposal should be sought' (ETUC *et al.* 2008c) and called upon Council and Parliament to take the concrete text proposals into account. It seems that this 'joint advice' was drafted without a clear mandate from some of the social partners' members on both sides, some of whom even opposed the result. The ETUC Executive Committee nevertheless retroactively approved the outcome of the talks.

Member States would have preferred formal negotiations between social partners, but finally also accepted the outcome of the informal talks. The 'joint advice' provided the working basis for the Council discussions. The social partners remained involved in the process by giving their views on Presidency text proposals and suggesting further changes which were again taken on board in the final draft.

The European Parliament's Employment Committee initially aimed at a more far-reaching reform of the EWC Directive and first resisted accepting the deal as such. However, the informal trilogue, with the help of the Commission, succeeded in bringing the European Parliament back to the social partners' compromise, when the text reached the plenary stage. Thus a first-reading agreement was reached within five months, which would most probably not have been possible without the social partners' active involvement and quasi-negotiations (Directive 2009/38/EC).

***A stronger role for the European Parliament?***

These two cases show that there has been a comeback for the legislative social dialogue in recent years after an exclusive focus on autonomous agreements in the first half of the decade. Admittedly the output has not yet attained the level of the late 1990s. At first glance, the main reason behind the revival of the social partners' legislative role seems to lie in the Commission's renewed activity in proposing labour legislation (which is of course relative, compared to past times).

This raises the question why the Commission has again put social issues higher on its agenda. Following the negative referendums on the draft Constitution in France and in the Netherlands and the difficult debate on the Services Directive, the Commission was criticised by many actors for putting business interests before social considerations. Pressure was growing from the Socialist and Green groups in the European Parliament for the EU to show its social face and improve workers' conditions. Working time, posting of workers, European Works Councils became symbolic files for which both the trade unions and the socialists pushed the European institutions, and in particular the Commission, to take action.

Towards the end of its mandate, the Commission became increasingly sensitive to this pressure and reacted accordingly. It committed itself vis-à-vis the European Parliament's Women's Rights Committee to propose new measures on reconciliation of work and family life. This has been one of the regular demands of the European Parliament (2007a), in particular a review of existing provisions on parental leave. This commitment led to the consultation of social partners in 2006 and 2007, building up realistic chances for new legislative proposals. It prompted employers to safeguard their previous parental leave agreement through negotiations.

Similarly, the European Parliament had on several occasions pushed for a reform of the EWC rules in order to strengthen the effectiveness of information and consultation of workers in transnational companies. In May 2007, it urged the Commission to set a timetable for the 'long-awaited revision of Directive 94/45/EC' in order to provide a coherent and efficient framework of law (European Parliament 2007b). On 1 May 2008 the ETUC, for which the EWC reform was one of the top priorities, launched a campaign for 'stronger European Works Councils' and brought Socialists and Greens behind them, building up additional pressure for Commission to come forward with a proposal.

These two exemplary developments show that the European Parliament, despite not having a formal role in the social dialogue according to the Treaty provisions, has become more influential in pushing social dossiers on the EU agenda, thereby also reactivating the legislative social dialogue. Whether this trend continues or not remains to be seen in view of a less left-leaning European Parliament following the June 2009 elections and the increased focus on growth and stability following the financial and economic crisis that happened around the same time.

Areas where the social partners could again become active as co-legislators, with the European Parliament pushing these dossiers, include working time and paternity leave. The Commission announced a new proposal on the revision of the Working Time Directive, after Council discussions on a previous proposal had failed in April 2009. Such a proposal needs to be preceded by a consultation of social partners under Article 154 TFEU, the second stage of which was launched in December 2010. The Commission's preferred outcome of the consultation would be negotiations and an agreement among the European social partners. However, ETUC already expressed its scepticism about the feasibility of a constructive dialogue on such a sensitive area, where Council was not able to agree even after five years of talks.

Paternity leave is another potential area where the European Parliament action could potentially result in legislative social dialogue. During the ongoing reform of the Pregnant Workers Directive, the European Parliament's Women's Rights Committee aimed at including new provisions on paternity leave into the existing one on maternity leave. Even if this plan might not succeed due to opposition in Council, the Committee is likely to keep pushing the Commission to come forward with new legislative proposals in this area. Depending on the likelihood of agreement on this file in Council at a given moment, employers and trade unions might seize the file after the compulsory consultation stage.

## Conclusion

Autonomous social dialogue and legislative dialogue do not exclude each other. In recent years they have been running in parallel. This was very important to ward off criticism, including from academics and from within the trade union movement, that softer autonomous agreements had replaced hard-law agreements implemented by Directive.

As regards the non-legislative dialogue, trade unions have been successful in obtaining a state of permanent dialogue with the employers' side. This might strengthen the development of a European system of industrial relations, where social partners regularly and institutionally address topics that are relevant to the labour market or individual employment relations.

On the other side, the level of activity of the legislative dialogue depends on the EU's level of ambition in the social domain. Without the threat of the legislative machinery starting to grind, employers still do not agree to establish hard labour norms at own initiative. While in the past it was clearly the role of the Commission to hold up that social ambition, this role might be shifting to the European Parliament. The Commission obviously retains its institutional function in supporting social dialogue, but the Parliament is gradually becoming an indirect promoter of the dialogue by putting forward political demands for a more social Europe.

The division of roles for both dialogues are also becoming clearer. Minimum standards in core labour law issues and social rights still cannot be established without relying on the mechanism of EU law. On the other side, a new field of activity has opened up for social partners to achieve a European model of employment relations through the convergence of working conditions and the definition of broader labour market objectives. In these cases, stringent legislation might be disproportionate and goals can better be achieved through autonomous agreements and other autonomous social dialogue instruments.

## Notes

1 The author is an official working in DG Justice of the European Commission. This chapter is written in his personal capacity and does not necessarily reflect the views of the European Commission.

2 Articles 138 and 139 EC Treaty before the entering into force of the Lisbon Treaty.

3 The subjects of these agreements are: telework (2002), work-related stress (2004), harassment and violence at work (2007) and inclusive labour markets (2010). These and the other social partner instruments mentioned in this chapter are available in the European Commission's database of social dialogue texts, http://ec.europa.eu/social/main.jsp?catId=521&langId=en, accessed 21 October 2011.

4 A new work programme for the period from 2011 is planned, but likely to be adopted after the new ETUC leadership will have been elected (at their Congress in May 2011).

5 Now referred to as 'Europe 2020'.

6 The European social partners delivered annual follow-up reports and final evaluation reports on both their frameworks of action. The final evaluations were adopted in 2006 and 2009 respectively.

7 While the regulation of a new form of work organisation like telework is rather straightforward and can be approached through traditional labour law tools and the concept of mutual rights and obligations in the employer-worker relationship, it is much more difficult to come

to terms with psychosocial risks like work-related stress which can have multiple causes and which are not easily tackled by a regulatory approach. Stress at work cannot simply be prohibited by law. It rather demands a preventive approach adapted to the individual working environment, focused on behavioural aspects and embedded in an overall policy of well-being at work.

8 This may also result from the fact that the stress agreement was already negotiated after the first-stage consultation by the Commission under Article 154 TFEU, since social partners did not await the second stage which is usually more concrete in terms of what the Commission expects as an outcome.

9 Clause 4(7) of the 1995 agreement reads: 'The signatory partners shall review the application of the agreement five years after the date of the Council decision if requested by one of the parties to this agreement.'

## References


*Council Directive 96/34/EC of 3 June 1996 on the Framework Agreement on Parental Leave.*

*Directive 2009/38/EC of the European Parliament and of the Council on the Establishment of a European Works Council or a Procedure in Community-scale Undertakings and Community-scale Groups of Undertakings for the Purposes of Informing and Consulting Employees.*

*Council Directive 2010/18/EU of 8 March 2010 Implementing the Revised Framework Agreement on Parental Leave.*

European Commission (2004), *Partnership for Change in an Enlarged Europe – Enhancing the Contribution of European Social Dialogue*, COM(2004) 557 final.

European Commission (2006), *A Roadmap for Equality between Women and Men 2006–2010*, COM(2006) 92 final.

European Commission (2007), *Communication from the Commission to the Council and the European Parliament Transmitting the European Framework Agreement on Harassment and Violence at Work*, COM(2007) 686 final.

European Commission (2008a), *Report on the Implementation of the European Social Partners' Framework Agreement on Telework*, SEC (2008) 2178.

European Commission (2008b), *Commission Document on Consultation of the European Social Partners [on European Works Councils]*, C/2008/660, 20 February 2008.

European Commission (2008c), *Proposal for a European Parliament and Council Directive on the Establishment of a European Works Council or a Procedure in Community-Scale Undertakings and Community-Scale Groups of Undertakings for the Purposes of Informing and Consulting Employees (Recast)*, COM(2008) 419 final.

European Parliament (2007a), *European Parliament Resolution of 27 September 2007 on Equality between Men and Women in the European Union – 2007* (2007/2065(INI)).

European Parliament (2007b), *European Parliament Resolution of 10 May 2007 on Strengthening European Legislation in the Field of Information and Consultation of Workers* (2007/2546(RSP)).

ETUC (2008), letter to Vladimír Špidla, 11 April 2008

ETUC, UNICE, UEAPME and CEEP (2004), *Framework Agreement on Work-related Stress*, 8 October 2004.

ETUC, BUSINESSEUROPE, UEAPME and CEEP (2008a), *Report on the Implementation of the European Autonomous Framework Agreement on Work-related Stress* adopted at the Social Dialogue Committee on 18 June 2008.

ETUC, BUSINESSEUROPE, UEAPME and CEEP (2008b), *Progress Report: Reconciliation of Professional, Private and Family Life*, 27 February 2008.

ETUC, BUSINESSEUROPE, UEAPME and CEEP (2008c), Joint advice by the Social Partners on the European Works Council 'Recast' Directive, 29 August 2008.

ETUC, BUSINESSEUROPE, UEAPME and CEEP (2009), *Work Programme of the European Social Partners 2009–10.*

MICHAEL KAEDING AND LUKAS OBHOLZER

# 3

# The EU and formalisation of sectoral social dialogue: lessons from the sector of central public administrations

## Introduction

European Commission entrepreneurship and the development of European social dialogue as an important tool of European governance have been closely intertwined. Since the Commission's 1998 initiative to formalise sectoral social dialogue committees (Commission Decision 1998/500), their number has surged to currently forty committees. Sectoral social dialogue committees are supported by the European Commission and produce outcomes of practical importance. Some 145 million workers are covered by the decisions, declarations and agreements of the European social partners (European Commission 2010). The formalisation of a social dialogue is contingent on the social partners' willingness and their fulfilment of three conditions: representativeness, adequate structures for effective participation, and a capacity to negotiate and adopt agreements (see Article 1 of Commission Decision 1998/500). They can discuss and agree on measures of varying degrees of bindingness with regard to their sector. But why are sectoral social dialogue committees formalised and how can we explain their outcomes? This chapter addresses the question as to what extent is the formalisation and conduct of sectoral social dialogue committees an autonomous process of the social partners as opposed to being driven by the European Commission.

The European Commission is considered to be at the 'very heart of the [European Union (EU)] system' (Nugent 2006: 49). This comes with considerable structural power and influence, for instance through agenda-setting, that grants the Commission a strategic advantage and leverage in the general policy making of the EU (Nugent 2001, Christiansen 2001). There are three functions which are of particular relevance for the analysis of the Commission's role in EU policy making: *initiation, mediation and mobilisation* functions (see Moravcsik 1999). Each of the functions facilitates an effective social dialogue and has the potential to further the Commission's preferences. By initiation, we refer to substantive input and agenda-shaping. Mediation denotes policy-shaping interventions inducing agreement in the dialogue. Mobilisation refers to the activation of social partners. In this chapter, we seek to apply these three functions as an analytical framework to the role of the Commission in the formalisation and conduct of sectoral social dialogue, i.e. outside normal policy making. In applying this framework, we will suggest that the Commission plays a pivotal role in sectoral social dialogue and, thereby, we will highlight the Commission's use of sectoral social dialogue as a tool for European governance.

We construct a crucial case study in order to test the role of the Commission in the formalisation and conduct of sectoral social dialogue. To this end, we draw on the recent test phase of a sectoral social dialogue in central public administrations, which culminated in the formalisation of the committee. This represents a least-likely case study (Przeworski and Teune 1970) for Commission influence in sectoral social dialogue. The Commission was represented by the Directorate-General (DG) Personnel and Administration (DG ADMIN, now DG Human Resources and Security) on the employer's side, and by DG Employment, Social Affairs and Equal Opportunities (DG EMPL, now DG Employment, Social Affairs and Inclusion) as the 'convenor'. This gives rise to the expectation that this ambiguity is accompanied by a more passive, impotent DG EMPL in the dialogue as it faces in-house constraints. However, the empirical evidence reveals that against these odds, DG EMPL was a key actor in the dialogue, and acted as a pivotal initiator, mediator and mobiliser in the discussions. Thus, the chapter shows that formalisation and dialogue outcomes are markedly driven by the Commission. This also implies that European social dialogue is a policy instrument for the Commission that provides legitimacy to its preferred policies rather than representing a mere forum for the autonomous interaction of the social partners.

The chapter is structured as follows. First, we will concisely outline the role of the Commission in European social dialogue. Before exploring the case study, we will outline the research design and methodology as well as the empirical data. The case study of the test phase of central public administrations drawing in parts on Kaeding (2008) will start off with a short introduction of the stakeholders involved in the process. We then reveal the changes during the test phase that the 'quasi-formalisation' entailed in terms of: institutions; the quality of the relations between the stakeholders; the efficiency of the structures with regard to outcomes. Throughout, we will analyse the impact of the Commission. A concluding section will discuss the role of the Commission in more depth.

## The European Commission and European social dialogue

In 1985, then Commission President Jacques Delors encouraged cross-industry European employers and trade union organisations to enter into an autonomous dialogue at European level. This so-called *Val Duchesse* process gained more importance with the Treaty of Maastricht and Amsterdam (1992 and 1997 respectively). European social dialogue became institutionalised as a means of consultation of the social partners on social policy initiatives and legislation at the European level (Art. 138 and 139 Treaty Establishing the European Communities (TEC)). The Treaty of Lisbon today explicitly recognises the role of social partners (Art. 152 Treaty on the Functioning of the European Union (TFEU)), the contribution of the tripartite social summit to social dialogue (Art. 152 TFEU), and the larger role for social partners at national level while Member States may entrust social partners with the implementation of directives or of a Council decision (Art. 153(3) TFEU). Thus, the importance of social dialogue for the European social model can be traced back to a Commission's initiative to mobilise the social partners at the European level.

During this process, the Commission has acted as an image-venue entrepreneur in 'reshaping the dominant "image" of EU social policy from one based on social rights to an alternative which emphasises that social policy contributes to stable economic growth and job creation' (Wendon 1998: 339). The Commission argued that European social dialogue complemented national industrial relations practices. Allowing the social partners to assist in the definition of European social standards, they were ascribed a vital role in the governance of the European Union. At the same time, however, the prominent role of the social partners boosted legitimacy of European social policy by relying on a pluralist conception of the EU. Thus, the Commission shaped the broad substantive orientation of dialogue. In addition, this chapter will show the extent to which the current sectoral social dialogue regime also allows the Commission to impact the substantive direction of sectoral social dialogue through its functions as initiator and mediator.

In 1998, the Commission decided to place more emphasis on sectoral social dialogue at European level and introduced the option of establishing sectoral social dialogue committees at the joint request of the European social partners. Sectoral social dialogue had existed before in various informal arrangements. The Commission's decision to formalise the dialogues struck the social partners as a surprise (Dufresne 2006) and provides a further example of the Commission's strategic leadership by implementing exogenous, top-down institutional change (Héritier 2007). The Commission's initiative thus led to the formalisation of all sectoral social dialogue arrangements at the European level as uniform 'Sectoral Social Dialogue Committees'.

The development that formal sectoral social dialogue has taken since the Commission Decision 98/500 is striking. At first sight, it seems to have blossomed as committees have mushroomed. Figure 3.1 depicts the increase in sectoral social dialogue committees since Commission Decision 1998/500. While twenty committees were formalised in the year following the Decision, the number of formalised committees had doubled until the end of 2010. Twelve of these committees are new, i.e. they had not existed as informal committees before 1998. This roughly reflects the pace at which informal committees had been established in the decade before. The Commission thus managed to mobilise social partners across key sectors to either move from an informal to a formal committee or to

**Figure 3.1 Quantitative Development of sectoral social dialogue since Commission Decision 98/500**

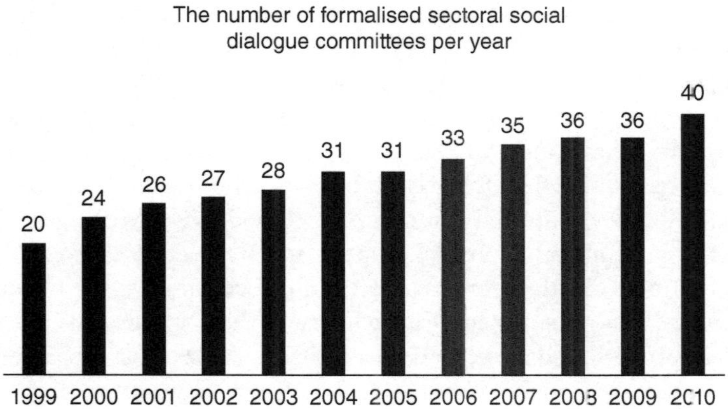


create new formal ones. Be it in spite of or because of the more comprehensive competencies of the formal committees (Branch 2005, de Boer, Benedictus and van den Meer 2005, Welz 2007) formal sectoral social dialogue, as initiated by the Commission, seems to be a success speaking for itself through sheer numbers (for further details on recent developments see Chapters 2 and 4).

However, in contrast to the steep increase in numbers, it is argued that quality of interaction and outcomes have not always followed suit. Keller (2003: 43–4) argues for example that the new social dialogue 'has not led to the hoped-for new quality of negotiated results' since 'the Commission has no means to convince sectoral social partners, especially employers' associations, to become engaged in "their" dialogue'. He also argues that the Commission's fragmented nature results in a lack of coherence impeding it from engaging in sectoral issues, while moreover subsidiarity is considered as a rationale for leaving sectoral initiatives (apart from health and safety) to the social partners. Similarly, Léonard (2008: 402) highlights that 'growing institutionalisation of the European sectoral social dialogue contrasts with a weak regulatory capacity, which is related to difficulty in producing binding norms, and implementing them'. After having created the formalised framework for the dialogue, the Commission apparently plays a more passive role. While the Commission now takes part in the meetings and subsidises sectoral social dialogue, it does not seem to successfully initiate activities, mediate between social partners or mobilise them. In the following, we will revisit these propositions.

## Research design

### *Case selection*

We assess the Commission's role in the process towards the formalisation of the hitherto informal European sectoral social dialogue in central public administrations. The public sector represents a key sector for 'smart, sustainable and inclusive growth' in Europe. It thus is a central success factor for Europe's economic and social model and its long-term sustainability given its importance in the context of public finance issues coupled with demographic trends. We have selected central public administrations as a critical case study (Eckstein 1975) for an analysis of the Commission due to the ambiguous role of the EU institution in this sector. On the one hand, the Commission's DG ADMIN is affiliated with the employers, and on the other hand DG EMPL acts as the convenor providing support to the committee. While DG ADMIN was hesitant with regard to the creation of a formal social dialogue in that it might be included, DG EMPL's general policy agenda is to promote and spread European social dialogue. The central public administration sector, therefore, represents a critical case for the Commission's role. With two DGs pursuing conflicting interests, the Commission's role has been ambiguous; promoting dialogue, on the one hand, while being subject of this test phase as an employer on the other hand. Therefore, the European social dialogue in central public administrations represents a least-likely case study (Przeworski and Teune 1970) for Commission influence on conduct and formalisation of a sectoral committee.

***Data***

In order to assess the so-called social dialogue Test Phase for Central Public Administrations this chapter draws on the evaluation of the first (Kaeding 2008) and second year (Ramböll 2009) of a test phase of an 'enhanced' (or formal) sectoral social dialogue. These consist of a range of research methods, both quantitative and qualitative. Based on a threefold methodological approach, including qualitative, quantitative and benchmarking methods, the findings and conclusions emerged from a sequential process of field and desk research, questionnaire surveys, and in-depth interviews.

Overall, the research strategy for the evaluation comprised four key stages: field research, document research, interviews, surveys and benchmarking. The first step to evaluating the first twelve months of the test phase involved 'shadowing' all meetings relevant to social dialogue. On the employer's side, we attended all Directors-General, Directors-General Troika, Troika Secretariat, Social Dialogue Steering Group, Human Resource Working Group as well as Social Dialogue Working Group and smaller Ad-hoc Working Group meetings with labour. In total, we observed twenty-two meetings directly related to the Social Dialogue Test Phase. This provided unique insights into the development and dynamics of the dialogue and into the impact of the Commission in this respect. Secondly, an early stage of the evaluation involved conducting a documentation review. This phase helped to collect useful information on the activities, management and governance of the Social Dialogue Test Phase for central public administrations and of European social dialogue issues more generally. In a third step, a total of sixty-eight in-depth interviews were carried out either face-to-face or by telephone, with different stakeholder groups: the social partners, including both European and national-level representatives of labour, the European Commission

(DG ADMIN and DG EMPL) and other stakeholders in European social dialogue (such as European Centre of Employers and Enterprises providing Public services (CEEP)). Last but not least, two questionnaires (in three languages) for different constituencies, and with a total of thirty-eight questions, were put online to survey the stakeholders' opinions. Responses from *all* stakeholders led to a final response rate for the survey of 70 per cent.

**Central public administration – a new kid on the block: from the early beginnings to an 'enhanced form' of European social dialogue**

In this section we briefly present the historical and regulatory context of social dialogue in central public administration and introduce the social partners with reference to the European Commission's role. Despite the fact that the EU does not have any concrete competences in this sector, there is a considerable amount of EU legislation with a direct effect on public services. Therefore, social dialogue is also not a new topic for EU central public administrations. In fact, members of the informal European Union Public Administration Network (EUPAN) have been concerned with the issue for almost twenty years. Since the early 1990s, European social dialogue for central government administrations has been on the agenda of Directors-General and Ministers responsible for public administration in the EU Member States, who constitute EUPAN (for a detailed historical overview see Mangenot and Polet 2004 and Demmke 2007).

During the test phase, the social partners sitting on the committee were the European Public Administrations Network (EUPAN) representing the employers, and the Trade Union National and European Delegation (TUNED) representing labour. Established in the late 1970s, EUPAN is a network of the ministries responsible for the civil service in the twenty-seven Member States, to which the Commission (DG ADMIN) is attached as a 'twenty-eighth employer' in an observer's role. The Directors-General provide leadership and supervision for the network. At the helm of the different groups is the country holding the Presidency in the Council of the EU that runs parallel to the EUPAN presidency. Continuity is safeguarded by troika systems including the one or two countries preceding and following the current Presidency. Three working groups assembling experts focussing on Innovative Public Services, e-Government, and Human Resources were complemented from 2008 by a Social Dialogue Group (see EUPAN 2008). This was split off from Human Resources Working Group as an autonomous group for the test phase (Kaeding 2008). With the decision on the formalisation of the dialogue, this group too was formalised as the EU Public Administration Employers (EUPAE) that comprised nine Member States (Belgium, Czech Republic, France, Greece, Italy, Luxembourg, Romania, Spain and the United Kingdom) in early 2011.

TUNED consists of the European Federation of Public Service Unions (EPSU) and the European Confederation of Independent Trade Unions (CESI). EPSU, the largest member of the European Trade Union Confederation (ETUC), represents public sector employees in several other formal sectoral social dialogues, in electricity, gas, hospitals, and, most notably, local and regional government. While a Congress meeting every four years adopts resolutions on the broad objectives, an executive committee and steering committee govern the organisation and its committees on the different dialogues (see EPSU 2009). CESI is the smaller, less representative of the two as a study reflecting the pre-enlargement situation showed (Marmont 2004). CESI tends to take a more pragmatic approach than the collective-bargaining focused EPSU. It has a similar governance structure consisting of a Congress meeting every four years, yearly board meetings and an executive board that is responsible for running the organisation and its specialist committees. Despite a long-running dispute between CESI and ETUC over the rights of representation of workers in the sector, the two confederations set up a joint structure – TUNED – in February 2005. On 25 May 2010, EPSU and CESI signed a revised cooperation agreement, which takes account of internal changes within CESI (European Federation of Public Service Employees is a member of CESI since 2009) and recent developments towards the establishment of a European sectoral social dialogue committee in central government administrations (EPSU and CESI 2010).

Jointly, they acquired a sufficient proportion to represent employees of the sector at European level, thus allowing trials in social dialogue in the central public administrations sector. The delegation is coordinated by EPSU. Plenary meetings and ad-hoc working groups enable the two parties to conduct and coordinate the work of the trade union delegation. EPSU is the designated contact with the Commission and with the employers' delegation in the meeting preparation phase, and keeps CESI regularly informed. TUNED represented trade unions from all twenty-seven Member States except for Slovenia and Poland.

The EUPAN resolutions reveal that despite some attempts by individual Presidencies, the progress regarding social dialogue made over the previous decades was rather sluggish and piecemeal. A new attempt to approach social dialogue was launched under the 2007 German Presidency, when Ministers adopted the so-called 'Action Plan on Social Dialogue'. This plan foresees a two-year test phase for an 'enhanced informal social dialogue'[1] exploring topics and work forms of formal social dialogue. The aim of the test phase would be to re-launch exchanges between EUPAN and TUNED by informally experimenting new forms of relations between them, similar to those in sectoral social dialogue committees.

## Assessing the test phase for a formalised European sectoral social dialogue for central public administrations

Overall, the twenty-four month period of 'enhanced' social dialogue for central government administration can be considered to have been successful and have brought progress in different fields when compared to the previous informal dialogue. The institutional changes brought about, the quality of relationships between stakeholders, and the output produced have been efficient and appropriate with the European Commission playing a distinct role. In the following, we will analyse these three fields with a view to the Commission's role as mediator, facilitator and mobiliser. However, it should be stated at this point that European social dialogue has again been brought to the top of the agenda of the social partners. The regular meetings at different levels between EUPAN and TUNED delegations represented exchanges on substantial issues of importance to employers and employees in the sector. Notwithstanding this progress, there are areas in which the performance of the test phase could be improved. There is room for clarification with regard to the Commission's (future) role in social dialogue for central public administrations, and achieving this would arguably contribute to uncovering the full potential of the sectoral dialogue.

***Institutional changes brought about***

The main institutional changes concerned work forms and organisational arrangements. Firstly, four important documents were adopted by EUPAN and TUNED, laying down the 'rules of the game' and specifying the topics to be addressed during the two-year test phase, as well as the indicators according to which the success of the test phase would be assessed. Rules of procedure and a joint 2008–09 work programme were adopted at the beginning of the Portuguese Presidency in summer 2007, with broad support from all stakeholders. The rules of procedure are modelled on and indeed closely follow those of other sectors, including railways, electricity and local and regional government, which had previously been identified as 'best practices' by the Commission. A more operational Trio Presidential work programme consisting of the coordinated input of three consecutive EU Presidencies (France, Czech Republic and Sweden) was drafted together with TUNED and the European Commission (DG EMPL), and was eventually adopted by EUPAN *and* TUNED members in May 2008, laying down the priorities until the end of 2009. It consisted of three themes, which responded to sector-specific questions as well as to the broader Commission European social dialogue agenda: sustaining efficient administration; building trust in central government administration; violence and harassment at work. Overall, the Commission functioned here as mediator between the stakeholders with regular input based on its experiences in other sectors and the cross-industry dialogue, thus shaping the definitive choice considerably.

Secondly, four new entities were created that provided forums for cooperation between the two sides of industry: the Directors-General plenary on Social Dialogue, the Social Dialogue Steering Group, the Social Dialogue Working Group, and Ad-hoc Working Groups to deal with specific issues whenever the need arises. The more extensive dialogue reflected in the organisational changes has predictably led to an increased workload for the actors on both sides. However, this did not negatively affect the attendance rate in the meetings among the well-resourced EUPAN members. Data on the level of participation for all four Social Dialogue

Working Group meetings during the first year for instance show that a very large number (97 per cent) of the employers were present. This is an exceptionally high figure in comparison to other well-established sectoral social dialogue committees, such as local government, electricity and rail transport. The figures for TUNED, however, look slightly different and provide evidence of the mobilising function of the Commission in establishing a dialogue that is comprehensive with regard to participation of the less well-resourced trade unions. Accordingly, TUNED participation was considerably higher when the Commission provided financial assistance. In addition to financial support, the language barrier was also an impediment to effective dialogue and inclusive participation. The Commission's provision of translation services thus facilitated participation. Despite mobilisation through the European Commission's substantial financial support, representatives from new Member States in particular were barely part of the steadily increasing TUNED delegation. Nevertheless, the mere willingness of the social partners to support a social dialogue is not enough for a dialogue to take place. Through financial support and provision of translation services, the Commission mobilises the social partners. By extension, since formal sectoral social dialogue takes places in this framework, we can categorise the Commission as an initiator of sectoral social dialogue.

Overall, the institutional changes have generally succeeded in meeting the specific objectives of the test phase, namely: exploring practices of formal social dialogue; experimenting with new forms of relations between stakeholders, similar to those in sectoral social dialogue committees; and exploring topics of formal social dialogue. The organisation of the process has been adequate since: its rules of procedure follow the good practice of other sectoral social dialogue committees and the European Commission's Decision 98/500/EC; the eighteen-month Trio Presidential work programme is clearly linked with the joint 2008–09 work programme and relevant activities at European and national levels. Interview data from EUPAN and TUNED members also show that the two chosen themes, 'work-related stress' and 'anticipation of change', are relevant, clear, detailed, of added value and appropriate. Hence, the test phase succeeded in creating a quasi-formal sectoral social dialogue.

Both EUPAN and TUNED members were committed to the test phase, agreeing that social dialogue for central public administration is an appropriate tool for sharing information and discussing issues of common concern. More than 80 per cent of EUPAN and TUNED members have increased their knowledge about and interest in European social dialogue. In particular, EUPAN and TUNED members together have been able to increase their knowledge on the perspectives of their European *and* national counterparts. In this respect, participation in the Commission's sponsored cross-sector workshop on third-party violence at work during the Slovenian Presidency proved to be very suitable. Over 60 per cent of EUPAN and TUNED members have learnt about broader European social policy legislation beyond the test phase experience of social dialogue, such as labour law directives, health and safety policy, issues of social inclusion and protection, equal opportunities and anti-discrimination.

***Quality of relationship between stakeholders***

In order to assess the quality of relationships between stakeholders in the Social Dialogue Test Phase, we examined relations between EUPAN and TUNED; between EUPAN/TUNED and the European Commission; and between EUPAN/TUNED and other actors in the European social dialogue. The analysis revealed much progress in improving the quality of relationships, thus suggesting that a formal sectoral social dialogue allows more constructive dialogue than the previous informal arrangements. This can be considered as counterintuitive as informal arrangements might be expected to allow for a more frank, unconstrained exchange.

Overall, employers and trade union representatives have succeeded in implementing an increasingly constructive dialogue. In total, 81 per cent of the stakeholders stated that the quality of the relations between them had improved over the first year of the test phase. This is mainly attributed to three developments: the intensification of contacts between EUPAN and TUNED (more than 60 per cent), the considerable improvement of the level of trust (more than 80 per cent), and the adoption of 'joint decisions' by consensus. Likewise, the test phase brought about more equitable relations between the social partners. While the internal coordination within TUNED appears to be more consensual compared with the informal EUPAN network, the Trio Presidential work programme – despite some divergence within EUPAN – was adopted by agreement. Employer and trade union representatives have also intensified their relationships with other actors of social dialogue; whereas contacts with the *national* counterparts have systematically increased, both among EUPAN and TUNED members (more than 60 per cent).

As regards to relations with the European Commission, views are also positive. Contacts have intensified, both with EUPAN and TUNED members (more than 30 per cent). Furthermore, the European Commission has increasingly become more actively involved by informing EUPAN and TUNED members about relevant developments on European social dialogue topics. This addresses a need highlighted by EUPAN and TUNED members. They identified several challenges as regards to their mutual relations. Next to the building of trust between parties, which has been considered essential, more than 60 per cent of EUPAN and TUNED members have identified the following key challenges: the need to increase knowledge about European Social Dialogue; the different levels of skills in delegations (language, group management, negotiation, diplomatic skills, etc.); the need to increase commitment by social partners; the unclear mandate of EUPAN; the representativeness of employers' and trade union representatives; and the diversity of national industrial relation systems. While some of these will prove to be long-term challenges, the Commission actively works towards alleviating the first two impediments.

With regard to the Commission's role, views have been mixed. As observer and facilitator the Commission is widely appreciated by EUPAN and TUNED members alike. However, these actors have different views about the European Commission's level of activism. Whereas some TUNED members would like the European Commission to become more involved as a policy initiator, most members of EUPAN welcome the European Commission's 'passive role'. This should not hide the fact that the Commission did initiate activities. For instance, some of the social partners participated in the cross-sector workshop on 'Third-party violence at work' in Brussels on 12 March 2008. Organised by the European Commission (DG EMPL) in cooperation with four sectoral social dialogue committees (local and regional government, hospitals, commerce and private security), the aim was to exchange specific country/sectoral examples to complement the Cross-Sectoral Autonomous Agreement on Violence and Harassment at Work. Three sectors – central public administration, electricity and education – were invited as observers to the workshop. Those attending the workshop considered the experience to be positive. The Commission's initiative allowed an increased number of contacts with other stakeholders in European social dialogue, and most importantly informed further discussions around the broader issue of 'violence and harassment at work and work-related stress' in the subsequent Social Dialogue Working Group meetings.

***Efficiency of structures: outcomes***

The institutional changes of the Social Dialogue Test Phase for central public administrations and the concomitantly changed relationships between the actors have proven to be productive and efficient. This holds both when compared to the output generated before the test phase *and* to that agreed on by other sectoral social dialogues. First of all, the test phase has produced two major outputs within a limited period of time due to the Commission's financial support: an application for a joint EU Project on 'Improving Trust'; and a Joint Position on work-related stress. In addition, EUPAN and TUNED have participated in one consultation process launched by the European Commission (DG EMPL) on the future of European social dialogue (amendment proposal to European Commission Decision 98/500).

Notwithstanding this progress, there are a number of areas in which the efficiency of structures could be further enhanced. Social dialogue is not an end in itself, but it is an instrument to promote social partners' goals and interests in a specific sector. Therefore, sector specificities need to be identified in order to gain high-quality output. A definition of priority areas would need to take into account national-level characteristics and activities such as the definition and the particularity of the central public administration sector. Depending on the Member State, the notion of central public administration may include or exclude certain subsectors (teachers, medical personnel, armed forces, police, prison officers, forestry workers, judicial personnel). In an ideal world, this identification of national level needs and realities would *precede* any definition of themes of common interest and action at the European level. In particular, this reveals to what extent the Commission has driven the social dialogue. While the topics have of course not been imposed by the Commission, we can appreciate to what extent the Commission's entrepreneurship steers the dialogue. Thereby, social dialogue becomes an instrument for governance of the European Commission, albeit it is eventually an autonomous process between the social partners.

The Trust Project was financed by the Commission and arguably came closest to a formalised form of social dialogue during the first twelve months of the test phase. In a relatively short period of time, both delegations together submitted their project 'Improving trust in central government administration through effective Social Dialogue', which was eventually approved by the European Commission (DG EMPL) on 29 June 2008. It covers all twenty-seven EU Member States, plus the Candidate Countries, and it is clearly linked to the Slovenian priority on trust, the Trio Presidential programme on anticipation of change and TUNED's consecutive priorities, such as the role of social dialogue, employees' rights and how to ensure quality change in public administration. Overall, both EUPAN and TUNED members evaluated the project very positively. A clear incentive for the application was the financial support of nearly €200,000 for travel, translation, and dissemination of results. On this basis, several follow-up measures were possible. It would be worth evaluating in more depth to what extent a selective allocation of funds by the Commission can function as a gate-keeping mechanism encouraging topics on the Commission's agenda.

At the same time, the project has shown that EUPAN and TUNED operate differently. While TUNED operates in a 'negotiation mode', the informal EUPAN network follows a 'discussion model', where members exchange experiences and thoughts on specific issues. This opened up room for the European Commission as a mediator between the two sides of the industry. Likewise, it became evident that EUPAN lacked a mechanism for defining clear mandates before meeting TUNED delegates. During the 'negotiation phase' of the Trust project with TUNED for example, the Slovenian Presidency suffered heavily from an unclear definition of mandate from its EUPAN colleagues. While TUNED spoke with 'one voice', EUPAN members transformed this meeting into a 'social multilogue'. An unclear EUPAN mandate delivered inefficient solutions, i.e. an uncoordinated, cumbersome, and complicated exchange with the TUNED delegation. It remains to be seen to what extent the newly founded employers' organisation EUPAE will be able to overcome this.

The second major output of the Social Dialogue Test Phase is the 'Joint Position of EUPAN and TUNED on work-related stress in central government administrations'. Adopted on 19 December 2008 under the French Presidency, it recognises that a good working environment is a precondition for healthy and attractive workplaces and for ensuring quality and efficiency in carrying out the job. Nonetheless, the text remains rather vague and unspecific towards the specific needs of the central public administration sector with regard to work-related stress. This, however, is in line with most of the other joint positions adopted in comparable sectors such as electricity, railways, and local and regional government. While follow-up monitoring actions were foreseen that might increase the awareness and understanding of work-related stress within central government administrations more specifically, the Joint Position is in line with a broader EU-level initiative on work-related stress. This underscores the inter-sectoral nature of sectoral social dialogue and the leadership of the Commission, which will be summarised in the conclusion.

## Conclusion: the European Commission as a strategic leader in sectoral social dialogue

During the test phase for an enhanced form of social dialogue for central public administrations the European Commission's role was central, despite its ambiguous role in the sectoral social dialogue committee. Being both a member of the EUPAN (DG ADMIN) and the promoter of European social dialogue in the EU (DG EMPL), the European Commission has been accelerating and constraining the formalisation of the social dialogue in a sector which is important in the implementation of any long-term EU economic and social strategy. Efficient public services are one of the pillars of social cohesion. Additionally, extensive, performing public services are an important *Standortfaktor* for Europe.

The European Commission has combined being a passive observer with being an active initiator, mediator and mobiliser. Data suggest that at the surface, the most tangible feature was the Commission's presence at all social dialogue related working group meetings in Ljubljana, Bled, Paris, Prague, Stockholm, Malmö and Brussels, as member of EUPAN (DG ADMIN), but also as 'observer' (DG EMPL). However, DG EMPL could clearly enlarge the margins of room for action by providing substantial financial assistance to run, for example, a joint EU project on 'Improving Trust'. The financial support helped mobilise the sectoral partners. Even though these initiatives, such as the consultation process launched by DG EMPL on the future of European social dialogue (amending proposal to European Commission Decision 98/500) were constrained by the actors and had to accommodate their interests to be successful, this also exemplifies the Commission's agenda-shaping role by acting as an initiator.

Moreover, the Commission was very successful in mediating between both sides when drafting a joint position on work-related stress, thus engaging in policy-shaping. It was the Commission's backstage assistance which eventually facilitated an agreement under the French Presidency. Interestingly, the Commission has always been perceived as a unitary actor. The assessment of the European Commission's conduct on the committee by the social partners reveals that many interviewees did not sufficiently distinguish between DG ADMIN and DG EMPL. Overall, the European Commission was seen more as a silent participant in social dialogue meetings, rather than an active mediator. Whereas EUPAN welcomed this, TUNED interview partners would have preferred to see the Commission play a more active role.

In addition to its mediating role, the Commission helped to link up with other (cross-) sectoral social partners (CEEP, Council of European Municipalities and Regions) in order to include additional stakeholders in the policy-making process and to build support coalitions. Given the omnipresent debate on the democratic deficit in the Commission, the institution thus seeks to bolster and legitimise its positions. Peters (2001: 90) has highlighted that a great deal of agenda-setting and policy entrepreneurship in the EU is the 'mobilisation of knowledge and political power', partly motivated by the lack of resources on the part of the Commission, in order to support the 'social and political construction of a policy' (*ibid.*: 78). Therefore, the Commission has engaged in what Mazey and Richardson (2001: 218) have termed the 'art of strategic group politics' in which the Commission can be conceptualised as a 'purposeful opportunist' seeking to expand and create policy domains, such as the extension of European social dialogue, while regulating the interactions with third parties to its own benefit.

More generally speaking, the test phase's interactions have been structured by rules and procedures similar to those of formalised sectoral social dialogue committees. Adopting Héritier's (2007) angle on institutional change, this has been a process driven both endogenously and exogenously. First, it has been agreed upon and has been implemented by the stakeholders following the Commission's model laid down in its Decision 1998/500. Second, however, this has been due to an exogenous environment providing strong incentives. Not only has the Commission acted as facilitator, the perceived exclusion from consultation has arguably been a key reason for the test phase. Moreover, it has been highlighted that the agreement on a test phase was the result of a long chain of events. The progress over two years in terms of working structures, practices and output has thus led to a formalisation of the social dialogue for central public administrations and has facilitated to closely focus attention on addressing the needs of its key stakeholders at the European level. The institutional changes highlighted here, the improvements in the relationships between the stakeholders and the output produced have provided an empirical rationale for the pursuit of formalisation of sectoral social dialogues by the social partners. Thus, they suggest a tentative answer to the question of why sectoral social dialogue committees are formalised. At the same time, we have shed light on the initiating, mediating and mobilising roles of the Commission in this formalisation and the conduct of the committee, thus presenting evidence of the key driving force that the Commission is in sectoral social dialogue. This has suggested the practical constraints to our understanding of sectoral social dialogue as an autonomous process between the social partners. While this is formally the case, the Commission in practice is a force to be reckoned with.

## Notes

1 Note that EUPAN used the term 'enhanced form of informal social dialogue' to not prejudge any outcome of the test phase.

## References

Branch, A. (2005), 'The Evolution of the European Social Dialogue Towards Greater Autonomy: Challenges and Potential Benefits', *International Journal of Comparative Labour Law and Industrial Relations* 21:2, 21–46.

Christiansen, T. (2001), 'The European Commission: Administration in Turbulent Times', pp. 95–114 in Richardson, J. (ed.), *European Union: Power and Policy-making*, London and New York: Routledge.

de Boer, R., Benedictus, H. and van den Meer, M. (2005), 'Broadening without Intensification: The Added Value of the European Social and Sectoral Dialogue', *European Journal of Industrial Relations* 11:1, 51–70.

Demmke, C. (2007), *Possibilities and Limitations of a Further Development of the Social Dialogue at the EU Level for the Public Services of the Member States - Social Dialogue within the Scope of EUPAN*, Maastricht: EIPA.

Dufresne, A. (2006), 'The Evolution of Sectoral Industrial Relations Structures in Europe', in Dufresne, A., Degryse, C. and Pochet, P. (eds), *The European Sectoral Social Dialogue: Actors, Developments and Challenges*, Brussels: Peter Lang, 49–82.

Eckstein, H. (1975), 'Case Study and Theory in Political Science', pp. 79–138 in Greenstein, F. and Polsby, N. (eds), *Handbook of Political Science*, Reading, MA: Addison-Wesley.

EPSU (2009), *Who are We?*, www.epsu.org/IMG/pdf/EPSU_sheets_090305_EN.pdf, accessed 1 August 2010.

EPSU and CESI (2010), *Cooperation Agreement between EPSU and CESI European Sectoral Social Dialogue in National Administration*, www.epsu.org/a/6574, accessed 10 April 2011.

EUPAN (2008), *The EUPAN-Handbook*, www.eupan.si/uploads/media/EUPAN_Handbook.doc, accessed 1 August 2010.

European Commission (2001), *European Governance - A White Paper*, COM (2001) 428 final.

European Commission (2010), *Commission Staff Working Document on the Functioning and Potential of European Sectoral Social Dialogue*, SEC (2010) 964 final.

Héritier, A. (2007), *Explaining Institutional Change in Europe*, Oxford: Oxford University Press.

Kaeding, M. (2008), *Mid Term Evaluation of the Social Dialogue Test Phase for Central Public Administrations*, Maastricht: EIPA.

Keller, B. (2003), 'Social dialogues - the State of the Art a Decade after Maastricht', *Industrial Relations Journal* 34:5, 411–29.

Léonard, E. (2008), 'European Sectoral Social Dialogue: an Analytical Framework', *European Journal of Industrial Relations* 14:4, 401–19.

Mangenot, M. and Polet, R. (2004), *European Social Dialogue and the Civil Services: Europeanisation by the Back Door?* Maastricht: EIPA.

Marmont, M. (2004), *Institutional Representativeness of Trade Unions and Employers' Organisations in the 'Central Public Services'*, Louvain: Institut des Services du Travail.

Mazey, S. and Richardson, J. (2001), 'Interest Groups and EU Policy-making: Organisational Logic and Venue Shopping', pp. 217–38 in Richardson, J. (ed.), *European Union: Power and Policy-making*, London and New York: Routledge.

Moravcsik, A. (1999), 'A New Statecraft? Supranational Entrepreneurs and International Cooperation', *International Organization* 53:2, 267–306.

Nugent, N. (2001), *The European Commission*, London: Palgrave.

Nugent, N. (2006), 'Political Dynamics in an Enlarged Europe', pp. 91–108 in Stephanou, C. (ed.), *Adjusting to EU Enlargement: Recurring Issues in a New Setting*, London: Edward Elgar.

Peters, G. (2001), 'Agenda-setting in the European Union', pp. 77–94 in Richardson, J. (ed.), *European Union: Power and Policy-making*, London and New York: Routledge.

Przeworski, A. and Teune, H. (1970), *The Logic of Comparative Social Inquiry*, New York: Wiley.

Ramböll (2009), *Evaluation of the Test-Phase of Enhanced Informal Social Dialogue for Central Public Administrations*, Stockholm: Swedish Agency for Government Employers.

Welz, C. (2007), 'The European Social Dialogue Under Articles 154 and 155 of the EC Treaty: Actors, Processes, Outcomes', unpublished Ph.D. dissertation. Nijmegen: Nijmegen School of Management, Radboud Universiteit.

Wendon, B. (1998), 'The Commission as Image-venue Entrepreneur in EU Social Policy', *Journal of European Public Policy* 5:2, 339–53.

*Evélyne Léonard, Emmanuelle Perin and Philippe Pochet*

# 4

# The European sectoral social dialogue as a tool for coordination across Europe?[1]

## Introduction

Since the 1960s, the European sectoral social dialogue has been bringing employer and trade union representatives from the different member states together around the table in Brussels, and in numerous multilateral contacts across the countries.

In 2011, the European social dialogue is not considered by many academics an arena for industrial relations in the 'classic' meaning of the term, since it rarely leads to 'hard' regulation and does not correspond to restricted notions of negotiation or collective bargaining leading to agreements that would generate enforceable rules, particularly on the core issue of wages and working conditions (see for instance De Boer, Benedictus and van der Meer 2005, Keller 2005, Ose 2011). Nevertheless, it is deemed to act as a different type of instrument, either as a political tool contributing to coordination with European policies (Dufresne and Pochet 2006), or as a socio-political process progressively developing and potentially contributing to the European integration and to the emergence of a multilevel system of industrial relations in the future (Marginson and Keune 2011).

At sectoral level, the forty committees active in 2011 bring together representatives from all over the European Union (EU) and produce a number of joint texts that may not be comparable to 'traditional' collective agreements as they exist at national level (Degryse and Pochet 2011).

This chapter analyses to what extent the European sectoral social dialogue actually acts as a networking platform and plays a coordinating role across the member states of the EU. In other words, to what extent are the European sectoral social partners able to unite, or at least combine, the interests of national constituencies who act in contexts that are economically, socially and politically very diversified, and who are embedded in different industrial relations regimes giving them different roles, capacities, objectives and strategies (Perin and Léonard 2011).

The question of coordination with the national constituencies also has two sides: firstly, 'upstream', when the European social partners have to try to integrate a diversity of interests among their own national members, to set up an agenda and to engage in discussions with the 'other side of industry' at European level; and secondly, 'downstream', when a given text has to be implemented or transposed in each national context. National members are embedded in their own institutional bodies and procedures that directly influence the implementation process and its feasibility, considering the weak degree of constraint involved in European sectoral social dialogue texts (Keller 2005). Even if it is not the main argument in this chapter (for a more in-depth analysis, see Ose 2011), the problem of implementing the agreed texts is one of the main challenges facing the social dialogue at both sectoral and cross-sectoral level.

This chapter focuses on the 'vertical' dimension of coordination as defined by Traxler (2002) in terms of relationships between the representatives involved in collective bargaining and their constituencies. For the European sectoral social dialogue, vertical coordination is constituted by the relationships between the European trade union and employer organisations participating in the sectoral committees with the national member organisations in the member states.

From a European perspective, this question is more complex than it seems: coordination is not an easy task when 'the two sides of the industry' have to represent member organisations from twenty-seven countries, who have a variety of resources, constraints and strategies, who are all embedded within highly differing institutional contexts and who face a variety of social, economic and political challenges. The outcomes are also very different from what the national industrial relations systems produce. Most of the respondents, when talking about the national systems of collective bargaining and the European social dialogue, refer to 'two parallel worlds'. The coordination must be seen, then, as a process rather than a stable framework.

In order to examine this question of coordination between the European sectoral social dialogue and the sectoral players in the member states, the chapter raises five sub-questions: firstly, how can we analyse theoretically the loose framework of an emerging multi-level institution (the sectoral social dialogue). Secondly, to what extent are European sectoral social partners able to federate national interests and constitute coalitions among their diverse national constituencies? Thirdly, what is the degree of the national members' commitment and participation in the European sectoral social dialogue committees? Fourthly, coping with heterogeneity and with various degrees of participation, how can the European sectoral social dialogue committees build up a common agenda and what is the content of this agenda? And finally, to what extent are European sectoral social dialogue committees capable of coordinating the national players when it comes to the key question of the implementation of joint texts in the member states?

The first section presents a brief overview of recent literature. We highlight the dynamics and tensions between the formal institutional framework and their interpretation by the key players. For this, it is necessary to build up a picture taking into account both the formal institutions and the actors at play.

The second section examines the variety of the European social partners' membership, considering the fact that heterogeneity in the membership constitutes, as such, a challenge for vertical coordination, since it makes it more difficult to unite a variety of interests and to find a common ground on which to start any dialogue.

In the third section, the chapter analyses whether the national organisations are committed to and participate in the European sectoral social dialogue, and to what extent. It shows that the national member organisations' degree of participation varies largely, from active involvement to simple absence.

Given the heterogeneity of the national interests that have to be represented in the European sectoral social dialogue, and given the various support from national members, can the European sectoral social dialogue committees build up a common agenda for discussion between employers and trade unions? Finding a common ground is a key issue for the European players, not only between management and labour, but also between the different national constituencies

The fourth section analyses results in term of joint texts and content of the work programmes defined by the committees for the years 2006–08, in order to understand on which topics and issues they can find leeway for coordination.

The fifth section then investigates the 'downstream' part, looking at the issue of the implementation of the European joint texts in the member states and the possibility for the European players to coordinate the implementation of their joint texts once a common agenda has led to the conclusion of a document, be it a set of recommendations or an agreement.

The chapter draws from two research projects conducted for the European Foundation for the Improvement of Living and Working Conditions, Dublin. The first one on 'New structures, forms and processes of governance in European industrial relations' (Léonard, Erne, Marginson *et al.* 2007) was conducted in 2006–07 and included semi-structured interviews with forty-nine respondents: European social partners, national players and academic experts. The second project focused specifically on the sectoral social dialogue (Pochet, Peeters, Léonard *et al.* 2009) and included in-depth interviews with forty-five sector-level respondents at European and national level. This project also included data from original databases including, amongst others, the sectoral committees' work programmes. Secondary data collected by the European Foundation (Glassner 2008, Traxler 2007) have also been used to examine specific sectoral cases.[2]

## The European sectoral social dialogue: institutions and players

The European sectoral social dialogue is rooted in the creation of the European Community. Between 2000 and 2010, several developments have resulted in changes in its institutional foundations, structures and scope: the inclusion of social dialogue, in general, in the Maastricht Social Agreement and, later, in articles 138 and 139 of the Treaty Establishing the European Community (EC Treaty); the transformation of older joint committees and informal work parties into homogenous 'sectoral social dialogue committees' by the Commission decision of 20 May 1998 (CEC 1998a, Pochet 2005a, 2005b, 2006a, 2006b); and the creation of new committees (up to thirty-six in 2008).

Certain important sectors have obtained recognition only recently: the chemical industry or local and regional government were both established in 2004, steel in 2006; four other sectoral committees have been set up since 2005 (hospitals in 2006; gas and catering in 2007; football in 2008). Three other sectors (non-ferrous metals, the automotive industry and cycling) have submitted a formal request to create a committee. The growing number of committees is in itself an indication of mounting interest. Another interesting indicator is the number of the documents adopted by the social partners, with almost 380 joint texts adopted by the social partners over the period 1999–2009 (see Figure 4.1).

**Figure 4.1: Number of documents per year (1999–2010) (418 documents)**

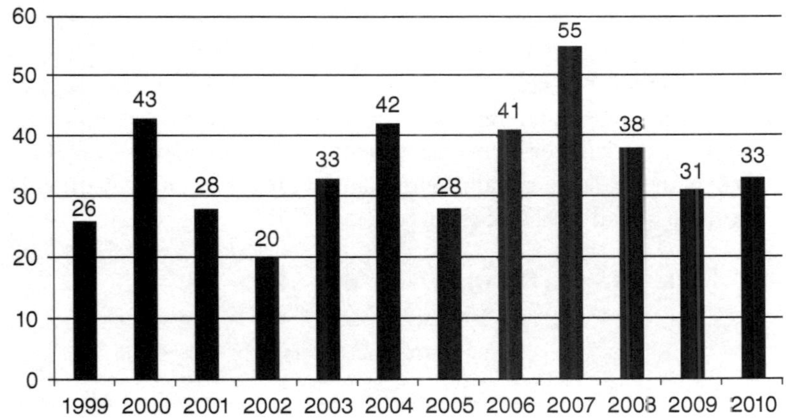


From a quantitative perspective, the number of committees and of texts indicates that much activity is taking place and that it leads to joint outcomes. However, this optimistic point of view must be tempered, since less than 2 per cent of the texts adopted at sectoral level are agreements with binding effect (Pochet 2005b, 2006b) and only 10 per cent are 'recommendations' which look like 'soft law' but recent research shows a trend toward more binding texts (Degryse and Pochet 2011).

If one looks at the legal and formal dimensions of the committees and their joint texts, they do not act as an industrial relations arena in the strict sense, defined as a set of practices and rules that regulate relationships between employees, employers and the state in companies, sectors or a whole country (Lallement 2008).

This does not mean however that they have no consequence, at the very least they offer a common lobbying platform oriented towards influencing European policies (Dufresne and Pochet, 2006). They could also, for example, play a role in exchanging ideas and experiences from different points of view, in 'capacity-building' initiatives in the new Member States (where sectoral bargaining is weak or non-existent).

According to Didry and Mias (2005), European social dialogue supports the building of new collective identities that transcend the traditional memberships with the objective to produce joint opinions and recommendations about labour issues in Europe. The actors involved in the European social dialogue form a network with transnational objectives. Trubek, Mosher and Rothstein (2000) argue the European social dialogue constitutes a good example of what they call a 'transnational advocacy network' able to form transnational multi-level labour regulation.

It is, as a network, that we will consider the ability of the European sectoral social dialogue to coordinate diverse national interests or in other words, from these interactions between the national social partners emerges a 'transnational network' with joint objectives on European social issues.

However, the social actors are not evolving in a vacuum. Their actions take place within particular and diverse national contexts. In order to examine the role that institutions play, but also how actors interact and coordinate, Mayntz and Scharpf (2001) provide an interesting starting point. They propose an integrative theoretical framework (actor-centred neo-institutionalism), combining actors and institutions, with a view to explaining regulation processes and self-organisation at play at macro-social level (see Figure 4.2).

**Figure 4.2 Mayntz and Scharpf's analytical model**

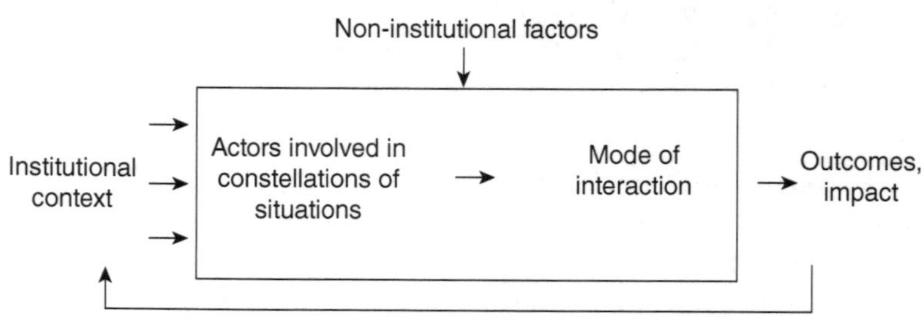


With this model, Mayntz and Scharpf conceptualise the relationship between institutions and social actors. They insist on the necessity of integrating all relevant players who intervene, directly or indirectly, in the field of social regulation. They remind us that, although a given institutional context defines limitations or opportunities for action, it does not determine the action itself. So, although each actor's actions are constrained or promoted by the institutional context, they are not entirely pre-determined. This explains why, in a similar institutional context, there are changes in the players' action, and why different actors can adopt diverging strategies in a common context. As a new framework is being created at European level, the institutional constraints are softened. At the same time, the creativity (and the freedom to innovate or to be path breaker) of actors is more important in shaping new institutions which are different from those at national level.

The analytical model proposed by Mayntz and Scharpf (2001) can be adapted to reflect the multi-level character of the European sectoral social dialogue. The system is a multi-level one in which institutions and players at European level intervene directly, but it also implies complex relationships including a variety of national organisations and institutional structures.

In analysing the context, the interplay between the European and national institutions and players must be taken into account. The relationship with the member states is a key issue, notably in terms of networking, coordination, mandate from national players to their European representatives, and implementation of texts. The relationships with the national institutions and the national-level sectoral players define a second complex set of constraints and opportunities for the European players.

As Béthoux, Jobert, Machu *et al.* (2008) note, the relevance of a specific arena of social dialogue mainly depends on the collective actors' capacity to structure themselves in this arena and to develop action at this level. This capacity, in turn, is determined by the actors' perception of the political, economic and social context at this level, and by the extent to which they find it a relevant and meaningful terrain in which to develop their own actions. In this sense, the relationships with the affiliates is a key dimension, since they will determine whether the constituencies will accept action at a given level, will support it and will give a mandate to their representatives to act at this specific level.

## Representing heterogeneous members

To what extent do European sectoral social partners have the capacity to federate national interests and constitute coalitions among their national constituencies in order to develop their own action and priorities at European level? Data on the demarcation of the sector in the member states therefore give an interesting indication of the degree of homogeneity or heterogeneity of a given sector across countries, and this indirectly indicates the degree of difficulty in defining a 'common ground' at European level.

The membership of each European sectoral social partner covers organisations in all member states, with a variety of sizes, roles, structure, etc. A first source of variation is the scope of the national member organisations: the different members do not necessarily cover the same sectoral perimeter. Traxler (2007) differentiates four types of situation:

- there is 'congruence', the perimeter of the organisations in a given country corresponds to the NACE demarcation;[3]

- case of 'sectionalism', the organisations' perimeter is narrower than the NACE demarcation;
- there is 'overlap' when the organisations cover not only the NACE perimeter but also parts of other sectors;
- finally, 'sectional overlap' refers to situations where the organisations cover parts of the NACE perimeter and parts of other sectors.

To illustrate this diversity, let us present very briefly and schematically the case of postal services which at first sight should be rather homogeneous.

In courier services, at European level, the definition of the sector is given by the codes NACE 64.1, including NACE 64.11, national post activities, and NACE 64.12, courier services other than national post activities.

Since the late 1990s, the sector has undergone major changes that directly affect its scope. Regalia (2007) particularly points to liberalisation, but also the diversification of operators and of their characteristics, the increase and diversification of the services provided, the definition of a universal guaranteed service, and the redefinition and harmonisation of regulations and operations in postal services, in accordance with European directives. In particular, liberalisation started after the 1997 directive, which constituted a major challenge: 'the sector is divided between a single main provider, mostly the former monopolistic public post companies, and various private companies that differ strongly in terms of their size and market shares' (Glassner 2008: 3).

Hence, the sector as such is undergoing deep transformation, and the European social partners – Union Network International (UNI-) Europa and Posteurop – have to face both heterogeneity and change.

As for trade unions in postal services, no national member organisation corresponds to the perimeter of the sector as NACE 64.1 defines it. In Bulgaria, Hungary and Poland, the trade unions represent a part of the sector as delineated by the NACE code; in most countries, they cover a larger perimeter, or a part of the sector plus parts of other branches (Glassner 2008 see also Figure 4.3).

Heterogeneity, however, is smaller on employer side, where the national members are mostly single companies that are the former monopolistic operators (Figure 4.4).

Again, although this clearly highlights the heterogeneity of the national situations, it also indicates that national members potentially represent different socio-economic realities and diversified interests that are difficult to combine in a coalition at European level.

On the employers' side, the national members of Posteurop are mostly individual companies that are the former monopoly postal firms. Employer organisation structures, therefore, do not correspond to what is traditionally called 'sectoral social partners'. There is also an asymmetry between the employers' representatives, who represent companies, and the trade unions that mostly represent the sector or parts of it. There is greater symmetry of employer organisations across countries than of trade unions, but this is associated with the prevalence of single-employer industrial relations in the former monopolistic enterprises.

**Figure 4.3 'Domain coverage' of trade unions in postal services**

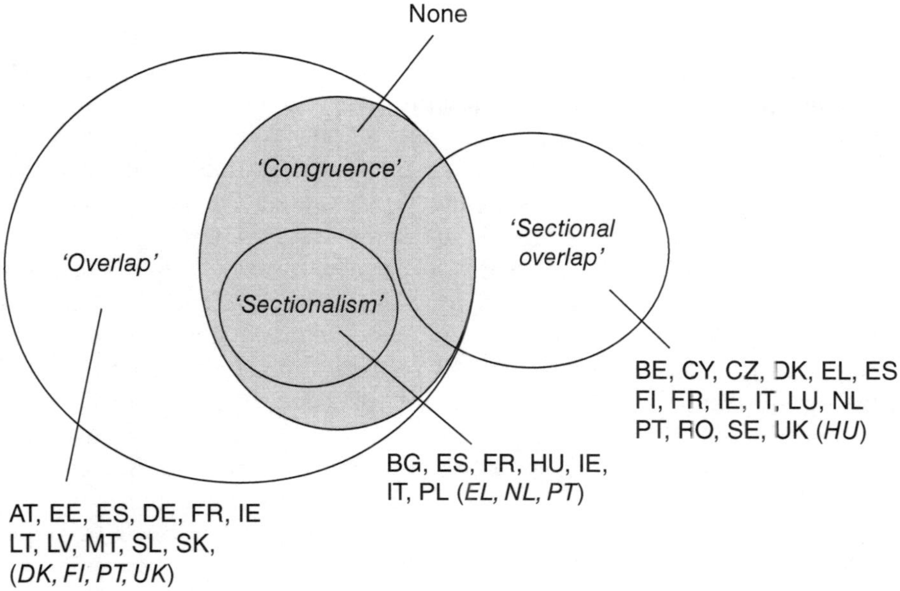


**Figure 4.4 'Domain coverage' of employer organisations in postal services**

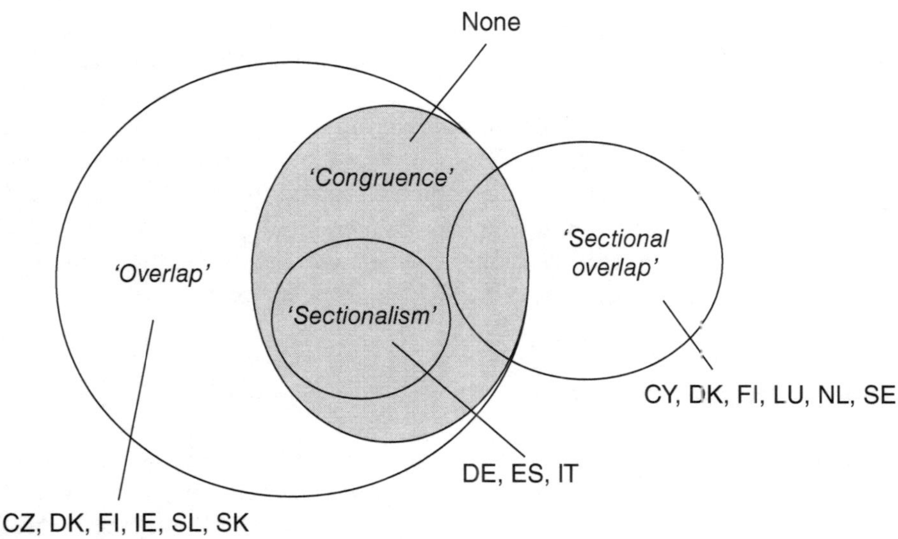


Nevertheless, heterogeneity generates greater difficulty in defining common positions within European associations. A founding member of the postal committee stated that 'The committee has been created in the context of sector liberalisation. The interests of PostEurop members were not the same in this context, and there was more divergence between countries than between trade unions and employers'.

Data in postal services display high coverage rates – over 50 per cent – in nearly all countries except Cyprus and Poland (Glassner 2008). Only in Denmark, Finland, Germany, Slovenia and Sweden is there a multi-employer bargaining (and to a lesser extent in Ireland). This clearly reflects the structure of the players themselves, in a sector where a single company plays the key role in social dialogue in most countries, leading to single-employer bargaining that, at the same time, covers a majority of the workforce in the sector (Glassner 2008).

To sum up, the European sectoral social partners do not only have to represent national member organisations that live in different countries and speak different languages. In addition, they represent member organisations that do not cover the same socio-economic reality, and that have different missions, different types of structures, and different roles in their domestic system of industrial relations.

Institutionally, they have to cope with path-dependency of domestic structures and bodies of industrial relations, which determine the role and 'domain coverage' of the member organisations. They also have to work with national member organisations whose resources, constraints and strategies vary greatly from one country to another.

The situation, however, differs from one sector to another, since the membership structure varies. Some have a more homogenous membership, with direct interlocutors in the sector or directly at company level (post and sugar, for instance); others are composed of 'social partner' structures that can play a role in collective bargaining at sector level but with a weak link to companies or workers (agriculture); others also consist of members who are not 'social partners' as such.

Therefore, defining a common interest does not only present a difficulty because European trade unions and employers have to cope with complex European issues and have different interests. It also involves much intra-organisational negotiation, in a context where it could be difficult to find common ground among national member organisations, which have different missions and interests because they act in sectors that are defined differently from one country to another, which are structured differently, and which play different roles.

## Different levels of participation

Beyond the formal organisation of the committee and the coordination role of the umbrella organisations, there are other factors likely to explain the national players' degree of involvement in a given committee's activity. From the results of the interviews conducted with national actors, one can identify three degrees of commitment in the committees:

- some national actors are central to the dynamics of the committee through proactive involvement;

- others also participate, but on a more 'ad hoc' basis and with a rather reactive position;
- the remaining group includes the absent players (for various reasons).

These categories have been proposed to illustrate the different types of involvement of the national actors within the committees. Nevertheless, they are not static, and actors are able to switch from one category to another one. As presented in our theoretical framework, the analysis of the action of actors is essential to understand the building of new and emerging institutions.

### *Committees' central players*

Some national players are closely involved in the decision-making process through their work in specific working groups or smaller group meetings. They bring their national inputs to the committee and usually have an underlying intention for the European social dialogue. Most of these actors are convinced of the necessity of transnational relationships and believe in the development of a European dimension in social matters.

Besides material reasons such as human and financial resources, which facilitate or favour active participation, the organisations' strategic and political objectives can explain the active presence and involvement of the actors. The impact of European integration on the sectors and the national context appear as factors likely to explain a large part of the strategies adopted by the actors and the reasons for their active commitment (Pochet, Degryse and Dufresne 2004).

A first set of objectives consists of trying to influence European policies and to act accordingly before any unilateral decision by the Commission. In agriculture, the social partners operate in a sector highly impacted by European policies, and one of the objectives frequently cited by the respondents is to act jointly or individually to try to influence the reform of the common agricultural policies. In postal services, the social partners intend to weight on the liberalisation process and to set common working conditions among the twenty-seven countries in order to prevent wage dumping and poorer working conditions, and to ensure the continued provision of universal postal services in each member state.

A second type of objective consists in transforming national activities into transnational ones, an objective indirectly linked to European integration policies and to globalisation of the markets. In postal services, as a consequence of the liberalisation, the former monopolistic groups tend to reorganise their activities on a transnational basis. This objective can be found in large postal companies such as Deutsche Post, La Poste, TNT or Royal Mail. On the trade union side, there is a concern to encourage the national trade unions to act at this transnational level to protect minimum standards of working conditions.

A third objective leading to commitment is to be informed about what the others are doing and to exchange experiences. This kind of activity generally involves informal bilateral cooperation between selected partners, besides meetings in the European sectoral social dialogue. According to the interviewees, informal relationships are more likely to develop among partners from countries with a close cultural background and comparable institutional structures. However these particular relationships also depend on the issues under discussion.

In more general terms, the national member organisations can also participate in order to express national positions, promote their national system and seek to influence the European social context.

So far, most social issues are strongly rooted in the national conception of the industrial relations systems. National players are attached to these specificities while the European integration phenomenon demands common instruments to solve common issues, which leads to a difficult articulation between national specificities and transnational movements.

***Observers on the periphery of the committees***

A second type of commitment is, rather, as an 'observer'. The 'observers' are not present regularly; they participate when they think that the issue at stake has a certain added value which makes it worthwhile facing some material obstacles, such as the lack of time or financial resources.

The interviews show that these seem to be more often representatives from smaller organisations and smaller EU 15 countries with scarcer human and financial resources. It can also be the situation of some organisations from the new member states that are not sufficiently structured or prepared to fully integrate the social dialogue committee.

***Committees absent***

This third type of participation covers heterogeneous national organisations that seem to have various reasons not to participate. The interpretation here is hypothetical, based as it is on what the more active members say about the others, because those 'absentees' could not be reached for interview for understandable reasons.

These organisations might first be interested in participating actively, but they face material obstacles: lack of the financial or human resources that are necessary to be present in Brussels, lack of knowledge of one of the working languages, weakly structured organisation with too few representatives. This situation may be the case for most organisations from the new member states that face a lack of resources to invest into European affairs and meetings.

Other elements of explanation can be found in the socio-cultural background of the post-socialist countries. Whereas a culture of social dialogue is well rooted in most Western countries, trade unions and the system of collective bargaining can be looked at with suspicion in post-communist regimes.

Finally, some organisations have limited or no interest in participating in the European social dialogue either because social affairs are not on their agenda or because European issues seem too ambitious and too far away from domestic preoccupations.

***Different degrees of room for manoeuvre***

Throughout the description of the three degrees of commitment, opportunities presented by – and constraints to – involvement and interest in the social dialogue committees can be identified.

Human and financial resources seem to be an important element because major organisations are more likely to be active than smaller organisations. However, the resources dedicated to this level of activity also depend on the organisation's interest to invest at this level.

The different degrees of participation can be explained, primarily, by the available human and financial resources. 'Richer' organisations can afford to have people working 'full-time' on these issues and representing their interests, whereas others may only intervene when it is essential to be present and to represent their interests via other organisations.

The national context also influences an organisation's participation. Organisations with resources to participate will generally come from corporatist countries with a high level of membership and opportunities to intervene in the national decision-making process. For instance, national context could explain the relative absence of British employers in some sectors, as they are not willing to be involved in social issues or social partnership.

The national institutional context is also an important factor for understanding the relative absence of most of the new member states (see also Ghellab and Vaughan-Whitehead 2003): in some countries or sectors, trade unions or employers' organisations are simply not organised or structured in a manner which would facilitate participation, and moreover 'soft' issues, such as training, are not a priority in the agenda of social partners.

The different degrees of participation are not static categories, and the actors can evolve from one situation to another according to the evolution of their own constraints, opportunities and (personal) interests and also depend on the issues discussed.

## Topics and issues

Defining a common agenda in the European sectoral social dialogue committees is not an easy task. It does not only imply discussions between employers and trade unions at the European level, but also much complex intra-organisation bargaining. What then are the topics that can lead to social dialogue in the sectoral committees?

An analysis of the topics covered by the joint texts signed from 1999 to 2010 (Figure 4.5, see also Pochet 2005b and 2006b), and of the content of work programmes for the year 2006, 2007 and 2008 for all committees (Table 4.1), gives an indication on the agenda that the sectoral committees are able to define.

The quantitative data demonstrate that the largest number of documents is devoted to economic and sectoral policies. It confirms the importance of joint

**Figure 4.5 Number of documents by topic (1999–2007)**

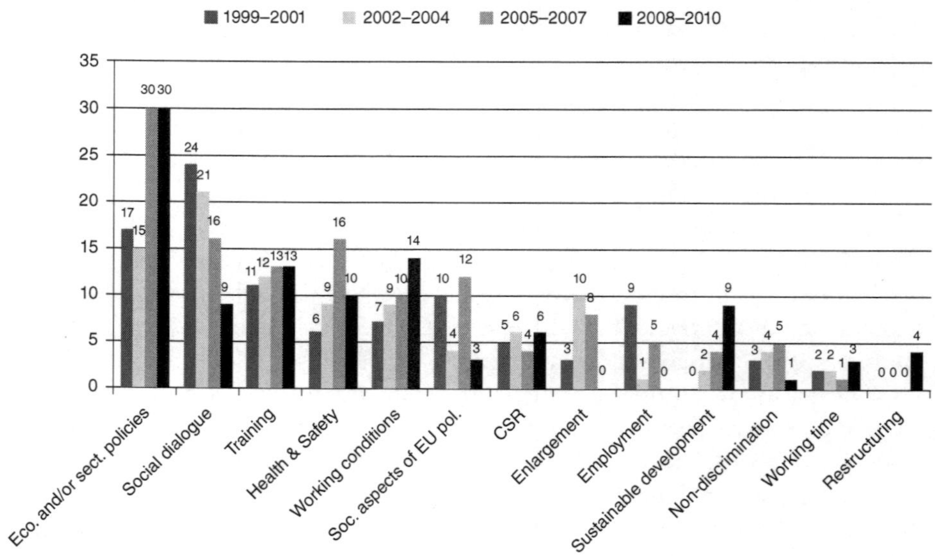


lobbying at EU level and trying to influence the legislative process at sectoral level. The importance of social aspects of Community policies (which cover the global social policies) has decreased in committees' agenda, in spite of many joint documents having been signed (see Figure 4.5). This topic is very much influenced by the EU agenda and by the revision of the Lisbon and European Employment Strategy attracting a lot of joint reactions. Consequently, the work programmes are not good indicators of the importance of these topics.

The importance of the topic of 'social dialogue' has clearly decreased, which can easily be explained by the fact that this topic is mainly dealt with under 'procedural text', i.e. the text generally adopted at the creation of the committee and defining the rules of the game. Only a few sectors have modified their original 'basic agreement'. Today, social dialogue in the new member states also attracts less interest than before as a specific topic for discussions. It is also illustrated by the fact that no text was adopted on enlargement (see Figure 4.5).

In parallel with the development of the so-called Copenhagen-Maastricht-Helsinki process on lifelong learning, training has gained in importance as a topic at European sectoral level (Léonard, Erne, Marginson *et al.* 2007). Training is a domain attracting more and more attention, and is on the agenda of twenty-one committees. This theme is often linked with demography and the fears of labour shortage in a near future.

What is more surprising is the relative stability in 'corporate social responsibility/codes of conduct/charter' over the years. This can partly be explained by the fact that, once adopted in a sector, new instruments do not need to be discussed later. The main concern, then, is the implementation of a given code or charter, which is reflected in the work programmes: when work programmes mention the topic 'Corporate Social Responsibility (code of conduct)', most of the time it concerns the follow-up of a code or charter previously adopted. In the audio-visual sector, for instance, the 2007 work programme provides for exchange of information on the subject; in footwear, the focus is on follow-up; in sugar, on report and communication on implementation.

By contrast, the number of texts dealing with sustainable development is increasing, owing to the global warming debate. The number of agreed texts has doubled (to nine) compared to the previous period (four) which was already double the previous three years (two) (see Figure 4.5).

Non-discrimination is another topic undergoing a slight rise in the joint texts until 2007 and this is also the case in the work programmes, even if only around one-third of the committees have this item formally on their agenda. Only one text has been adopted since 2007.

Working conditions are still an important issue. A glance at the work programmes shows that flexicurity is now a theme under discussion in different committees (banking, construction, private security, temporary agency work), a development which hardly comes as a surprise. Working time, a topic strongly linked to the working time directive, is now a very marginal topic.

Interestingly, adaptation to change and restructuring issues were very rarely addressed in common texts, but these topics are already in the work programme of a growing number of committees and some joint texts have been adopted recently.

Health and safety issues are being tackled with increasing frequency. The increased production of joint texts is mirrored by an increasing number of committees that have the topic on their agenda. In all, twenty sectors have health and safety discussions on their agenda (compared with fourteen joint texts adopted over the last three years). Among the sectors, construction and the extractive industry have a broader agenda.

Overall, in terms of topics covered, the quantitative data show the diversity of themes discussed, many of them directly related to the EU agenda. The majority of documents are 'common positions' addressed to the European institutions with a view to influencing EU policy makers. In other words, one important function of social dialogue consists in the joint lobbying of the EU. But new themes are also emerging at EU level: lifelong learning, non-discrimination, flexicurity or at a lesser extent, sustainable development.

The diversity of circumstances, issues and dynamics is one explanation of the difficulties involved in building a well-structured system of industrial relations at Community level. It seems, however, that several sectors have reached a critical point. In some, social dialogue appears purely formal, with no actual impact at EU or national level. Those sectors that adopted 'recommendations', which could also be described as 'soft law' are all facing the same problems: how should these texts be implemented nationally and monitored at EU level? What linkage should there be between the European and national sectoral levels? These questions are addressed in the next section.

**Table 4.1 Themes and topics of committees' work programmes, 2006–08**

| *Theme* | *Keyword* | *agriculture* | *audiovisual* | *banking* | *catering* | *chemical industry* | *civil aviation* | *cleaning industry* | *commerce* | *construction* | *electricity* | *footwear* | *furniture* |
|---|---|---|---|---|---|---|---|---|---|---|---|---|---|
| *economic and/or social policies* | *adaptation to change* | | x | x | | | | | | | x | x | |
| | *Sectoral policies* | | | | x | | x | x | | | | x | x |
| | *EU policies, legislative developments* | | x | | | | x | x | | | x | | |
| *Social dialogue (SD)* | *SD (in general)* | | | | x | | | x | x | | | x | |
| | *SD in NMS* | | x | x | | | | | | | | x | x |
| *training* | *LLL/ education/ vocational training* | x | x | x | x | x | x | | | | | x | x |
| *health and safety* | *accidents/ alcohol/best practice/NO2 /MSD/etc.* | x | | | x | x | x | | x | x | x | | x |
| *social aspects of EU policies* | *undeclared work* | | | | | | | x | | x | | | |
| | *future of the industry* | | | | | | x | | | | | | |

| *Theme* | *Keyword* | *gas* | *horeca-tourism* | *hospitals* | *inland waterways* | *insurance* | *live performance* | *local/regional government* | *mines* | *personal services* | *postal services* | *private security* | *professional football* |
|---|---|---|---|---|---|---|---|---|---|---|---|---|---|
| *economic and/or social policies* | *adaptation to change* | x | | | | x | | x | | | | | |
| | *Sectoral policies* | x | | | | | | | | x | x | x | |
| | *EU policies, legislative developments* | x | x | | | x | x | x | x | | | | |
| *Social dialogue (SD)* | *SD (in general)* | | | X | | | | | | | x | | |
| | *SD in NMS* | | | X | x | x | x | x | | | | | |
| *training* | *LLL/ education/ vocational training* | | x | X | | | x | x | | x | x | x | |
| *health and safety* | *accidents/ alcohol/best practice/NO2 /MSD/etc.* | x | x | X | | | x | | x | x | x | x | |
| *social aspects of EU policies* | *undeclared work* | | x | | | | | | | | | | |
| | *future of the industry* | x | | | | | | | | | | | |

| *Theme* | *Keyword* | *railways* | *road transport* | *sea fishing* | *sea transport* | *shipbuilding* | *steel* | *sugar* | *tanning and leather* | *telecoms* | *temporary agency work* | *textiles/clothing* | *woodworking* |
|---|---|---|---|---|---|---|---|---|---|---|---|---|---|
| *economic and/or social policies* | *adaptation to change* | x | | | | x | x | x | | | | x | |
| | *Sectoral policies* | x | | | | x | x | x | x | | x | x | x |
| | *EU policies, legislative developments* | x | x | x | x | x | | x | | x | x | x | |
| *Social dialogue (SD)* | *SD (in general)* | | | x | | | x | | x | | x | x | |
| | *SD in NMS* | x | | x | | | | | x | x | | x | x |
| *training* | *LLL/ education/ vocational training* | x | x | x | x | | x | | x | x | x | x | x |
| *health and safety* | *accidents/ alcohol/best practice/NO2 /MSD/etc.* | | x | x | x | | x | | x | x | | | x |
| *social aspects of EU policies* | *undeclared work* | | | | | | | | | | | | |
| | *future of the industry* | | | | | | | | | | | | |

| | | | | | | | | | | | | | | | | | | | | | | | | | | | | | | | | | | | | | |
|---|---|---|---|---|---|---|---|---|---|---|---|---|---|---|---|---|---|---|---|---|---|---|---|---|---|---|---|---|---|---|---|---|---|---|---|---|---|
| | *impact on employment* | x | | | | | | | | | x | | | | | | | | | | | | | | | | | | | | | | | | | | |
| *working conditions* | *working conditions (in general)* | | | | | | | | x | | | | | | x | X | x | | | | | x | | x | | x | x | | x | | | | | | | | |
| | *flexicurity* | | | x | | | | | | x | | | | | | | | | | x | | | | x | | | | | | | | | | | x | | |
| | *working time* | | | | | | x | x | | | | | | | | | x | | | | | | | x | | | | | | | | | | | | | |
| *enlargement* | *enlargement (in general)* | | | x | | x | | | x | x | | | | x | | | | x | x | | | | | | | | x | x | | | | | | | x | x | |
| *employment* | *employability/ employment* | x | | | | x | | | | | x | | | | | X | | x | | | | | | | | x | | x | x | | | | | | | | |
| *CSR* | *CSR: best practice (code of conduct)* | | x | | x | | | x | | | | x | | | | | | | | | | | | x | | | | | | | | x | x | x | | x | |
| | *CSR (in general)* | | | x | x | x | x | | x | | x | | | | x | X | | | | | x | | x | | | | | | | | | x | | x | | x | |
| *non-discrimination* | *gender equality /diversity /equal opportunities* | | x | | x | | | | x | | x | | | | | X | | | | x | | | | x | | x | x | | | | | | | x | x | | |
| | *sexual harassment* | | | | | | | | | | x | | | | x | | | | | x | | | | | | | | | | | | | | | | | |
| *sustainable development* | | | | | | | | | | | | | | | | | | | | | | | | | | | | | | | | | | | | | |
| | *environment* | | | | | | | | x | | | | | | | | | | | | x | | | | | | | x | | | x | | | | | | x |
| *others* | *migrants, seasonal workers, self-employed, temporary workers* | x | | | | | | | x | x | | | | | x | | | | | | | | | x | | | | | | | | | | | x | | |
| | *social security* | | | | | | | | | x | | | | | | | | | x | | | | | | | | | | | | | | | | | | |

Source: OSE's database

## Implementing common guidelines or practices

Implementation in the member states is a key question and decisive as regards to the European sectoral social dialogue capacity to regulate employment relationships, be it in a 'soft' or a 'hard' manner. Again, beyond the formal classification and the official provisions in the texts, it is interesting to look at the coordination that takes place, in any, with the national members for the implementation of texts.

In terms of follow-up procedures at European level, we have distinguished different techniques that can be grouped under five categories:

- A written survey among members: very often verification of national implementation is done through a questionnaire sent to the national affiliates. This questionnaire is generally a joint questionnaire: in other words, it can be completed by both sides of industry at national level, or each side may choose to send its questionnaire back to its European body. The EU secretariats have to mobilise and personally call their affiliates for a return, which is generally well below 50 per cent.
- Annual or periodic reports: to ensure good results, these should be considered as strategic by both parties. It often consists of an oral report by the parties in a plenary meeting. In a sense, they are tools meant to show that 'something has happened' at national level and that the soft law approach is more than window dressing. Each affiliate is supposed to present its achievements at national level.
- Presentation of good practices: this is often linked to a charter or corporate social responsibility text, and to the importance of the enterprises in the sector. A typical example is the charter of the sugar sector reviewed each year; in this approach, both sides agree on selected good practices related to one or more provisions of the charter.
- Conferences or websites: the follow-up can also occur through the organisation of a public event and creation of a common website. In such cases, compliance with the provision of the texts is supposed to increase as a result of better visibility.
- Finally, new texts or new initiatives: the follow-up can also be another text or initiative. Very often, the dialogue on a topic is dynamic, each step leading incrementally to another. The follow-up provision is then more of a pretext to further the dialogue than an object per se. In other words, the main objective of the follow-up process is to reinforce the consensus among members and partners rather than a real exercise of implementation.

In many cases, different procedures are foreseen and these categories are not mutually exclusive. There is an ongoing discussion between the social partners on how to improve the existing procedures and practices.

To complete the interviews with the European players, interviews were conducted with affiliates at national level. Although they are not representative of all situations in the different countries, they give an insight on how the national players envisage implementation from their domestic point of view.

According to these interviews, the implementation of texts largely relies on the initiatives of the European peak organisations and on the goodwill of the national members. The latter is in turn influenced by the nature of the text (type of commitment or issue), by the domestic regulatory framework, and by the experience that a given organisation has in the domain covered by a given text.

Does that mean that implementation does not take place? Up to now, few studies have reported on the implementation of the European sectoral social dialogue texts within the member states. Murhem (2006), when examining the situation in Sweden, remarks that the 'no' answer from the trade unions cannot be considered as evidence that the sectoral texts have not been implemented in Sweden. Their perception of implementation and of the impact of the texts on workers' daily lives can be different from the expected results of the joint texts and will depend on their own goals regarding social dialogue.

The perception of implementation and of the impact of the texts in workers' daily lives can differ from the expected results of the joint texts and will depend on their own particular goals regarding social dialogue. Besides, each text has different objectives and the impact at national level can be indirect, and therefore hard to assess.

It is extremely difficult to appreciate the impact of the texts in the member states, because of the lack of a regular monitoring and ranking process and because of the nature of the texts themselves, voluntarily defined in a broad sense in order to be adaptable to any institutional and cultural context (Weber 2010). Very often, the implementation makes no reference to the EU text, which complicates the tracing of the impact of the European texts.

However, respondents quasi-unanimously agreed that the joint texts and the presentation of good practices offer opportunities to learn from one another and to examine how social partners across Europe are dealing with such issues. This process fosters cooperation, as well as informal contacts among different actors who share common initiatives. It also opens up new ways of thinking.

Another opportunity offered by the texts is that, even in countries in which the social partners, and especially trade unions, are largely powerless to intervene in the national legal framework, the social actors can use the European texts as a mean of exerting pressure or at least of increasing the awareness of the government or other actors about a particular issue. Implementation may then not be as 'patchy' as it seems, since non-formal or less visible processes are at play.

## Conclusion

From our analysis and research, it is clear today that sectoral social dialogue has no power to enforce compliance among the national members, but this does not mean that it has no influence. Social dialogue as such requires coordination, particularly when it leads to defining a common agenda at European level, discussing joint texts, and trying to implement them in the member states.

In a way, social dialogue fosters coordination. It gives an arena and resources for the actors to build up new forms of collective action. Common socio-economic issues and European integration provide common issues for the national actors to tackle, however without a concrete place where to meet together, coordination is hard to realise. European sectoral social dialogue committees provide such arenas to meet and to exchange ideas that contribute to the constitution of a new collective identity transcending the traditional boundaries. Moreover, it leads to dialogue between trade unions and employer organisations on concrete issues that are specifically addressed at a European level and to the production of joint texts including agreements.

Actors are working on two parallel levels and their national contexts constrain their actions at a supranational level. It is then important to consider the strategies of the national social partners within the framework of their industrial relation system and to consider the European sectoral social dialogue partly as a product of the diverse national strategies.

As Mayntz and Scharpf (2001) have described, the European sectoral social dialogue has its own institutional context, defined by the European regulation and rules that organise the European social dialogue, such as the Articles 138 and 139 EC. However, the actors' actions and the interplay between them determine how it works in practice. The specificity of the European sectoral social dialogue is that it gathers constituencies from twenty-seven countries. The national member organisations are all embedded within particular national institutions, and they also have their own interests and strategies towards the European sectoral social dialogue. In that sense, the European sectoral social dialogue is really constituted of 'actors involved in constellations of situations' to use Mayntz and Scharpf's terms. Therefore its capacity to produce outcomes must not be assessed only against its institutional framework, nor by a simple comparison with the traditional national-level industrial relations systems (Marginson and Sisson 2004). One can only understand this capacity to produce outcomes by examining how the 'constellation', involving the actors and their respective institutions, works.

If we look at the upside of the European sectoral social dialogue, it is necessary for the European social dialogue to be able to coordinate the diverse national interests and build up common transnational interests. However, industrial relations systems in Europe are not homogeneous and workers and employer representatives not covering the same socio-economic reality, they do not play the same role nor do they have the same structure from one country to another.

All actors are not able or willing to be active in the same way in the social dialogue. Some are more involved than others, according to their respective national strategies, resources and room for manoeuvre. To simply gather trade unions and employer federations from twenty-seven countries is as such an incredible challenge. Besides, to find common grounds to discuss or even to negotiate is extremely difficult. The diversity of languages and cultures makes the tasks of European umbrella organisations a real conundrum. However, a diversity of themes, including many directly related to the Commission agenda, is discussed and results in joint texts.

These outcomes could remain strictly formal without any impact, if coordination does not include the implementation of the texts at the national level.

On the downside, committees of European sectoral social dialogue organise different types of follow-up procedures but at the end, implementation mostly depends on the initiatives of the national organisations. Again, the national players' resources, expectations and strategies towards the European sectoral social dialogue inevitably differ.

Finally, it appears joint texts and presentation of good practices offer opportunities to actors to learn from each other, to exchange ideas and to transfer their knowledge to others. In this way, the European sectoral social dialogue acts as a coordinator.

## Notes

1 Parts of this chapter have been revised and included in Léonard, E., Perin, E. and Pochet, P. (2011), 'The European Sectoral Social Dialogue: Questions of Representation and Membership', *Industrial Relations Journal*, 42(3), 254–72.
2 This paper is inspired by the report for the European Foundation on the dynamics of the European sectoral social dialogue (Pochet *et al.*, 2009).
3 NACE Codes refer to the Statistical Classification of Economic Activities in the European Community (Nomenclature statistique des activités économiques dans la Communauté européenne).

## References

Béthoux, E., Jobert, A., Machu, L., and Mias, A. (2008), 'Introduction. Le dialogue social dans l'espace européen: branches, entreprises, territoires', pp. 13–23 in Jobert, A. (ed.), *Les nouveaux cadres du dialogue social: l'espace européen et les territoires*, Brussels: P.I.E.-Peter Lang.

CEC (1998a), *Commission Decision 98/500/EC of 20 May 1998 on the Establishment of Sectoral Dialogue Committees Promoting the Dialogue between the Social Partners at European Level*, OJ L 225, 12 August, 27–8.

De Boer, R., Benedictus, H. and van der Meer, M. (2005), 'Broadening without Intensification: The Added Value of the European Social and Sectoral Dialogue', *European Journal of Industrial Relations* 11(1), 51–70.

Degryse, C. and Pochet, P. (2011), 'Has European Sectoral Social Dialogue Improved since the Establishment of SSDCs in 1998?', *Transfer* 17(2), 145–57.

Didry, C. and Mias, A. (2005), *Le moment Delors, Les syndicats au coeur de l'Europe sociale*, Brussels: P.I.E.-Peter Lang.

Dufresne, A. (2006), 'Sectoral Employer Strategies in the EU: Lobbying by Partners?', pp. 249–79 in Dufresne, A., Degryse, C. and Pochet, P. (eds), *The European Sectoral Social Dialogue: Actors, Developments and Challenges*, Brussels, PIE-Peter Lang.

Dufresne, A. and Pochet, P. (2006), 'Introduction', pp. 49–81 in Dufresne, A., Degryse, C. and Pochet, P. (eds), *The European Sectoral Social Dialogue*, Brussels: P.I.E.-Peter Lang.

Ghellab, Y. and Vaughan-Whitehead, D. (eds) (2003), *Sectoral Social Dialogue in the Future EU Member States: The Weakest Link?*, Geneva: ILO.

Glassner, F. (2008), *The Social Partners and their Representativeness: Post and Courier Services*, Dublin: European Foundation for the Improvement of Living and Working Conditions.

Keller, B. (2005), 'Europeanisation at Sectoral Level. Empirical Results and Missing Perspectives', *Transfer* 11(3), 397–408.

Lallement, M. (2008), *Sociologie des relations industrielles*, Paris: La Découverte.

Léonard, E., Erne, R., Marginson, P. and Smismans, S. (2007), *New Structures, Forms and Processes of Governance in European Industrial Relations*, Luxembourg, Office for Official Publications of the European Communities.

Marginson, P. and Keune, M. (2012), 'European Social Dialogue as Multi-Level Governance: Towards More Autonomy and New Dependencies', in Barbier, J.-L. (ed.), *EU Law, Governance and Social Policy*, European Integration Online Papers (EIOP) 76(4), http://eiop.or.at/eiop/texts/2012-004a.htm.

Marginson, P. and Sisson, K. (2004), 'European Integration and Industrial Relations, Multi-Level Governance in the Making', Basingstoke: Palgrave Macmillan.

Mayntz, R. and Scharpf, F. (2001), 'L'institutionnalisme centré sur les acteurs', *Politix* 14(55), 95–123.

Murhem, S. (2006), 'Implementation of the Sectoral Social Dialogue in Sweden', in Dufresne, A., Degryse, C. and Pochet, P. (eds), *The European Sectoral Social Dialogue: Actors, Developments and Challenges*, Brussels: P.I.E.-Peter Lang.

OSE (2011), 'European Social Dialogue: state of pay and prospects', *Final Report*, ETUC, Brussels, January, www.etuc.org/IMG/pdf/Dialogue_social_2010_Rapport_OSE_CES_EN.pdf.

Perin, E. and Léonard, E. (2011), 'European Sectoral Social Dialogue and National Social Partners', *Transfer* 17(2), 159–67.

Pochet, P. (2005a), 'Le dialogue social dans le secteur du textile et des vêtements: l'expérience européenne', in Sajhau, J.-P. (ed.), *Promoting Fair Globalization in Textiles and Clothing in a Post-MFA Environment*, Report for discussion at the Tripartite Meeting on Promoting Fair Globalization in Textiles and Clothing in a Post-MFA Environment, Geneva, International Labour Organisation, Geneva, 60–4.

Pochet P. (2005b), 'Sectoral Social Dialogue? A Quantitative Analysis', *Transfer* 11(3), 313–32.

Pochet, P. (2006a), 'A Typology', pp. 109–30 in Dufresne, A., Degryse, C. and Pochet, P. (eds.), *The European Sectoral Social Dialogue: Actors, Developments and Challenges*, Brussels, PIE-Peter Lang.

Pochet, P. (2006b), 'A Quantitative Analysis', pp. 83–108 in Dufresne, A., Degryse, C. and Pochet, P. (eds), *The European Sectoral Social Dialogue: Actors, Developments and Challenges*, PIE-Peter Lang, Brussels.

Pochet, P., Degryse, C. and Dufresne, A. (2004), *Rapport final 'Dialogue social européen'*, Contrat VC/2003/0440, Brussels: Observatoire social européen.

Pochet, P., Peeters, A., Léonard, E. and Perin, E. (2009), *Dynamics of the European Sectoral Social Dialogue*, Dublin: European Foundation for the Improvement of

Living and Working Conditions.
Regalia, I. (2007), *Industrial Relations in the Postal Sector.* Dublin, European Foundation for the Improvement of Living and Working Conditions, www.eurofound.europa.eu/eiro/studies/tn0704018s/tn0704018s.htm, accessed 19 April 2012.
Traxler, F. (2002), 'Wage Policy, Bargaining Institutions and Monetary Policy: Empirical Findings and Policy Implications for European Monetary Union', pp. 111–30 in Pochet, P. (ed.), *Wage Policy in the Eurozone*, Brussels, P.I.E.-Peter Lang.
Traxler, F. (2007), *Representativeness of the Social Partners: Agriculture,* Dublin, European Foundation for the Improvement of Living and Working Conditions, 2007, www.eurofound.europa.eu/docs/eiro/tn0608017s/tn0608017s.pdf, accessed 19 April 2012.
Trubek, D.M., Mosher, J., and Rothstein, J.S. (2000), 'Transnationalism in the Regulation of Labor Relations: International Regimes and Transnational Advocacy Networks', *Law & Social Inquiry* 25(4), 1187–211.
Weber, S. (2010), 'Sectoral Social Dialogue at EU Level – Recent Results and Implementation Challenges', *Transfer* 16(4), 479–507.

Évélyne Léonard and André Sobczak

# 5

# European social dialogue and transnational company agreements

## Introduction

In recent years, in parallel to the European cross-industry and sectoral social dialogue, many developments have happened at the company level, illustrated by the multiplication of transnational company agreements.

The developments at these different levels have led to debates on their respective importance, status and significance. These developments suggest that new forms of joint regulation may currently be emerging across or above the traditional national systems of industrial relations, in parallel to the increasing internationalisation of markets and companies. Yet it is clear, at this stage, that there is no transnational system of industrial relations that would be comparable to national systems (Marginson and Sisson 2004).

The developments at the various levels are very different: the forms of European social dialogue at the sectoral level are strongly grounded in institutional settings and closely related to the European political agenda, while transnational company agreements, on the other hand, stem mainly from managerial initiatives within large multinational companies, apparently beyond any institutional context.

The question of the relationships between the different forms of transnational social dialogue may seem purely theoretical since, so far, there is no formal hierarchy or structure that would articulate the three levels – cross-industry, sector and company. However, the parallel developments and the potential connections between the players involved may suggest that links do exist.

This chapter intends to show that the development of transnational company agreements is not disconnected from other levels of social dialogue in the European Union (EU). More generally, it discusses and compares the recent developments in the different spheres of transnational social dialogue, in order to address the key questions of the potential development of industrial relations above or across countries and, conversely, of the emergence of joint regulation processes with an international dimension.[1]

The first section of the paper reviews the major debates on transnational company agreements. It analyses the potential coordination of collective bargaining across borders, the importance and the regulatory capacity of the European social dialogue, as well as the legal nature and status of transnational company agreements.

Examining empirical data, the second section compares the two spheres where employers and worker representatives signed most joint texts over the last decade: the European sectoral social dialogue and transnational company agreements. In particular, it examines the players involved and the issues discussed at both levels. The comparison intends to highlight the potential links between the two levels, in order to see whether they are separate routes of regulation defined in the broadest sense, or whether they share common features and can be articulated.

The third section finally comes back to the issues of coordination and joint regulation at the transnational level, elaborating on the question as to whether the different forms of transnational social dialogue are complementing each other or compete with each other.

## Regulation by transnational company agreements?

The growing importance of multinational corporations raises important challenges for the regulation of employment relations, for at least three reasons (Murray and Trudeau 2004). Firstly, taking advantage of the mobility of capital and acting in different markets around the world, those companies use management practices that cross the borders and make it difficult for local players and domestic regulation to weight on wages and working conditions in the subsidiaries. Secondly, multinational companies favour changes towards global production systems with transnational production flows that result in complex international structures with unbalanced power relationships between demand and supply within the company, leading to in-company competition and 'coercive comparisons' between subsidiaries (Marginson and Sisson 2004). These, in turn, put pressure on wages and working conditions and reduce the capacity of established industrial relations bodies to regulate them. Thirdly, this movement takes place within broader trends characterised by the influence of neo-liberal ways of thinking and the decline of the regulatory capacity of the State in post-Fordist regimes (Murray and Trudeau 2004). In a word, as Papadakis (2008) notes, globalisation has generated a mismatch between the scope of the activities of global actors such as multinational enterprises and the scope of action of social actors such as trade unions and the State.

In such a context, the recent and rapid increase of the number of transnational company agreements may appear as a response, since they define joint provisions that are negotiated between management and trade unions and that apply to all subsidiaries of the multinational companies (Sobczak 2007). These agreements

**Table 5.1 Transnational company agreements applicable worldwide**

| | | | Signatories on worker side | | | |
|---|---|---|---|---|---|---|
| *Company* | *Country* | *Year* | *International trade union federation* | *European trade union federation* | *European Works Council* | *National trade union federation* |
| Accor | France | 1995 | UITA | - | no | no |
| Anglogold | South Africa | 2002 | ICEM | - | no | no |
| Arcelor Mittal | Luxembourg | 2005 | FIOM | FEM | no | no |
| Ballast Nedam | Netherlands | 2002 | IBB | - | no | no |
| BMW | Germany | 2005 | FIOM | - | yes | no |
| Bosch | Germany | 2004 | FIOM | - | yes | no |
| Brunel | Netherlands | 2007 | FIOM | - | no | yes |
| Carrefour | France | 2001 | UNI | - | no | no |
| Chiquita | USA | 2001 | UITA | - | no | no |
| Club Méditerrannée | France | 2004 | UITA | - | no | no |
| Daimler Chrysler | Germany | 2002 | FIOM | - | yes | no |
| Danone | France | 1988 | UITA | - | yes | no |
| Danske Bank | Denmark | 2008 | UNI | - | no | yes |
| EADS | Netherlands | 2005 | FIOM | FEM | yes | no |
| EDF | France | 2004 | ICEM/ISP/ OIEM/ FMTI | - | no | yes |
| Endesa | Spain | 2002 | ICEM | - | no | yes |
| ENI | Italy | 2002 | ICEM | - | no | yes |
| Euradius | Netherlands | 2006 | UNI | - | no | yes |
| Faber Castell | Germany | 2000 | IBB | - | no | yes |
| Fonterra | New Zealand | 2002 | UITA | - | no | yes |
| France Télécom | France | 2006 | UNI | - | no | yes |
| Freudenberg | Germany | 2000 | ICEM | - | no | yes |
| GEA | Germany | 2003 | FIOM | FEM | yes | no |
| H&M | Sweden | 2004 | UNI | - | no | no |
| Hochtief | Germany | 2000 | IBB | - | no | yes |
| IKEA | Sweden | 1998 | IBB | - | no | no |
| Impreglio | Italy | 2004 | IBB | - | no | yes |
| Inditex | Spain | 2007 | FITTHC | - | no | no |
| ISS | Denmark | 2003 | UNI | - | no | no |
| Italcementi | Italy | 2008 | IBB | - | no | yes |

| Company | Country | Year | Signatories on worker side: International trade union federation | European trade union federation | European Works Council | National trade union federation |
|---|---|---|---|---|---|---|
| Lafarge | France | 2005 | IBB/ICEM | - | no | no |
| Leoni | Germany | 2003 | FIOM | FEM | yes | no |
| Lukoil | Russia | 2004 | ICEM | - | no | yes |
| Merloni-Indesit | Italy | 2001 | FIOM | - | no | yes |
| Metro | Germany | 1999 | UNI | - | yes | no |
| NAG | Australia | 2006 | UNI | - | no | yes |
| Nampak | South Africa | 2006 | UNI | - | no | no |
| Norske Skog | Norway | 2002 | ICEM | - | no | yes |
| OTE | Greece | 2001 | UNI | - | no | yes |
| Portugal Telecom | Portugal | 2006 | UNI | - | no | yes |
| Prym | Germany | 2004 | FIOM | - | yes | no |
| PSA Peugeot Citroën | France | 2006 | FIOM | FEM | no | yes |
| Quebecor | Canada | 2007 | UNI | - | no | no |
| RAG | Germany | 2003 | ICEM | - | no | yes |
| Renault | France | 2004 | FIOM | - | yes | no |
| Rheinmetall | Germany | 2003 | FIOM | FEM | yes | no |
| Rhodia | France | 2004 | ICEM | - | no | no |
| Röchling | Germany | 2004 | FIOM | FEM | yes | no |
| Royal BAM | Netherlands | 2007 | IBB | - | no | no |
| SCA | Sweden | 2004 | ICEM | - | yes | yes |
| Schwan Stabilo | Germany | 2005 | IBB | - | no | yes |
| Securitas | Sweden | 2006 | UNI | - | no | yes |
| Skanska | Sweden | 2001 | IBB | - | no | no |
| SKF | Sweden | 2003 | FIOM | FEM | no | no |
| Staedler | Germany | 2006 | IBB | - | no | yes |
| Statoil | Norway | 1998 | ICEM | - | no | yes |
| Telefonica | Spain | 2000 | UNI | - | no | yes |
| Umicore | Belgium | 2007 | FIOM/ICEM | - | no | yes |
| Vallourec | France | 2008 | FIOM | - | yes | no |
| Veidekke | Norway | 2005 | IBB | - | no | yes |
| Volker Wessels | Netherlands | 2007 | IBB | - | no | no |
| Volkswagen | Germany | 2002 | FIOM | - | yes | no |
| WAZ | Germany | 2007 | FIJ | FEJ | no | no |

appear as a new instrument for social dialogue that could favour new forms of social regulation at global level, although their numerical importance remains limited (Telljohann, da Costa, Müller *et al.* 2009). In a 'Commission staff working document' on 'The role of transnational company agreements in the context of increasing international integration' of July 2008 (SEC[2008] 2155), the European Commission identified 147 joint texts that have been negotiated in 89 companies, most of which have been signed since 2000.

At first sight, there is no connection between transnational company agreements that have, in principle, an international scope, and the European social dialogue. However, a closer examination is needed, since a large part of those agreements have a European dimension (see also Telljohann *et al.* 2009). The working document of the European Commission mentions that, among these texts, 76 are applicable only to subsidiaries located on the European territory, whereas 59 are applicable globally, and another 12 contain provisions that either apply to the whole world or to the European continent. The exact figure varies from one study to another, because a given agreement may not necessarily define precisely where it is applicable, and because the boundary between worldwide agreements and European ones is often unclear. In addition, according to the Commission, the total number of texts is probably higher, since some texts do not circulate outside the company.

In a study conducted in 2008–09 for the French DARES, we identified 63 joint texts that are applicable worldwide (Sobczak and Léonard 2009). Table 5.1 indicates where they have been signed and whether they have been signed with an international trade union federation, a European trade union federation, the European works council, or national trade unions.

The vast majority of these agreements are signed in companies that have their headquarters within the EU, and in particular in Germany (27% of texts) and France (17%).

To date, at international level, there is no legal framework to regulate this type of text, which raises a number of questions regarding the status of the signatories and the nature of the provisions.

On the employer side, being signed by the top management at the headquarters of the company, the texts reflect the situation of the economic power and the managerial hierarchy within the company, but this goes against the principle of legal independence of each subsidiary. From a nationally based legal point of view, the employer is the subsidiary, and the headquarters do not have the status of the employer for each of the subsidiaries. Therefore, legally, the headquarters do not have the capacity to negotiate, with the status of the employer, for the subsidiaries.

On the worker side, all transnational company agreements that have a worldwide scope are signed by at least one international trade union federation. The most active ones are in metalworking, the chemical industry, construction and services. By the end of the year 2008, among the international trade union federations, only two – Education International, and International Transport Workers'

Federation – had signed no transnational company agreement. Again, the status of the signatories on the worker side is unclear, since international sectoral federations act, in each case, at the level of a single company, and often with no formal mandate from the national trade unions.

In terms of content, almost all agreements cover fundamental rights as they are defined by ILO's conventions. This again raises question on their regulatory capacity, since they do not cover the traditional dimensions covered by collective agreements, such as wages and working conditions. Moreover, they do not necessarily add original provisions to what is already present in international rules.

Many transnational company agreements are applicable in the context of the EU. According to the European Commission (CEC 2008a), there are more 'European-wide' than 'worldwide' agreements. Most of the texts that are applicable within the EU have been signed in companies that have their headquarters in the EU. However, building on the obligation to set up a European works council, even American companies have signed agreements that only have a European scope.[2]

The context of what we may call 'the European texts' is generally more focused, and several companies have negotiated successive texts to cover different subjects, or to bring more precision to terms already defined in a former text. The 62 European texts considered in the study for DARES have been signed in 31 companies only (see Table 5.2).

France is widely represented as the country of origin of the multinational companies signing European-wide agreements (with 21 texts out of 62). More surprisingly, USA-based companies are also very active (with 20 texts out of 62).

As at the international level, in the European context, the legal status and nature of those texts remain uncertain.

On the employer side, the signatories are the headquarters of the company, which raises the same questions on the status as employer. On the worker side, the European Works Councils (EWC)[3] have signed 48 of the European-wide agreements and, in most of the cases, the EWC is the only signatory party. In comparison, European trade union federations have only signed 15 texts.

The signature of such texts by the EWCs raises several questions. When the text is applicable to subsidiaries and, sometimes providers, in countries outside the EU, the legitimacy of the EWC is questionable, since it only represents European constituencies. When the agreement is applicable in the EU only, there is still the problem that the composition of the EWC, comprising worker representatives, does not guarantee the representation of national trade unions, who in most Member States are the only ones authorised to negotiate collective agreements. More generally, so far the EWCs have no legal capacity to negotiate collective agreements. This situation has led to debates on the possible creation of an optional framework for transnational company agreements within the EU (see Ales, Engblom, Jaspers *et al.* 2006, Bé 2008). Yet, there is no agreement on the issue so far.

Given the uncertainty of the legal status of transnational company agreements, their application is also unclear. If, on the employer side, the implementation can be conducted by the hierarchy, the autonomy of the local players and the

**Table 5.2 Transnational company agreements that are applicable within the European Union**

| | | | *Signatories on worker side* | | | |
|---|---|---|---|---|---|---|
| *Company* | *Country* | *Year* | *International trade union federation* | *European trade union federation* | *European Works Council* | *National trade union federation* |
| | | 2005 | - | - | no | yes |
| Air France | France | 2005 | - | - | no | yes |
| | | 2007 | - | - | yes | no |
| Arcelor Mittal | Luxembourg | 2002 | - | - | yes | no |
| | | 2004 | - | - | yes | no |
| Areva | France | 2006 | - | FEM | no | no |
| Axa | France | 2005 | UNI | - | no | yes |
| Bouygues | France | 2001 | - | CES | yes | no |
| Club Méditerranée | France | 2001 | - | - | yes | no |
| Daimler Chrysler | Germany | 2006 | - | FEM | yes | no |
| | | 1988 | UITA | - | no | no |
| | | 1989 | UITA | - | yes | no |
| Danone | France | 1989 | UITA | - | yes | no |
| | | 1997 | UITA | - | yes | no |
| | | 2001 | - | - | yes | no |
| Dexia | Belgium | 2002 | - | - | yes | no |
| Diageo | United Kingdom | 2002 | - | - | yes | no |
| | | 1996 | - | EMCEF | no | yes |
| ENI | Italy | 2001 | - | - | - | yes |
| | | 2003 | - | - | yes | no |
| Etex | Belgium | 2002 | - | - | yes | no |
| | | 2000 | - | - | yes | no |
| Ford | USA | 2000 | - | - | yes | no |
| | | 2003 | - | - | yes | no |
| | | 2004 | - | - | yes | no |
| | | 2002 | - | - | yes | no |
| GE Plastics | USA | 2003 | - | - | yes | no |
| | | 2004 | - | - | yes | no |
| | | 2000 | - | FEM | yes | no |
| | | 2001 | - | - | yes | no |
| | | 2001 | - | - | yes | no |

| | | | Signatories on worker side | | | |
|---|---|---|---|---|---|---|
| *Company* | *Country* | *Year* | *International trade union federation* | *European trade union federation* | *European Works Council* | *National trade union federation* |
| General Motors | USA | 2002 | - | FEM | yes | no |
| | | 2004 | - | FEM | yes | no |
| | | 2007 | - | FEM | yes | yes |
| | | 2007 | - | FEM | yes | no |
| Generali | Italy | 2006 | - | - | yes | no |
| Geopost | France | 2005 | UNI | - | no | yes |
| If Insurance | Sweden | 2006 | - | - | no | yes |
| Marazzi | Italy | 2001 | - | - | yes | no |
| | | 1998 | - | - | yes | no |
| | | 1998 | - | - | yes | no |
| Philip Morris | USA | 2001 | - | - | yes | no |
| | | 2001 | - | - | yes | no |
| | | 2002 | - | - | yes | no |
| | | 2005 | - | - | yes | no |
| Porr | Austria | 2004 | - | - | yes | no |
| RWE | Germany | 2007 | - | - | yes | no |
| Schneider | France | 2007 | - | FEM | no | no |
| | | 1999 | - | - | yes | no |
| Solvay | Belgium | 2002 | - | - | yes | no |
| | | 2003 | - | - | yes | no |
| Suez | France | 2007 | - | CES | yes | no |
| | | 2004 | - | EMCEF | no | no |
| Total | France | 2005 | - | EMCEF | no | no |
| | | 2007 | - | EMCEF | no | no |
| Unilever | Netherlands | 2001 | - | - | yes | no |
| | | 2004 | - | - | yes | no |
| Vinci | France | 2003 | - | - | yes | no |
| Vivendi | France | 1999 | - | - | yes | no |
| | | 2005 | - | CES | no | no |

status of the text in the domestic regulatory system are key dimensions in the implementation.

In sum, the potential capacity of transnational company agreements to regulate work and employment in multinational companies is highly uncertain: the asymmetry between management and labour in those companies makes it difficult to conduct collective bargaining in the traditional meaning of the term; the mandate of the signatory parties is not formally established; the content is very different from collective agreements; the implementation is based on the company's hierarchy but may be difficult to conciliate or harmonise with domestic regulatory systems.

However, they can be considered as a move towards transnational industrial relations since they represent a form of joint regulation, especially when compared to the unilateral codes of conduct that only stem from managerial initiatives (see Schoemann, Sobczak, Voss *et al.* 2008).

According to Simons (2004), the efficiency of those instruments could be much improved if they were complementary to other forms of social regulation and particularly, to forms that are more independent from managerial initiatives. This is particularly true in the European context. On the one hand, the European dimension is important in a large part of transnational company agreements, because many signatory companies are based in the EU and sign European-wide agreements, or because the EWC or European trade union federations play an important role. On the other hand, in the specific context of the EU, transnational company agreements take place in an institutionalised context where, by contrast to the international level, the conditions of cross-industry, sectoral and company-level social dialogue are clearly defined.

## Interactions between transnational company agreements and other levels of European social dialogue

The interaction between the different levels is a very classical question in industrial relations. Yet the question is particularly relevant when it concerns transnational social dialogue: within national systems, players and bodies are well established and fairly stable, whereas the players at transnational level have a shorter history and often less stability, the institutional bodies are not clearly established as soon as one looks beyond the European area and, moreover, the legal status of the outcomes is not established.

Considering the potential connections, the various levels require an examination of the relationships between the players involved in the different bodies, the scope of regulation that is covered, the effectiveness of the outcomes, even if the literature generally considers the different types of texts as 'soft' rather than 'hard' regulation. In theory, when examining the three levels of industrial relations – cross-industry, sector and company – and the different geographical fields – international, European and national – there could be twelve types of interactions. Considering all of them would not only be fastidious, but irrelevant. On the one hand, at the international level, the cross-industry and the sectoral activities are practically nonexistent. On the other hand, other studies have already analysed different types of links, particularly between the articulation between the European level and national industrial relations (see for instance Pochet, Léonard, Perin *et al.* 2009, Marginson and Sisson 2004).

The study we conducted in 2008 for the DARES thus mainly focused on connections between transnational company agreements and the institutionalised European social dialogue and, in this area, with the European sectoral social dialogue. Therefore, this section focuses on these connections.

Publications on transnational company agreements rarely mention the activities of European sectoral social dialogue committees, and reciprocally. However, confronting the literature and data on the two levels is relevant both from a theoretical and from a practical point of view. The two levels raise similar questions, notably on the potential development of transnational joint regulation, and the answers to those questions for one level may be relevant for the other. In practice, the two levels coexist and, as Jagodzinski (2007) notes, there must be at least partial overlap between them.

When examining the two levels of transnational social dialogue, the first obvious observation is that the institutional context is totally different. Whereas company-level bargaining is marked by legal uncertainty, the European sectoral social dialogue, by contrast, benefits from a clearly established institutional framework that is defined by Articles 154 and 155 Treaty on the Functioning of the EU (TFEU) (previously 138–9 of the EC Treaty). The sectoral social dialogue takes place in committees that are formally installed and recognised by the European Commission according to explicit criteria (in particular, the representativeness specified by CEC (1998).

As for the players involved, more connections appear, since the European trade union federations play an important role in the European sectoral social dialogue, but also in the negotiation of transnational company agreements (see Table 5.3). The literature on transnational company bargaining generally insists on the asymmetry between the parties involved: on one side, the management of a single company; on the other, the sector-level trade unions, either at the international or the European level (Daugareilh 2005, Jagodzinski 2007, Papadakis 2008, Sobczak 2007). While Jagodzinski considers that this asymmetry does not raise any particular difficulty, others note that it is contradictory with the traditions of national industrial relations systems where both players are constituted within the remits of the company (Daugareilh 2005, Sobczak 2007).

On the employer side, in principle, transnational company agreements involve the management of a single company, whereas the European sectoral committees involve sectoral federations. However, this must be nuanced for some sectors where European employers' associations represent national constituencies that are, directly, large companies. This is the case, for instance, in the electricity sector, where national members are very large companies that play an active role at the European sectoral level. In such cases, the same players act at the two levels. The French electricity company EDF, for instance, has signed a transnational company agreement and is highly involved as the French representative in the European sectoral social dialogue.

On the trade union side, the symmetry is more important, since European sectoral trade union federations are members of the European sectoral committees

**Table 5.3 Participants in transnational company agreements and in European sectoral social dialogue committees**

| | *Transnational company agreement* | *European sectoral social dialogue* |
|---|---|---|
| employers | One or more representatives of the multinational company headquarters, including, in some cases, representatives of subsidiaries | One or more of the 53 European sectoral employer associations, or European branch of international federations, representing their national constituencies |
| trade unions | Four possibilities (Alès *et al.*, 2006): a) one or more international sector-level trade union federations; b) members of the European works council of the company; c) national trade union associations; d) a combination of various of these players | Sectoral trade union federations, of European branch of international trade union federations, representing their national constituencies |
| status | On management side, no employer status as such; on worker side, no formal capacity to negotiate for the MNC, representativeness and mandate not clearly established | Associations recognised according to criteria defined by the European Commission |
| role | Negotiation, signature | From information to collective bargaining |

and often play an active role in negotiating and implementing transnational company agreements. To date, European trade union federations have signed European-wide agreements, but also global texts. Table 5.4 clearly indicates that European Metalworkers' Federation (EMF) and, to a smaller extent, European Mine, Chemical and Energy Workers' Federation (EMCEF) play a key role at both levels.

The active role played by EMF in transnational company agreements reflects the Federation's strategy, deployed since the mid-1990s, to coordinate the different levels of social dialogue in Europe (Pulignano 2010). According to Pulignano, the EMF's objective is to avoid, as much as possible, social dumping and competition between the countries as well as negative pressure on wages and working conditions. One of the tools developed to support this strategy is an internal procedure set up in February 2006 to coordinate the negotiation with multinational

**Table 5.4 Participation of European trade union federations, as signatory parties, in transnational company agreements**

| *Company* | *Country of origin* | *Sector* | *Year* | *Title* | *Scope* | *European trade union federation involved* | *Role* |
|---|---|---|---|---|---|---|---|
| Air France | France | transport | 2001 | Social Charter | Mixed | ETF | Representative of ETUC, Co-signature with EWC |
| Arcelor-Usinor (Mittal) | Luxembourg | steel | 2005 | Global agreement | Global | EMF | Co-signature, with involvement of EWC |
| Areva | France | metalworking, energy | 2006 | Group agreement | European | EMF | Signature, with involvement of EWC |
| Daimler Chrysler | Germany | automobile | 2006 | Principles | European | EMF | Mandate towards EWC |
| EADS | Netherlands, (France, Spain) | aerospace industry | 2005 | Framework agreement | Mixed | EMF | Co-signature |
| ENI | Italy | energy | 1996 | Agreement | European | EMCEF | Co-signature |
| GEA AG | Germany | engineering | 2003 | Declaration | Global + EWC | EMF | Co-signature |
| General Motors | USA | automobile | 2000 | Framework agreement | European | EMF | Co-signature |
| General Motors | USA | automobile | 2002 | Agreement | European | EMF | Co-signature |
| General Motors | USA | automobile | 2004 | Framework | European | EMF | Co-signature |
| General Motors | USA | automobile | 2007 | Orientations | European | EMF | Co-signature |
| General Motors | USA | automobile | 2007 | Agreement | European | EMF | Co-signature |
| PSA Peugeot | France | automobile | 2006 | Global agreement | Mixed | EMF | Co-signature |
| Rheinmetall | Germany | defence, automobile | 2003 | Code of conduct | Global + EWC | EMF | Co-signature |
| Röchling | Germany | automobile, plastics | 2004 | Code of conduct | Global + EWC | EMF | Co-signature |
| Schneider | France | electrical devices | 2007 | European agreement | European | EMF | Co-signature |
| SKF | Sweden | metalworking | 2003 | Code of conduct | Global + EWC | EMF | Represented by signatory |
| Total | France | oil, energy | 2004 | Agreement | European | EMCEF | Co-signature |
| Total | France | oil, energy | 2005 | European agreement | European | EMCEF | Co-signature |
| Total | France | oil, energy | 2007 | European agreement | European | EMCEF | Co-signature |

Source: CEC 2008b; list of agreements as established in July 2007

**Table 5.5 Topics in the texts**

| *Topic* | *Global company agreements (n=63)* | *European-wide company agreements (n=62)* | *Joint texts of the European sectoral social dialogue* (1999-2007, n=295) |
|---|---|---|---|
| AIDS | x | | |
| corporate social responsibility | x | x | x |
| employment | x | x | x |
| equal opportunities, non-discrimination | x | x | x |
| EU enlargments | | | x |
| financial participation | | x | |
| freedom of association and trade union recognition | x | | |
| health and safety | x | x | x |
| prohibition of child labour | x | | |
| prohibition of forced labour | x | | |
| protection of data | | x | |
| restructuring | x | x | |
| social and economic policies | | | x |
| social and political aspects of EU | | | x |
| social dialogue | x | x | x |
| subcontracting | x | x | |
| sustainable development, environment | x | | x |
| training | x | x | x |
| wages | x | | |
| working conditions | x | x | x |
| working time | x | | x |

Source: CEC 2008b, for data on transnational company agreements
Source: Pochet *et al.*, 2009, for data on the joint texts of the European sectoral social dialogue

companies. The procedure intends to make sure that, when a transnational company agreement is discussed, trade unions are involved and not the EWC, because the latter has no mandate for collective bargaining.

The role played by management, on one side, and by sectoral trade union federations, on the other side, reflects a more general asymmetry in their action, as Marginson notes (in Léonard, Erne, Marginson *et al.* 2007: 53).

> A striking feature of these autonomous processes in the Europeanisation of industrial relations is the asymmetry in focus in the predominant level of activity for employers and trade unions (Marginson and Sisson 2004; Marginson and Schulten 1999). For employers, although employer organisations do engage in cross-border information exchange and learning at sector level, the primary focus is at multinational company (MNC) level … For trade unions, the primary focus has been at sector level coming in the shape of initiatives aimed at sharing bargaining information across borders and ultimately at coordinating bargaining agenda and outcomes.

The topics covered can also indicate that there are connections between transnational company agreements and the European sectoral social dialogue.

It is not easy to compare the issues covered by the two spheres, because classifications used to identify the topics differ and, also, because a given text can cover several topics. In addition, data are partial since they only reflect the issues on which an agreement has been concluded, and not all the subjects that

**Figure 5.1 Topics covered in the different levels**

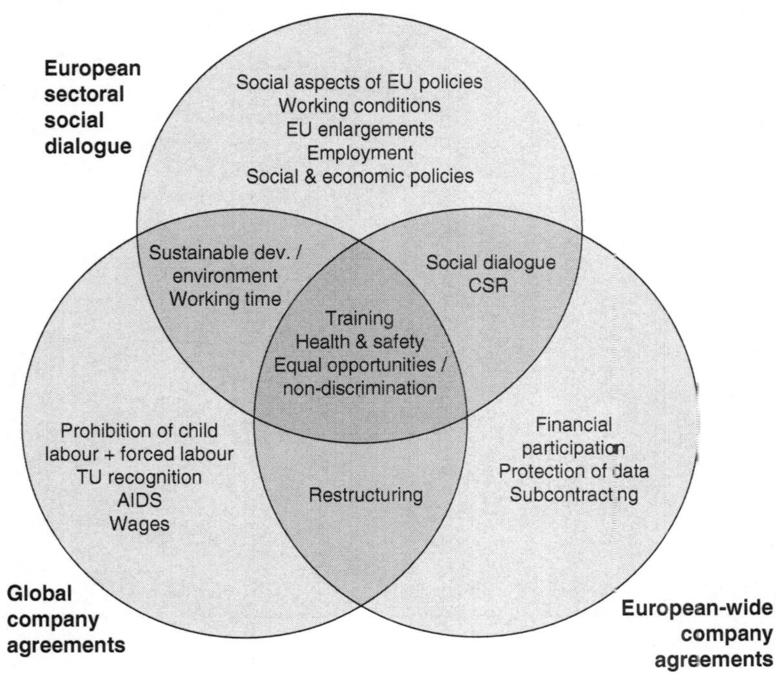

**Table 5.6 Occurrence of topics covered in the texts at the different levels**

| *Topics (by decreasing degree of presence in the texts from the European sectoral social dialogue)* | *Global transnational company agreements (n=63)* | *European-wide transnational company agreements (n=62)* | *Joint texts from European sectoral social dialogue* |
|---|---|---|---|
| | *% of texts on the topic* | *number* | *number* |
| social and economic policies | | | 55 |
| social dialogue | 100 | 11 | 53 |
| training | 61 | 3 | 33 |
| health and safety | 87 | 8 | 29 |
| social and political aspects of EU integration | | | 28 |
| working conditions | 72 | | 26 |
| EU enlargements | | | 19 |
| employment | 15 | | 15 |
| CSR | 98 | 7 | 14 |
| equal opportunities, non-discrimination | 98 | 2 | 12 |
| sustainable development, environment | 64 | | 6 |
| working time | 62 | | 5 |
| prohibition of child labour | 95 | | |
| prohibition of forced labour | 95 | | |
| freedom of association and trade union recognition | 100 | | |
| financial participation | | 2 | |
| protection of data | | 7 | |
| wages | 72 | | |
| restructuring | 15 | 20 | |
| AIDS | 13 | | |
| subcontracting | 80 | 3 | |

are discussed between management and labour. It is nevertheless interesting to compare the issues that are dealt with, and to identify whether they are specific to each level (see Table 5.5).

Figure 5.1 shows which issues are discussed in all three spheres or are in the intersection between two spheres.

The data indicate that several topics 'travel' across the spheres: corporate social responsibility, working conditions, health and safety at work, employment and training. One can add equal opportunities and non-discrimination if we consider this as a single issue. Other issues are present both in the European sectoral texts and in global transnational company agreements with a global scope: sustainable development and working time.

Some issues, by contrast, appear as being specific to a given level. Topics that are directly related to European integration, such as the social aspects of European integration, employment policies or social and economic policies, are specifically treated in the European sectoral committees. On the other hand, an interest in fundamental rights is more frequent at company level. Two issues are only included in company agreements with a European scope: financial participation and data protection, probably in relation to European regulation.

Table 5.6 examines the presence of the different issues according to their degree of occurrence in the texts. It confirms that training and health and safety are important in all three spheres. It also confirms that equal opportunities and non-discrimination are important, but at a lesser extent.

Even if the texts cover common issues, the data indicate that each level has its specificity (see also Table 5.7):

- logically, only texts from the European sectoral social dialogue cover issues that are directly related to European policies;
- worldwide company agreements focus primarily on fundamental rights as defined by the International Labour Organisation's conventions;
- European-wide company agreements cover, as sectoral texts do, principles and procedures organising the relationships between management and worker representatives, that is, social dialogue as such.

The data indicate that each of the levels tends to concentrate on a small number of issues, and these do not include the traditional 'hard' topics of collective bargaining, such as pay and working time. Therefore, while the geographical scope covered is very broad, the scope of contents treated is in fact narrow. Several reasons may explain this situation: first, social dialogue at transnational level is generally very complex. Second, the players can leave the negotiation without serious negative consequences. Third, the national players are often reluctant to delegate a negotiating power to their international representatives.

Finally, in terms of implementation of texts, apart from the specific agreements on the installation of a EWC or on the definition of the place of the workers in the European Company Statute, transnational company agreements have no legal status, whereas sectoral joint texts are regulated by the Articles 154 and 155 TFEU and by Commission communications. Even if the committees do not

**Table 5.7 Relative occurrence of topics, for each level**

| *Global company agreements (n=63)* | | *European-wide company agreements (n=62)* | | *Joint texts of the European sectoral social dialogue (1999-2007, n=295)* | |
|---|---|---|---|---|---|
| *Topics, by decreasing occurrence* | *Relative occurrence of topics (%)* | *Topics, by decreasing occurrence* | *Relative occurrence of topics (%)* | *Topics, by decreasing occurrence* | *Relative occurrence of topics (%)* |
| CSR | 12 | Restructuring | 32 | social and economic policies | 19 |
| trade union recognition | 12 | social dialogue | 17 | social dialogue | 18 |
| non-discrimination | 12 | health and safety | 13 | training | 11 |
| prohibition child labour | 11 | protection of data | 11 | health and safety | 10 |
| prohibition forced labour | 11 | CSR | 11 | social and political aspects of eu | 9 |
| health and safety | 9 | training | 5 | working conditions | 9 |
| wages | 8 | subcontracting | 5 | EU enlargments | 6 |
| training | 7 | non-discrimination | 3 | employment | 5 |
| sustainable development | 7 | financial participation | 3 | CSR | 5 |
| working time | 7 | / | / | non-discrimination | 4 |
| restructuring | 2 | / | / | sustainable development | 2 |
| AIDS | 2 | / | / | working time | 2 |
| | 100 | | 100 | | 100 |

Source: CEC 2008b, for data on transnational company agreements.
Source: Pochet et al. 2009, for data on the joint texts of the European sectoral social dialogue; percentages from this report.

systematically apply the typology of cross-industry and sectoral texts established by the Commission (CEC 2008a), this typology proposes categories that differentiate the type of implementation and follow-up. There is no equivalent for texts negotiated at the company level. The latter have a vast majority of titles – code of conduct, guidelines, procedure, framework agreement, common principles, global agreement, declaration, joint opinion, etc. – and, moreover, there is a lack of criteria to determine the type of implementation that they imply.

The practical implementation process also differs: company agreements can be implemented by the hierarchy within the multinational, whereas the implementation of sectoral texts depends on a Council decision or on the State and social partners in the Member States. In all cases, however, translation and transposition of a sectoral text give way to a degree of uncertainty on the implementation in all Member States (Keller 2003). However, even within the hierarchical system of the multinational, there is a degree of uncertainty. Within the EDF group, for instance, the implementation of the transnational agreement on corporate social responsibility (CSR) involves indicators and a compulsory reporting process for all subsidiary managers, but the implementation is not fully monitored and the situations varies from one country to another. As is the case for sectoral agreements, the degree of constraint does not go much beyond the voluntarism of local players (Pichot 2008).

## Complementary or competing levels?

Transnational company agreements may appear as being specific, separate from the other levels of European social dialogue. They are not integrated in a defined institutional framework. They involve 'asymmetrical players': managers with no formal mandate as the employer on one side and, in most cases, international trade union federations, on the other. A number of the topics that they cover are specific, such as, for instance, fundamental rights, restructuring, subcontracting or financial participation. Their implementation mainly depends on hierarchies within the signatory companies.

However, they also share some common features with the joint texts issued by the European sectoral social dialogue committees: they share common issues, such as corporate social responsibility, social dialogue, training, health and safety, non-discrimination. In terms of implementation, if the two types of texts formally have different institutional backgrounds, they share a high degree of uncertainty as to their respective transposition and impact. Moreover, beyond simple common features, there are connections mostly linked to the role played by the European trade union federations and, to some extent, the EWCs.

If there are connections between levels, different scenarios are possible. Firstly, transnational company agreements can be seen as the expression of a general trend towards decentralisation of industrial relations at the company level, related to a relative decline of collective bargaining at the cross-industry and the sectoral level. In such a case, the development of transnational social dialogue at the company level may appear as the sign of a growing role for the company, even at an international level (Lallement 1996), rather than the branch or cross-industry level. Secondly, transnational company-level agreements could constitute the 'single-employer' layer in a structured system of industrial relations with three inter-related levels: cross-industry, sector and company. Thirdly, there is an intermediary scenario in which transnational company agreements would be autonomous, specific, but would also have interactions and some overlapping with the other levels of social dialogue and, specifically, with the European social dialogue.

The data indicate that there is a 'partial overlap' (Jagodzinski 2007) between the two spheres of social dialogue, but also some 'porosity', according to the term used by Daugareilh (2005), with common players and similar issues covered. This supports the third scenario.

Accordingly, in the European context, do transnational company agreements and the European sectoral social dialogue complement each other, or compete with each other? They may be competing if company agreements are meant to avoid other sources of regulation, resulting then clearly in employer-led initiatives. In this case, the company level appears as a specific field of action that can be a 'decentralised version' of transnational social dialogue, at the expense of the sectoral level. Considering them as purely specific and totally separate from other sources of regulation would support this perspective. However, partial overlap between topics and players indicates that they share similar challenges. The central one is the regulation of employment relations in multinational companies. In a context of globalised employment relations, they are alternative strategies of regulation. At this stage, only in cases where there is explicit coordination by a European trade union federation or by the involvement of the same players, on trade union or on employer side, at the two levels, can they clearly be complementary. In any case, clarifying the status of transnational company agreements is a condition to the recognition of the company as a relevant level of social dialogue within the EU. And, in addition, their links with other levels need to be specified.

## Notes

1 This chapter is largely based on a study conducted in 2008 for the research unit of the French Ministry of Labour (*Direction de l'Animation de la Recherche, des Etudes et des Statistiques* (DARES)) in the context of a conference organised by the French Presidency of the European Union, 13–14 November 2008, www.travail-emploi-sante.gouv.fr/IMG/pdf/dares_rapport_final_final.pdf, accessed 2 April 2012.

2 To date, there is no specific legal framework for transnational company agreements signed at European level, with two exceptions: the Council Directive 94/45/EC of 22 September 1994 on the establishment of a European Works Council or a procedure in Community-scale undertakings and Community-scale groups of undertakings for the purposes of informing and consulting employees; Council Directive 2001/86/EC of 8 October 2001 supplementing the Statute for a European company with regard to the involvement of employees.

3 The Council Directive 94/45/EC of 22 September 1994 'imposes a works council or an information and consultation procedure in Community-scale undertakings and Community-scale groups of undertakings on the basis of an agreement negotiated between employees' representatives forming a special negotiating body and the central management of the undertaking. It also defines the procedures for the operation of this body.' (http://europa.eu/legislation_summaries/employment_and_social_policy/social_dialogue/c10805_en.htm, accessed 24 September 2010).

## References

Alès, E., Engblom, S., Jaspers, T., Laulom, S., Sciarra, S., Sobczak, A., and Valdés Dal-Ré, F. (2006), *Transnational Collective Bargaining: Past, Present and Future*, Brussels: European Commission, http://ec.europa.eu/employment_social/labour_law/docs/transnational_agreements_ales_study_en.pdf, accessed 11 December 2008.

Bé, D. (2008), 'A Report on the European Commission Initiative for a European Framework for Transnational Collective Bargaining', pp. 221–36 in Papadakis, K. (ed.), *Cross-border Social Dialogue and Agreements: An Emerging Global Industrial Relations Framework?*, Geneva: International Labour Office.

CEC (1998), *Commission Decision 98/500/EC of 20 May 1998 on the Establishment of Sectoral Dialogue Committees Promoting the Dialogue between the Social Partners at European Level*, OJ L 225 of 12 August 1998, 0027–0028.

CEC (2008a), *Mapping of Transnational Texts Negotiated at Corporate Level, Brussels: European Commission*, EMPL F2 EP/bp 2008 (D) 14511.

CEC (2008b), *Document des services de la Commission. Le rôle des accords d'entreprise transnationaux dans le contexte d'une intégration internationale croissante, Bruxelles : Commission des Communautés européennes*, SEC (2008) 2155.

Daugareilh, I. (2005), 'La négociation collective internationale', *Travail et Emploi* 104, 69–84.

Jagodzinski, R. (2007), 'Involving European Works Councils in Trans-National Negotiations: A Positive Functional Advance in their Operation or Trespassing?', *Industrielle Beziehungen. Zeitschrift für Arbeit, Organisation und Management* 14(4), 316–33.

Keller, B. (2003), 'Social Dialogue at Sectoral Level: The Neglected Ingredient of European Industrial Relations', pp. 30–57 in Keller, B. and Platzer, H.-W. (eds.), *Industrial Relations and European Industrial Integration: Trans-and Supranational Developments and Prospects*, Ashgate, Aldershot.

Lallement, M. (1996), *Sociologie des relations professionnelles*, Paris: La Découverte, Coll. Repères.

Léonard, E., Erne, R., Marginson, P. and Smismans, S. (2007), *New Structures, Forms And Processes of Governance in European Industrial Relations*, Research report for the European Foundation for the Improvement of Living and Working Conditions, Luxembourg: Office for Official Publications of the European Communities.

Marginson, P. and Schulten, T. (1999), 'The "Europeanization" of collective bargaining', *European Industrial Relations Observatory Online*, Ref: TN9907201S.

Marginson, P. and Sisson, K. (2004), *Europeanisation, Integration and Industrial Relations. Multilevel Governance in the Making*, Basingstoke: Palgrave Macmillan.

Murray, G. and Trudeau, G. (2004), 'Une regulation sociale de l'entreprise mondialisée? Introduction', *Relations Industrielles/Industrial Relations* 59(1), 3–14.

Papadakis, K. (ed.) (2008), *Cross-Border Social Dialogue and Agreements: An Emerging Global Industrial Relations Framework?*, Geneva: International Institute for Labour Studies/International Labour Organisation.

Pichot, E. (2008), 'Les opportunités et les questions ouvertes par le développement d'accords d'entreprise transnationaux', *Cahiers de la Fondation 'Europe et Société'*, October 2007–September 2008 (69–70), 35–40.

Pochet, P., Léonard, E., Perin, E. and Peeters, A. (2009), *Dynamics of the European Sectoral Social Dialogue*, Luxembourg: Office for Official Publications of the

European Communities, www.eurofound.europa.eu/publications/htmlfiles/ef0898.htm, accessed 23 September 2009.

Pulignano, V. (2010), 'Syndicats et coordination des négociations collectives en Europe' , in Arcq, E., Capron, M., Léonard, E. and Reman, P. (eds), *Dynamiques de la concertation sociale*, Brussels: CRISP.

Schoemann, I., Sobczak, A., Voss, E. and Wilke, P. (2008), *Codes of Conduct and International Framework Agreements: New Forms of Governance at Company Level, Report to the European Foundation for the Improvement of Living and Working Conditions,* Luxembourg: Office for Official Publications of the European Communities.

Simons, P. (2004), 'Corporate Voluntarism and Human Rights: The Adequacy and Effectiveness of Voluntary Self-regulation Regimes', *Relations Industrielles/Industrial Relations* 59(1), 101–41.

Sobczak, A. (2007), 'Legal Dimensions of International Framework Agreements in the Field of Corporate Social Responsibility', *Relations Industrielles/Industrial Relations* 62(3), 466–91.

Sobczak, A. and Léonard, E. (2009), *Dialogue social transnational: Quelles interactions entre différents niveaux?*, Rapport de recherche pour la DARES, Ministère du Travail, Paris.

Telljohann, V., da Costa, I., Müller, T., Rehfeldt, U. and Zimmer, R. (2009), *European and International Framework Agreements: Practical Experiences and Strategic Approaches*, Dublin: European Foundation for the Improvement of Living and Working Conditions, www.eurofound.europa.eu/publications/htmlfiles/ef08102.htm, accessed 24 September 2009.

# PART II

## The EU as driver of institutional change in industrial relations at the national level

*Valeria Pulignano and Norbert Kluge*

# 6

# The European dimension of employee involvement: articulating between local practices and supranational structures

## Introduction

Employee involvement (EI) at company level is an important feature of the established industrial relations systems in Europe. It can take the form of procedures for informing employees, institutions ensuring their consultation, and even participation at boardroom level. Gradually the EU has also become involved in regulating EI at company level. European Directives have been aimed at ensuring a minimum level of worker involvement in companies across all Member States, and have paid particular attention to creating forms of EI in transnational companies operating within the EU.

In the first section of this chapter we provide an overview of the European legal framework for EI. However, Europeanisation of EI does not simply emerge by adopting common rules at the European level, but depends on how local actors develop their own bottom-up action in relation to the legal framework provided by the EU. In the second section we look at the rather sceptical expectations on the extent to which a real Europeanisation of EI could emerge.

In the third section we analyse how far concrete practices for EI emerging at the transnational company level can contribute to Europeanisation. Concretely, it attempts to shift attention from the macro structures, such as institutional arrangements and regulatory initiatives, to the micro effectiveness of the practices for employee involvement developed at the transnational level. Specifically, with regard to European Works Councils (EWCs), this chapter proposes to distinguish between EWC practices determined by regime competition, EWC practices helping to develop joint interests, and pro-active EWC practices.

## European regulation of employee involvement at company level

A series of EC-driven initiatives regarding employee involvement was launched from the 1970s onwards. These initiatives mainly took the form of directives, which sought to set out a comprehensive framework for worker participation throughout Europe (Ahlering and Deakin 2005). This would be achieved, on the one hand, by providing minimum standards for employee involvement that would apply to companies in all the Member States, and on the other hand by providing rules for such involvement in transnational companies acting (partially) within the EU.

However, EU regulation in the field of information for employees' representatives and consultation represents a political compromise. Not only do the opposing interests between the social partners need to be bridged, but often strong internal debates within the various parties also have to be overcome. Rules and provisions for employee participation are deeply rooted in national legislation and cultural settings and experiences. Therefore, the importance and extent of becoming involved in company decision-making and control has been fundamentally contested internally within the affiliations of both European trade unions and European employers' federations.

Not surprisingly EU regulation on employee involvement took many years to get adopted. Prominent forerunners were the first draft proposal of a European Company Statute (1970); the Fifth Directive (1972); and the Vredeling Directive (1980). All these initiatives later were enriched by other measures and resulted in the adoption of Directives. There are currently some fifteen Directives that govern the involvement of employee representatives at company level in some form or another (Gold 2010). The most notable initiatives are the 1994 and 2009 Directives on European Works Councils (EWCs); the 2002 Information and Consultation of Employees Directive (ICE); and the 2001 European Company Statute (ECS) Directive. The others cover the extension of the rights for employees' participation in specific cases, such as collective redundancies within companies, health and safety issues, and the restructuring of companies including the transfer of undertakings, cross-border mergers, and take-over bids, Table 6.1 provides an overview of the most important Directives.

EU legislation for participation at both transnational and national level was required because 'no common minimum rules applied to European companies for timely and appropriate information and consultation' (Quintin 2003: 5). By setting minimum standards, the law lessens competition between firms in respect of information, consultation and participation arrangements. It creates a baseline standard which contributes to a single or universalist regulatory environment (Streeck, 1995). Whereas *transnational* structures for the representation and participation of the employees are conceived as the most appropriate instrument for labour to respond to the process of economic internationalisation and 'coercive comparisons' by multinational firms (Coller 1996),[1] the rationale of setting up *national-level* employees' information, consultation and participation rights is consistent with the process of domestic adaptation to European regional

**Table 6.1 Overview of the relevant EU directives regulating employee involvement**

| *Directive* | *Content* | *Date of proposal* | *Date of adoption* | *Not adopted* |
|---|---|---|---|---|
| European Company/ Cooperative Statute Directive (2001/86/EC)/ (2003/72/EC) | Employee involvement in the European Company (Societas Europaea, SE)/ Cooperative (SCE) | 1970 | 8 October 2001 | |
| Fifth Directive of European Company Law | Governing employees board-level representation | 1972. In 1983 an amended version was presented | Still pending, but effectively closed by the adoption of the SE regulation | X |
| European Works Council Directive (1994/45/EC) | Information and Consultation of Workers at transnational level | Proposed first as the Vredeling Directive in 1980.; the first proposal of the ECW Directive followed on 5 December 1990 | 22 September 1994 | |
| Information and Consultation of Employees Directive (ICE) (2002/14/EC) | Information and Consultation of Workers at national level (providing with minimum requirements and definitions) | 11 November 1998 | 23 March 2002 | |
| Recast European Works Council Directive 2009/38/EC | Revision of the European Works Councils Directive | Revision should have occurred by September 1999 | 6 May April 2009 | |
| Cross-border Mergers or 10th Directive 2005/56/EC | To facilitate mergers across European borders. With regard to employee board-level representation, the directive refers to the mechanism used in the European Company (SE) legislation | 18 November 2003 | 26 October 2005 | |
| Takeover directive 2004/25/EC | To establish rules for safeguarding i.e. shareholders protection and information and consultation rights of employees in the case of cross-border takeovers | 25 February 2003 | 21 April 2004 | |

Source: Own elaboration

integration more generally. The distinction between the two rationales guiding the EU intervention on transnational and national statutory arrangements for employee involvement is reflected in both the origins and the evolution of the different European directives dealing with both national and cross-border level representation issues. The origins of the ECS Directive can be traced back to 1959. The ECS was a proposal for a voluntary system of board-level representation with an accompanying European works council for companies that chose to register at the community level (Schwimbersky and Gold 2009). The first proposal for the ECS Directive borrowed from the German system of co-determination and specified a range of issues on which information, consultation and co-determination rights should be made available to employee representatives, with information rights available on longer-term issues of business strategy and co-determination rights applying to some welfare, recruitment and training matters. Yet, in spite of the existence of some form of board-level representation in several European countries (e.g. Germany, France, the Netherlands, and Luxembourg) the ECS proposal failed to gather enough support from the Member States (Waddington 2010). It was not until 2001 that the ECS was adopted. For a long time, the debate on the ECS evolved alongside the parallel proposal for a Directive on European company law dealing with board-level employee representation. This latter Directive, the so-called 'Fifth Directive' should have been adopted together with the ECS Directive. As opposed to the ECS proposal, the Fifth Directive was intended to harmonise systems of corporate governance within countries in companies with 500 or more employees. Debates amongst the Member States, employers' organisations, and trade unions ranged from the size threshold of the workforce (companies with 500 employees) through the means of selection of the employee representatives, to the principle of board-level representation. As a consequence, the Fifth Directive was not adopted.

In order to achieve further progress in this particular field of EU legislation, the issue of information and consultation provisions available to workers within multinationals was separated from the issue of board-level representation. This mirrors the 1980 Vredeling Directive, which was originally proposed by the Directorate General of the Commission for Social Affairs. The starting argument was the acknowledgement that in multinationals, managerial decision-making often took place in locations that were outside the scope of national legislation covering workers' involvement, thus weakening the effect of such national legislation. In order to remedy this deficiency, the Vredeling Directive proposed that central management should inform the local management at subsidiary level, who in turn should inform employee representatives about plans regarding plant closures, transfers and production, fundamental changes in purpose or organisation, and the commencement of long-term cooperation with other undertakings. While the European Trade Union Confederation (ETUC) welcomed the proposal, the employers' confederation of Europe (the former UNICE, now termed Business Europe) opposed it in the light of its legal basis and the challenges it created for business and competitiveness in Europe. However, discussions on a new proposal of the directive were initiated first and foremost by the Commission in the Val Duchesse meeting between the social partners in 1985. After a series of failed tentative attempts to meet the objectives of information and consultation raised in the Directive, in 1991 the Commission submitted an amended proposal which was put to the Council. The UK government was the only Member State to oppose this measure. Invoking the Social Protocol of the Maastricht Treaty, in 1993 the Commission submitted the proposed directive to the social partners encouraging them to use negotiation as an alternative to legislation. As the negotiation failed, the Commission stepped in, and the proposals were finally adopted as the EWC directive (94/45/EC) in September 1994. The EWC directive requires that all companies which employ more than 1,000 employees, of whom at least 150 are employed in each of two Member States, are legally obliged to establish a forum or procedures for informing and consulting their employees across Europe, if requested by employees (Hall 1994). Recent data from the European Trade Union Institute in Brussels indicate that there are currently 995 active EWCs established in almost 931 multinationals (ETUI, *Benchmarking Social Europe*, 2011). Several studies have illustrated the problematic outcomes regarding the EWCs. In particular, EWC agreements revealed a crucial question concerning the timing of information and consultation. The timing, form and content must enable employee representatives to examine in detail the repercussions of a proposed measure, allowing for consultation and dialogue. Despite the contrasting positions of the social partners at the EU level and contradictory expectations, the Commission announced in October 2007 in its work programme for 2008, that a revision of the EWCs directive was scheduled for 2008. The Commission was forced to make use of its right to intervene by pushing the social parties to reach an agreement. Within less than a year of the launch of the legislative process in February 2008, the Recast Directive was accepted by the Council of the European Union on 17 December 2008. In spite of the scepticism, the Recast Directive is seen as introducing advancements to the previous legislation. In particular, Jagodzinski (2009) identifies five areas of improvement: the transnational and timeless character of information and consultation; the comprehensiveness and quality of information which allows preparation for consultation; the obligations on central and local management to transmit information required for commencing negotiations by an EWC; the empowerment of a EWC to hold a follow-up meeting without management to enable discussion of the content and quality of the plenary meeting and draw up strategies on the basis of the information received from management; and the mandatory content of EWC agreements.

In 2002, the EU adopted the Directive 2002/14/EC on the national rights for information to employees and consultation, which was drafted in fairly broad terms, and therefore allowed Member States considerable flexibility regarding the practical arrangements for the implementation of its provisions (Carley and Hall 2009). The large range in flexibility of options allowed by the Directive firstly contributed to a cooling down of the climate of tension between national governments, employers' organisations and trade unions with regard to the introduction of binding rules concerning employee involvement (EI). However, the vagueness of certain provisions culminated in demands for the revision of some aspects of the Directive (e.g. the definition of information and consultation, timeliness of information and consultation, definition of establishments and undertakings, and provisions governing confidentiality) which are perceived as not functioning well (Gold 2010).

## Why the Europeanisation of employee involvement is difficult to realise

The EU's gradualist approach to mandating the participation of employee representatives in Europe via Directives has contributed to developing expectations of the realisation of a genuine transnational space for employee involvement by both social scientists and policy makers. However, several problems have been identified (Cressey 2009). Firstly, there is the problem of fragmentation (Gold 2010), due to the mismatch between the EU legislation and the cross-national diversity of industrial relations systems. These systems differ widely across the EU Member States[2] and are averse to change. Differences in systems of EI across the EU are not only due to different national regulations, but are also dependent on a variety of company structures, sectoral differentiation, traditions, and trade union ideology (Hall and Marginson 2005, Pulignano 2007). Likewise, Keller and Werner (2009) point to the fragmentation of participation arrangements within a European Company (Societas Europea or SE) as a result of sector-based and power relations factors inside the Special Negotiation Body.

In such a diverse environment, it is difficult to ensure uniform compliance and/or enforcement of transposed measures. Several studies have highlighted the variation of compliance regimes across the EU (e.g. Falker, Treib, Hartlapp *et al.*, 2005). Further analysis is needed regarding the procedures available to employee representatives to claim rights in cases of non-compliance, the effectiveness of the enforcement agencies, and the possible sanctions that could be imposed in each Member State.

As a result some may argue that Europeanisation of workers' involvement will never occur. Streeck (1997), for instance, showed clearly that EWCs are an extension of national systems of participation. For example, with regard to a German multinational company, co-determination rights within German company law will apply only to its German workforce even if the majority of the workforce is outside Germany, and the EWC will co-exist alongside the central works council, which is likely to be better resourced and closer to the management. Moreover, the process of widening the EU has reinforced trends towards even greater fragmentation given the weak and non-homogeneous institutional and structural arrangements for employee participation that exist within those countries, which do not conform to the norm of coordinated arrangements typical of Western economies (Marginson 2006). Alarmed by such a prospect, some commentators have underlined the necessity of EU-level intervention to establish and entrench the core institutional architecture of industrial relations in new member states, arguing that relying on internal dynamics within these societies will not suffice (Mailand and Due 2004).

However, while European-wide intervention is crucial in influencing national behaviour by eliciting EI, the success of Europeanisation depends on an interaction between vertical (top-down) and horizontal (bottom-up) developments (Marginson 2006: 11). At the end of the day, it is ultimately the employers and employees who are in a position to put concepts into practice or not. We will, therefore, focus on the various practices and specific modes of interplay between the different policy actors and levels of action. More specifically, it means focusing on the existing experiences and practices adopted at the transnational level with regard to EI.

In the next section we will present and discuss some evidence of transnational experiences with regard to employee involvement at the company level in Europe, namely EWC and SE agreements. They illustrate the capacity local policy actors have to fill in the institutional EU framework by identifying their role and functions within these institutions. Despite the obstacles for Europeanisation to occur, as identified above, we demonstrate that these experiences have contributed – in more or less positive ways – to constructing the first pillar of transnational employee representation and a collective voice at the company level in Europe.

## Articulation of social interests in a transnational and multi-level governance system of EI in Europe: what do practices tell us?

In the light of a series of case studies (carried out in 2006–07 and updated in 2008) into EWCs and SE agreements, we assess the extent and types of real practices for workers' involvement developed within transnational institutional structures. We illustrate that some of these practices have helped to develop a proactive and joint agenda between management and employees. This does not mean to deny the value of the academic argument addressing the problematic functioning of transnational employee representation structures. In contrast, it argues that it is not possible to objectively and unequivocally evaluate complex transnational institutions for employee involvement with a simple judgement of 'successful or unsuccessful' that is solely based on an attempt to quantify the impact of a relatively weak EU regulatory setting with regard to information provided to employees and their participation. A more systematic analysis is needed of the experiences characterising the existing transnational institutions for statutory employee involvement. This requires an assessment of the extent of Europeanisation by firstly examining the different practices developed at the local level under the EU regulatory framework, and secondly identifying the diverse conditions sustaining the functioning of these practices. This presupposes a more complex and articulated (bottom-up and top-down) approach rather than a simple unidirectional one.

First of all, let us restate some important facts. As the result of European regulation of EI, more and more employees have come under the umbrella of a transnational body representing their interests. This means more and more representatives (12,000–14,000 delegates, according to a very recent ETUI estimate)[3] at the European cross-border level have dealt for the first time with topics of transnational importance, such as internationalisation, regime competition, and cross-border restructuring. Figures about the spread of EWCs give a clear picture in this regard (see Figure 6.1).

By taking a bottom-up perspective, one can question if the pessimistic expectations regarding the Europeanisation of EI are fully justified or if the glass may look fuller than is expected. This means questioning, for example, whether EWCs and SE works councils with the opportunity to also represent employee interests in company boardrooms have the potential for dynamic and positive development, especially when seen from the position where company developments become visible rather than from a higher perspective. It has to be recognised that every case is unique and that each agreement on EI represents the result of a compromise reached through negotiations between management and the special negotiating body representing employees. A study into the adaptation by the parties, relevant at both the group level of the company and the workplace level, in the context of a comparatively highly formalistic and legalistic model of interest representation and co-determination such as in Germany, illustrates the fact that there are various facets of practical implementation. This study was developed jointly by the Hans-Bockler Foundation and the Bertelsmann Foundation (1998). It focused on the use of co-determination law in the transformed post-Fordist workplaces in Germany at the end of the 1990s, and gives an example of the heterogeneity of practices developed locally by the social actors (management and employee representatives) under the same umbrella of national law on co-determination. The study found that despite conforming to national legislation on co-determination, practices of labour relations varied very much in accordance with the company and workplace requirements. Thus, one can conclude that the exercise led to better adaptation to the new climate of decentralised decision making typical of the new post-Fordist regime of production. Hence, a similar logic may help to explain here, in the light of the empirical data, the resort to local practices and the importance of local experiences while assessing the effects of Europeanisation with regard to EI more generally.

In this light, we looked at EWCs by differentiating between three basic types of EWC practices: EWCs driven by regime competition; EWCs based on cross-border commonalities and the joint interests of management and employees; and pro-active EWCs based on strong trade unions. This classification is based on an evaluation of the functioning and dynamics typical of existing EWCs (for more details, see Voss, Kluge, Kollewe *et al.* 2010). The type of EWC based on regime competition is strongly characterised by growing internationalisation and the relocation threat to national labour regimes. This type of EWC practice mirrors the characterisation as a vehicle for the international competition of labour

**Figure 6.1 Development of EWCs over the years**

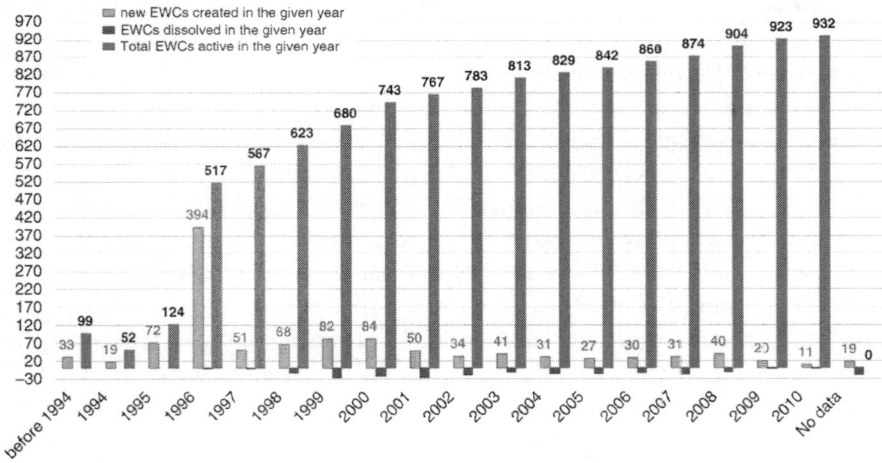


regimes (Hancke 2000). Among the features characterising this type of EWC, we note difficult relations with management and minimalist, or even obstructive, behaviour on the part of management towards the EWC; difficulties in defining common cross-border interests within the EWC and the absence of any strategy or agenda for EWC policy, resulting in generally passive behaviour in the context of restructuring or other issues; and a lack of, or very weak, integration in the relevant national industrial relations systems. This type of EWC can be described as having minor impact in relation to overall company-wide institutions and structures of interest representation, social dialogue and EI. The EWC experiences of Siemens, Electrolux and Bosch, for example, illustrate this type of EWC. Several conditions coincide, undermining the dynamic functioning of EWCs in these cases: very high diversity in company structures in terms of corporate divisions, composition of the workforce, and local labour relations; a decentralised corporate HR culture with highly decentralised autonomy and control of local management over labour relations; a high degree of internationalisation of production and corporate functions; and the EWCs' structure and practice being predominated by headquarters (e.g. the cases of Siemens and Bosch, with a strong German group works council with strong institutions, representation interests, and co-determination in the home country).

The EWC practice based on joint and common social interests is typical of those EWCs characterised by a search for commonalities in European interest representation to define joint ideas and strategies at the EU level. Examples are Deutsche Telekom, the Belgian KBC Bank, the French Sanofi-Aventis group and the Hungarian MOL. In contrast to the first type of EWC, these companies established EWC structures comparatively late. For example, Deutsche Telekom and MOL established their EWCs in 2004 and although the EWC at KBC bank was formed in 1996, it was mainly related to the development of group-wide interest representation and coordination structures within various undertakings in Belgium. Similarly, Sanofi-Aventis (established in 2005 through the merger of the French Sanofi-Synthelabo and French-German Aventis) is an example of a corporate culture characterised by growing internal diversity, integrating very diverse parts into a common corporate identity. An interesting feature of this type of EWC is the fact that management uses the EWC as an instrument for supporting the creation of a corporate identity and achieving consensus. Very illustrative of this are the Belgian KBC and Deutsche Telekom cases, where management were confronted with the task of implementing corporate identity through massive re-branding processes and tried to use the European institutions to help in integrating their foreign subsidies into the parent company.

Finally, the last type refers to those EWCs strongly involved in company development, in particular in the context of transnational restructuring. We refer mostly to those French (e.g. Danone, PSA Peugeot-Citroen, Renault and Total), German (e.g. Deutsche Bank), and US (e.g. GM and Ford) multinationals, where transnational framework agreements (see Chapter 5) were negotiated after the mid-1990s. Key features include strong trade union involvement, EWC practice integrated in national structures and organisations for interest representation and EI, and efforts to support national participation. Table 6.2 presents a summary of the type and the content of the EWCs practices.

Empirical findings show that proactive EWCs and EWCs with commonalities and joint interests are in general better prepared to cope with challenges, both at group and local level, than are those EWCs driven by regime competition. There is a clear correlation between early, effective EWC involvement and pro-active EWC practices at headquarters level. In terms of information, consultation and participation, it is possible to identify certain factors contributing to the development of good EWC practices. Among these factors, a European collective identity seems crucial (Knudsen, Whittal and Huijgen *et al.*, 2007). This is an important challenge facing EWCs. In fact, current studies demonstrate that very few EWCs have been able to develop a common sense of purpose that stretches beyond national borders. Kotthoff (2006) refers to this as the 'day-to-day Europeanization' of employee representatives' work. Therefore, one of the most important preconditions for creating cross-border reflections is intensified communication. It is no surprise that an increase in the number of possible meetings was one of the major demands of the Recast 2009 EWC directive.

Consistent with the variety of EWC practices examined above, a similar evaluation of SE agreements compiled by the ETUI in Brussels reveals that the overall quality of agreements differs significantly from an employee perspective, including both rather good and definitely deficient ones (Stollt and Kluge 2011). Case studies of these first 'big shots' of European companies (SE), such as BASF, Allianz, Fresenius, Elcoteq and MAN, suggest that the overall results reached in most of these SEs represent good reference points from an employee perspective in the way they have contributed to establishing and reinforcing employee representation rights. They have also proved to serve as new benchmarks for renegotiations of

**Table 6.2 Summary of the type and the content of the EWCs practices**

| *Typology of EWCs practices* | *Content of the EWCs practices* |
|---|---|
| EWCs driven by regime competition | Minimalist and obstructive behaviour by management; no common interests among EWC representatives; no strategy or agenda for EWC policy; very weak integration of EWC employee representatives in the respective national industrial relations systems. |
| EWCs based on commonalities and joint interests | Commonalities in European interest representation to define joint ideas and strategies at the EU level; management use of EWC as an instrument supporting the creation of a corporate identity and achieving consensus. |
| Proactive EWCs | Strong trade union involvement in EWC; EWC practice integrated in national structures and organizations of interest representation and obligatory workers involvement (OWI), as well as efforts to support national participation. |

Source: Own elaboration based on Voss, Kluge, Kollewe *et al.* (2010)

EWC agreements (Knudsen, Müller and Rehfeldt 2008). The possibility of representation in the company boardroom of an SE can be seen as a particularity of employee interest representation at transnational level, which has never featured in Europe's worker life previously. As a result, by October 2010 some 80 employee representatives were sitting on the supervisory or administrative board of 31 SEs, coming from a total of 10 different countries. Moreover, in many cases the creation of an SE has led to an internationalisation of the board, thereby indirectly spreading participation rights in Europe. This working together represents a major challenge for the employee representatives and trade unions involved (especially if in some of the countries concerned, board-level participation is largely absent by law). However, undoubtedly there is also considerable potential in the developments fostered by the SE, such as the possibility for employees to benefit from a new forum for continuous exchange and cooperation. Accordingly, European trade unions have asked for a European mandate, which would mean that employee board representatives could go beyond acting in the interests of their national workforce. In a recent resolution, ETUC member organisations unanimously committed themselves to securing a high degree of board-level participation in negotiations within SEs. Therefore, they supported the principle in accordance with which board representatives have a mandate to represent the interests of all employees. A European Worker Participation Fund has been created. It is financed by obligatory contributions made by employee representatives on SE boards and it will be used to promote activities related to worker participation in general, and to supporting workers' board-level representatives in SEs in particular.

## Conclusion

In this chapter we have analysed how the EU got involved with regulating EI at company level, and we discussed the extent to which real practices fill in the European legal framework for EI. Europeanisation depends greatly on how positively employee representatives, trade unions, and management in different organisational and national contexts view the results of negotiations, and how they act upon institutional structures by using them as resources (or constraints) while making sense of European law. It is more and more in the mindsets of interest representatives that cross-border operations have become a feature of their everyday life, wherever they are located. This is also the case in the context of the current economic crisis.

Evidently, in countries with balanced labour relations (i.e. in Germany, Austria and also France) it was possible to rapidly devise alliances between the two industrial parties mostly supported by governmental measures in order to provide company management with the space and flexibility to react to radical cuts in demand without making their qualified workforce immediately redundant. In particular, temporary reductions of wages and short-term work agreed as measures of urgency by trade unions were also often initiated and hedged by works councils in order to protect employment. However, we have also to admit that transnational statutory bodies for interest representation were only involved in this process at a later stage. The whole processes around overcoming the crisis showed how relatively underdeveloped the Europeanisation of such social issues still is. In the light of abrupt demands putting labour relations under pressure, it was all about trust and reliance on proven practices. However, in contrast to the past, the transnational quality of the social consequences was recognised by the involved parties. Thus, more than before, EWCs were also involved and considered to have contributed to post-crisis solutions. However, it is too early to draw proper conclusions regarding the further development of EI at transnational level and its division of tasks and interplay with the national or local level.

## Notes

1 'Coercive comparison' is used to describe the behaviour of multinationals to diffuse the most efficient employment practices across borders, by comparatively assessing the performance of local plants.
2 Traditionally we distinguish between systems with strong legal foundations (as in Germany), systems where trade unions are social partners (as in the Nordic countries), systems based on voluntary agreements and company-based power structures (as in the UK), and systems

governed by politics and the State (as in France and other southern European countries) (Gold 2010).

3 See Jagodzinski, R. and Pas, I. (2010), ETUI, EWC database, April.

## References

Ahlering, B. and Deakin, S. (2005), 'Labour Regulation, Corporate Governance and Legal Origin: A Case of Institutional Complementarity', Working Paper no. 72/2006, University of Cambridge.

Carley, M. and Hall, M. (2009), *The Impact of the Information and Consultation Directive on Industrial Relations,* European Industrial Relations Observatory, www.eurofound.europa.eu/eiro/studies/tn0710029s/tn0710029s.htm, accessed 2 October 2010.

Coates, D. (1980), *Labour in Power?*, Longman: London.

Coller, X. (1996), 'Managing Flexibility in the Food Industry: A Cross-national Comparative Case Study in European MNCs', *European Journal of Industrial Relations* 2(2), 153–72.

Cressey, P. (2009), 'Obligatory Workers Involvement (OWI)', pp. 139–59 in Gold, M. (ed.), *Employment Policy in the European Union: Origins, Themes and Prospects*, Basingstoke: Palgrave.

ETUI (2010), *Benchmarking in Europe*, Brussels.

Falkner, G., Treib, O., Hartlapp, M. and Leiber, S. (2005), *Complying with Europe: EU Harmonisation and Soft Law in the Member States*, Cambridge: Cambridge University Press.

Featherstone, K. and Radaelli, C.M. (eds) (2003), *The Politics of Europeanization*, Oxford: Oxford University Press.

Graziano, P. and Vink, P.M. (eds) (2007), *Europeanization. New Research Agendas*, London: Palgrave Macmillan.

Gold, M. (2010), 'Obligatory Workers Involvement (OWI) at the European Union Level: Was it Worth the Wait? The Concept of "Functional Equivalence" Revisited', unpublished paper.

Gumbrell-McCormick, R. and Hyman, R. (2010), 'Works Councils: The European Model of Industrial Democracy?', pp. 286–314 in Wilkinson, A., Gollan, P., Marchington, M. and Lewin, D. (eds), *The Oxford Handbook of Participation in Organizations*, Oxford: Oxford University Press.

Hall, M. (1994), 'Industrial Relations and the Social Dimension of European Integration', pp. 281–311 in Hyman, R. and Ferner, A. (eds), *New Frontiers in European Industrial Relations*, Oxford: Blackwell.

Hall, M. and Marginson, P. (2005), 'Trojan Horses or Paper Tigers? Assessing the Significance of European Works Councils: Participation and Democracy at Work', pp. 204–21 in Harley, B., Hyman, J. and Thompson, P. (eds), *Participation and Democracy at Work*, Basingstoke: Palgrave Macmillan.

Hancké, Bob (2000), 'European Works Councils and Industrial Restructuring in the European Motor Industry,' *European Journal of Industrial Relations* 6(1), 33–57.

Hyman, R. (2010), 'British Industrial Relations: The European Dimension', pp. 54–80 in Colling, T. and Terry, M. (eds), *Industrial Relations. Theory and Practice*, Oxford: John Wiley & Sons.

Jacobi, O. (1998), 'Contours of a European Collective Bargaining System', *Transfer* 4(2), 299–309.

Jagodzinski, R. (2009), 'Recast Directive on European Works Councils: Cosmetic Surgery or Substantial Progress?', *Industrial Relations Journal* 40(6): 534–45.

Jagodzinski, R. and Pas, I. (2010), European Trade Union Institute, EWC database, April.

Keller, B. and Werner, F. (2009), 'Arbeitnehmerbeteiligung in der Europa ischen Aktiengesellschaft (SE): empirische Befunde und (un-)erwartete Konsequenzen', *WSI-Mitteilungen* 62(8), 416–24.

Kluge, N. (2004), 'Workers' Involvement in Europe – A Still Unfinished Jigsaw', pp. 115–36, in Jorgensen, H., Baerentsen, M. and Monks, J. (eds), *European Trade Union Yearbook 2003/2004*. ETUI: Brussels.

Knudsen, H., Whittal, M. and Huijgen, F. (eds) (2007), *European Works Councils and the Problem of European Identity*, London: Routledge.

Knudsen, H., Müller, T. and Rehfeldt, U. (2008), 'Converting MAN B&W Diesel AG into MAN Diesel SE – Negotiations and the Agreement on Employee Involvement', Brussels: ETUI, www.worker-participation.eu/European-Company/SE-COMPANIES-News/Case-studies/Converting-MAN-B-W-Diesel-AG-into-MAN-Diesel-SE-negotiations-and-the-agreement-on-employee-involvement, accessed 27 October 2010.

Kotthoff, H. (2006), 'Lehrjahre des Europäischen Betriebsrats. Zehn Jahre transnationale Arbeitnehmervertretung', Berlin: edition sigma.

Marginson, P. (2006), *Between Europeanisation and Regime Competition: Labour Market Regulation Following EU Enlargement*, Warwick Papers in Industrial Relations, 79, February.

Marginson, P. and Sisson, K. (2004), *European Integration and Industrial Relations*, Basingstoke: Palgrave Macmillan.

Patmore, G. (2010), 'A Legal Perspective on Obligatory Workers Involvement (OWI)', pp. 76–104 in Wilkinson, A., Gollan, P., Marchington, M. and Lewin, D. (eds), *The Oxford Handbook of Participation in Organizations*, Oxford: Oxford University Press.

Platzer, H-W. (1998), 'Industrial Relations and European Integration: Patterns, Dynamics and Limits of Transnationalisation', pp. 81–120 in Lecher, W-E. and Platzer, W-H. (eds), *European Union – European Industrial Relations?*, London: Routledge.

Pulignano, V. (2007), 'Co-ordinating across Borders: The Role of European Industry Federations within EWCs', pp. 74–93 in Knudsen, H., Whittal, M. and Huijgen, F. (eds), *European Works Councils and the Problem of European Identity*, Routledge: London.

Pulignano, V. and Kluge, N. (2007), 'Employee Involvement in Restructuring: Are We Able to Determine the Price?', *Transfer* 13(2), 225–40.

Quintin, O. (2003), 'High Performance Workplaces: Information and Consultation Rights for UK Workers Conference', presented at a conference organised by the TUC, January, London.

Schwimbersky, S. and Gold, M. (2009), 'New Beginning or False Dawn? The Evolution and Nature of the European Company Statute', pp. 41–66 in Gold, M., Nikolopoulos, A. and Kluge, N. (eds), *The European Company Statute*, Oxford: Peter Lang.

Stollt, M. and Kluge, N. (2011), 'Potential of Employee Involvement in the SE to Foster the Europeanization of Labour Relations', *Transfer* 17(2), 181–91.

Streeck, W. (1995), 'Neo-Voluntarism: A New European Social Policy Regime?', *European Law Journal* 1, 31–59.

Streeck, W. (1997), 'Neither European Nor Works Councils: A Reply to Paul Knutzen', *Economic and Industrial Democracy* 18(2), 325–37.

Voss, E., Kluge, N., Kollewe, K. and Wilke, P. (2010), 'Behind the Curtains – the Relevance of European Works Councils for Industrial Relations in an Enlarged Europe', pp. 17–46 in Struck, O. (ed.), *Industrial Relations and Social Standards in an Internationalised Economy*, Munich: Rainer Hampp Verlag.

Waddington, J. (2010), *European Works Councils. a Transnational Industrial Relations Institution in the Making*, Routledge: London.

*Nieves Pérez-Solórzano Borragán and Stijn Smismans*

# 7

# The EU and institutional change in industrial relations in the new Member States

## Introduction

Although the Treaty on the Functioning of the European Union (TFEU) provides explicit competence for the EU to promote social dialogue only in relation to the European level, the Union has also encouraged such dialogue at the national level. This has particularly been the case in relation to the development of industrial relations systems in the candidate and New Member States (NMS). In this chapter we will first look at why the EU got involved with industrial relations (IR) in the enlargement countries. It is argued that a developed social dialogue is considered a stabilising factor for economic and social cohesion in these countries and in the single market, as well as a necessary condition for the European social dialogue to function effectively. The (lack of) strong industrial relations infrastructure in the countries of Central and Eastern Europe (CEE) has proven particularly challenging in this respect. Social dialogue has therefore been proposed to the candidate countries as a criterion to join the EU.

There are, however, inherent limits to how social dialogue can be set as a conditionality requirement for EU membership; due to a lack of a single industrial relations model and a coherent normative theory; and because of the principle of autonomy of industrial relations and a weak binding acquis communautaire on IR. In the following section, we show how the EU, and in particular the European Commission, has nevertheless aimed at steering IR in the NMS, giving a maximalist interpretation to the 'social acquis', mainly by reference to the 'administrative' or 'institutional acquis' needed to implement it. In this way, the Commission aimed to strengthen the IR infrastructure in the candidate countries, although it was more a practice of persuasion than a stringent condition to join the EU. Having an established IR infrastructure has never been a stringent condition for membership in a way that political and judiciary institutions and principles of free market economy, for instance, have been.

The inherent limits in requiring such an infrastructure and the fact that IR systems cannot simply be established by decree but require bottom-up development imply that the EU has paid particular attention to providing funding for capacity building. The last part of this chapter analyses how the EU has provided support for capacity-building for IR in the NMS. With the support of the European and national social partners organisations the social partners' representatives in the candidate and new Member States are expected to learn from their counterparts in the old Member States.

## Why the EU got involved in promoting IR in candidate and new Member States

### *The state of industrial relations in CEE*[1]

There are significant differences between the various CEE States (the EU10) in the way industrial relations are structured. It is beyond the scope of this chapter to deal with all these countries separately. However, one can identify some common characteristics that make social dialogue and social partnership in these countries considerably distinctive from that in the old Member States (Mailand and Due 2004), which may explain why the EU has been concerned with promoting social dialogue at the national level particularly in the context of enlargement. Industrial relations in the EU10 are characterised by the weakness of the social partners and the strong dominant position of the State; a preference for national-level tripartite action and the absence or underdevelopment of social dialogue at sectoral and company level (Pérez-Solórzano Borragán 2006). This state of affairs is explained by the 'reaction to and a legacy of the communist system of the past, and as the expression of a highly individualistic neo-liberal approach' (Weiss 2004: 7) but also by the very dynamics of post-communist politics that brought about the decline of trade unions that lost membership, density, workplace influence and bargaining power (Ost 2011: 169).

Trade unions have moved from a monistic system controlled by the communist party to a situation of economic pluralism where they are unable to achieve representation in the small enterprises that have proliferated since economic liberalisation. This is problematic in terms of the representativeness and salience of trade unions as these small enterprises are at the core of the new free market economy and employ the largest share of the labour force. At the company level this translates into very limited direct workers' participation in consultative forums such as works councils. This absence of sufficient workplace representation is one of the factors explaining the low levels of unionisation,[2] a dynamic that is also evident in the EU15[3] but that is more exacerbated in the EU10. Employers' organisations face similar challenges with very low levels of membership particularly amongst the small business entrepreneurs in the private sector, although membership density is higher than that of the trade unions. The employers' organisations also often lack the authorisation of their affiliates to undertake binding commitments. They focus their efforts on lobbying policy rather than developing dialogue with trade unions (European Foundation for the Improvement of Living and Working Conditions 2008: 12). Both trade unions and employers' organisations lack sufficient resources and organisational capacity. While the available financial resources are sufficient to maintain daily operations, there is not sufficient funding to allow social partners to pursue crucial aspects of capacity building such as modernisation, education or the development of international partnerships (European Foundation for the Improvement of Living and Working Conditions 2008: 15). Social partners often lack sufficient expertise and knowledge about the relevant employment legislation to meaningfully engage in social dialogue although the situation is worse among trade unions.

As a consequence, the government retains a dominant position within the weakly developed industrial relations systems of the EU10. Collective bargaining takes place mainly at the level of national tripartite action. With the exception of Hungary,[4] the national economic and social councils are the main structures in which tripartite social dialogue takes place in the EU10. However, such councils have an advisory function, dealing with issues such as minimum wages, pensions, taxation, employment politics and legislation, and administration of social insurance systems and vocational training programmes (European Foundation for the Improvement of Living and Working Conditions, 2008: 7), but are not suited for adopting binding cross-sectoral agreements. Even in countries where social pacts have been concluded, such as Hungary or Poland, the commitment to implementation is very low.

Collective bargaining in the EU10 in fact affects a very small proportion of workers, around 37 per cent, as opposed to 72 per cent in the EU15. Only Slovenia has a solid infrastructure for the adoption of bipartite binding cross-sectoral agreements. At the sectoral level the situation is even more problematic, with most countries having a weak sectoral dialogue, and others lacking such a dialogue altogether. Company-level collective agreements are more important than sectoral collective agreements, but are most common in medium to large enterprises, particularly in the larger formerly state-owned enterprises (European Foundation for the Improvement of Living and Working Conditions 2008: 75, Vaughan-Whitehead 2007: 57).

### *Why the state of IR in CEE is a matter of concern for the EU*

The industrial relations systems in CEE were a cause of concern for the EU at the time of enlargement and remain a challenge today. Firstly, although industrial relations systems vary considerably from country to country, most old Member States consider social partnership an important aspect of social cohesion in modern democracies. The absence of well-developed industrial relations systems is perceived as being at the expense of the stability of the politico-economic system. Secondly, the involvement of employers' organisations and trade unions in aspects of policy making is also thought to increase governability, not only in terms of social and political stability but also in terms of better policy implementation.

Social partners play an important role in the implementation of several policies in particular in the economic and social domain. In some of the old Member States the social partners have, for instance, been assigned a role as service provider in the distribution of welfare benefits, or ensure the control and monitoring of health and safety protection. Thirdly, in the same way that social partners can play a role in the implementation of national policies, they are equally expected to contribute to the implementation of the acquis communautaire. Without the involvement of the social partners, the implementation of the acquis communautaire risks being limited to the transposition of European regulation into national legislation without being put into practice. Weiss points to 'the legalistic approach still commonly found in the CEE States, whereby a problem is regarded as having been solved if a law or regulation has been passed to deal with it' (Weiss 2004: 10). European social policy legislation frequently assigns a role for the social partners to implement European legislative provisions by way of bipartite action allowing for tailor-made solutions. While such European legislation generally leaves the initiative of social partners as an option rather than an obligation, the absence of strong bipartite structures to take up this option reduces much of the European legislator's flexibility, placing the final responsibility entirely with the national governments. Moreover, European policy making is increasingly relying on policy instruments, such as the Open Method of Coordination, which depend on the involvement and persuasion of stakeholders, rather than on prescriptive rules that can be sanctioned in court. If these stakeholders, such as the social partners in relation to employment policy, are not effectively organised to ensure their involvement bottom-up, such types of 'persuasive policy-making' risk remaining ineffectual.

Finally, the weakness of IR in the (new) Member States did not only constitute a risk for socio-economic stability and a problem for the successful implementation of the acquis communautaire in these countries. The EU's engagement with promoting social dialogue in the NMS was also inspired by the fact that their weak IR systems may undermine the social dialogue at the European level. The weak organisational features of the social partners in CEE undermines the representativeness and capacity for action of the European social partners and puts into doubt the representative nature of their collective agreements. At the same time, the weak IR infrastructure in CEE makes the implementation of European collective agreements more problematic. This is particularly the case for autonomous agreements, when implementation is left to the voluntary means of IR, although experience with the first autonomous agreements shows some remarkable willingness of several NMS to compensate for their weak IR infrastructure by implementing such European autonomous agreements by legislative action (see Chapter 2).

## The difficulties in setting requirements for IR in the candidate countries

While the state of IR in the countries of CEE was surely a concern for the EU, it was less clear how and to what extent the EU could formulate the existence of a functioning

IR system as a requirement for EU membership. More particularly, it is unclear what the 'template of IR' that could be set as example or benchmark would be.

Industrial relations systems in the EU15 have developed within the specific historical context of the nation state and show important differences in balances between tripartite and bipartite action, and between cross-sectoral, sectoral and company-level IR structures. Although it is possible to identify different country groups showing common features – namely, the Nordic, Rhineland, Latin and Anglo-Saxon groups – each industrial relations system is unique. Therefore there is not a commonly agreed model of IR in the EU that may become a template for the EU10 to imitate or transpose.

While this is also the case when it comes to providing the EU10 with templates for political, administrative or judicial systems, the social dialogue suffers from particular normative limitations due to the absence of a coherent normative theory on the desirability and format of IR. The EU's Copenhagen criteria, for instance, require a candidate country to have stable institutions guaranteeing democracy, the rule of law, human rights and respect for and protection of minorities. While there are different ways to comply with such requirements – either through a presidential or a parliamentary system, a majoritarian or proportional electoral system – the commitment to the rule of law, human rights, multi-party system, free and fair elections are all part of a long-standing and extensive tradition of democratic thought and theory. However, in the case of IR such common ground is absent. IR systems have developed as a matter of fact without strong accompanying normative theoretical arguments. Although in most of the EU15, the role of trade unions and employers' organisations in governing socio-economic issues and in dealing with labour market issues within a certain autonomous remit is generally accepted as unopposed and complementary to modern democratic regimes, their role is accepted rather as a matter of fact than as a matter of theory.[5]

In the absence of clear and agreed theoretical considerations on the desirability and format of social dialogue and social partnership, the task to persuade the EU10 to comply with the industrial relations traditions of the old member states may prove to be more difficult than persuading them to implement criteria of democratic organisation. Vague Commission statements on social partnership being a common tradition or an 'expression of European democracy'[6] may not be sufficient.

The desire for democratic reform – and economic prosperity – has been central to the demise of communist rule. In this way, the bottom-up demands coincide with the criteria set by the EU. Such coincidence cannot be assumed in relation to systems of industrial relations. The idea of social dialogue and partnership is not inherent in the common package of democratic thought that inspired changes in CEE. Rather, some aspects of social dialogue and partnership might remind people of the communist past they wanted to get rid of. Requirements for worker consultation at enterprise level, for instance, are often received with some reluctance, as they may be perceived as re-establishing communist 'worker-control'. While the free market ideology may fit well with the basics of democracy, there is no automatic evidence for the new Member States that social partnership would equally fit that picture. Moreover, the state of industrial relations in Western Europe points to a 'post-industrial' order where trade unionism, collective bargaining and institutionalisation of the employment relationship are in decline. Thus the EU10 have neither a normatively agreed model nor an obvious leading model of IR to imitate (Meardi 2007: 504).

The absence of a clear template for IR, and of an agreed normative discourse to justify it, is coupled with a weak European legal framework for IR at the national level. As we will analyse in more detail in the following section, enlargement conditionality has foremost been constructed on the requirement to implement the EU's acquis communautaire, i.e. the entirety of EU law's binding provisions. However, in relation to IR infrastructure at the national level, the EU's binding acquis is limited. Although the EU has been given the competence to adopt Directives in the field of 'representation and collective defence of interests of workers and employers, including determination' (Article 153 TFEU) such action is extremely difficult as it requires unanimity in the Council, which is nearly impossible to reach given the divers approaches to IR in the Member States. Hence, the legally binding acquis on IR is mainly limited to provisions on information and consultation of workers at company level, for which the Treaty allows qualified majority voting (Article 153 TFEU). There is thus no established binding acquis to impose a particular and overall structure of IR at cross-sectoral, sectoral and company level.

The absence of such a detailed template is obviously also due to the nature of IR. Industrial relations constitute a complex social reality which relies largely on bottom-up processes from civil society. IR cannot simply be created by legal decree. Although State intervention is needed to provide some institutional framework within which industrial relations can operate, the latter is also precisely established to create some autonomy from State intervention and it can only operate as far as the societal forces can provide the bottom-up dynamics for it.

Faced with these limitations, the EU has developed a two-track approach to IR in the candidate and New Member States. On the one hand, and despite the lack of a full and legal template, the European Commission has attempted to influence IR in the candidate countries by presenting social dialogue as part of a broad interpretation of the 'social acquis', which we will analyse in the next section. On the other hand, the EU has aimed at contributing to the bottom-up building of an IR infrastructure by supporting capacity-building initiatives for social partners during and after accession, which will be analysed in the final section of this chapter.

## Social dialogue as conditionality for enlargement: the Commission's maximalist interpretation of the 'social acquis'

Despite the lack of a clear template for IR, the EU, and in particular the European Commission have tried to influence the shaping of IR in the candidate countries in the context of the enlargement conditionality process. The EU's traditional method of enlargement would require the candidate country to adopt the acquis communautaire, i.e. the entirety of European binding norms. In the context of the enlargement to the EU10, the EU developed a more extensive and complex set of conditions for the candidate countries going beyond ensuring the transposition of the legal acquis. The new 'enlargement acquis' includes conditions 'partially designed to address transformation problems and weaknesses of the candidates' (Dimitrova 2002: 175), and refers in particular to an 'administrative acquis', i.e. a set of institutions and administrative structures needed to successfully implement the legal acquis, even if there is no explicit legally binding requirement for such institutional infrastructure. In this manner the EU has been able to exercise a substantial influence over the socio-economic and political systems of the countries of CEE as the attractiveness of membership has allowed the Union 'to pursue broader political goals through its enlargement policy' (Sedelmeier 2011). However, going beyond the legal acquis, the enlargement requirements become increasingly prone to discretion by the EU institutions. The Commission in particular can act here as a policy entrepreneur in framing the criteria for enlargement. This is exactly what happened in relation to the criteria for an IR framework at the national level. The Commission has acted as a decisive policy entrepreneur going beyond the criteria for enlargement set by the Council and giving a pro-active teleological interpretation to the EU's legal framework in this field. We will first clarify that requirements for IR have never been part of the core political and economic conditions for enlargement. Moreover, such requirements received only minor attention in the EU's screening of the 'administrative acquis'. It has mainly been the Commission's DG for Employment and Social Affairs which has aimed to frame requirements regarding IR institutions as part of the 'social acquis'. However, as that social acquis does not include many legally binding provisions regarding IR at the national level, the Commission has developed an extensive interpretation of the social acquis, referring to an institutional or administrative acquis implicitly required to implement the European social policy provisions.

***No mention of IR in the political and economic criteria for EU membership***

The European Council at Copenhagen in 1993 laid down three groups of conditions for the countries of CEE to join the EU, namely:

- stability of institutions guaranteeing democracy, the rule of law, human rights and the respect for and protection of minorities (the political criteria);
- the existence of a functioning market economy as well as the capacity to cope with competitive pressure and market forces within the Union (the economic criteria);
- the ability to take on the obligations of membership, including adherence to the aims of political, economic and monetary union. This criterion refers to the implementation of the acquis communautaire.

An initial reading of the accession criteria shows that the establishment of social dialogue and industrial relations systems at the national level is hardly a priority for accession. Although social dialogue has an important role in socio-economic governance of modern democracies, it has not been included among the political criteria. As argued above, while it is difficult to deny the importance of interactions between government and social partners and the autonomous governance action that the latter may develop, their role has not been thought through in terms of democratic theory. As a consequence, the enlargement criteria do not include social dialogue among the political criteria against which a well-structured screening exercise takes place.[7]

Neither did social dialogue become part of the economic criteria for membership, which have been further defined in Agenda 2000 for the existence of a functioning economy. These criteria include institutional requirements as an enforceable legal system, a consensus about economic policy, and a sufficient amount of human and physical capital. Despite the strong interrelation between economic governance and systems of industrial relations, and social partners' role in providing consensus on economic policy and building social capital for economic governance, these economic criteria have not explicitly included conditions on industrial relations.

Absent from the political and economic criteria explicitly defined by the European Council, the IR requirements only enter the enlargement criteria by way of the third Copenhagen criterion, namely the implementation of the acquis communautaire, and more precisely by a very entrepreneurial interpretation of the social acquis by the European Commission.

***IR has only a minor place in the screening of the administrative acquis***

The 1995 Madrid European Council stressed that it is not enough for the candidate Member States to transpose European legislation into national laws, but they need to also ensure that the administrative and judicial infrastructure to implement the acquis communautaire exists. The administrative capacity condition for accession means that a candidate country must bring its institutions, management capacity and administrative and judicial systems up to Union standards with a view to implementing the *acquis* effectively in good time before accession. The administrative acquis, also termed 'institutional and administrative acquis' since 1997 (European Commission 1997) has been characterised by a lack of clarity about what it specifically implies and what its measurement criteria are (see Tulmets 2005, Dimitrova 2002, Malovà and Haughton 2002). This is due particularly to the EU lacking the specific sets of enforceable rules and a specific administrative and institutional model to transfer to the candidate countries given the variations between different member states. At the general level, this requires a well-functioning and stable public administration built on an efficient and impartial civil service, and an independent and effective judicial system to effective apply the acquis communautaire. In practice it also requires 'a sectoral capacity' to implement the acquis in each policy area and the development of European integration coordination structures (Dimitrova 2002: 179).

The systematic assessment of the candidate countries' administrative and institutional capacity takes place in the framework of the Commission's Regular Reports. To identify possible criteria, the Commission drew on a number of sources, in particular the OECD's SIGMA baseline assessment tool and its own framework developed in the *Agenda 2000* and its *Guide to the Main Administrative Structures Required for Implementing the Acquis* (updated in 2005). However, the concept of administrative and institutional acquis, which is more extensive than the legally binding acquis, opens the door to the Commission's discretion, and the formulation and implementation of criteria which have neither been explicitly defined through democratic procedure, nor been applied to screen the old Member States' compliance. To safeguard its position, the Commission states in the front page of its Guide that it is an 'informal working document for guidance only' and it specifies in its introduction that 'it should not in any way be construed as committing the European Commission'(European Commission 2005). However, the template put forward is systematically used in assessing candidate countries' progress towards membership.

The guide for administrative reform to implement the acquis focuses on the necessary administrative set-up of public authority. Interactions between public administration and civil society actors, or more broadly, governance mechanisms relying on private actors obtain only marginal attention in the document. As a result, social dialogue mechanisms, with their traditional dimension of autonomous bipartite interaction, are not considered a central issue of concern. Social dialogue appears only as an issue in the screening process on the 'administrative acquis' under the chapter regarding 'social policy and employment'. Most of this chapter, again, focuses on how *public authorities* [our emphasis] should adapt to implement the European social acquis, for instance, by creating labour inspectorates to control the implementation of health and safety regulation, or by setting up an 'equality body' to implement Directive 2002/73/EC to ensure equality between men and women.

The guidelines for administrative reform only mention social dialogue in one paragraph stating in very general terms that 'there should be representatives of the two sides of industry, including social partners' organisations', 'in view in particular of their role in the elaboration and implementation of Community legislation', but that 'it is entirely for each Member State to decide which structure it will use, provided that the effect of implementing the requirements of the *acquis* is achieved' (European Commission 2005: 64). Focused on the reform of public authorities, the administrative acquis guide fails to give any indication on how social partners could or should play a role in national cross-sectoral, sectoral and company-level bargaining.[8] Neither does it specify what the implementation of the (social) acquis would entail in terms of national IR infrastructure.

### *IR as a central part of an extensive interpretation of the social acquis*

While the separate screening process for the administrative acquis hardly dealt with IR, other actors within the Commission have been more explicit in defining social dialogue as part of the 'social acquis' and in particular the 'administrative or institutional acquis' needed to implement it. The DG Employment and Social Affairs has repeatedly stated that social dialogue is an integral part of the acquis communitaire. In its 1998 Communication on the social dialogue it argued that the incorporation of the social dialogue procedure in the EC Treaty by the Treaty of Amsterdam 'consolidates the position of the social dialogue as a major component in Community social policy which new Member States have to take into account in incorporating the acquis communautaire into their legislation' (European Commission 1998: 20). In a guidance document for the preparations for enlargement, the same DG distinguishes between a legislative and an institutional basis for the social dialogue as part of the Community acquis.[9]

The legislative dimension is further clarified in the document, providing (non-exhaustive) examples of the legal acquis that include obligation for consultation of the social partners. However, cases of legal obligations are (mainly) limited to requiring consultation of workers at company level.[10] One can rightly argue that European legislation provides important binding requirements that structure industrial relations at company level (such as the EWC Directive and the Information and Consultation Directive 2002.). This social legal acquis must without any doubt be implemented by the EU10. However, there is no European legislation with legally binding requirements structuring industrial relations above the company level. There is no legal requirement to create an infrastructure for bipartite negotiation at national cross-sectoral or sectoral level.

The Commission in its guidance document attempts to create such a requirement by referring to the concept of 'institutional acquis'. The document argues that the social dialogue 'should be regarded as an integral part of the institutional *acquis*' for several reasons:

1 Many directives specify that they may be implemented in the Member States by agreements between the social partners (option also provided by the Treaty)
2 The social dialogue procedure of Articles 154–5 TFEU
3 The role of the social partners in the employment strategy
4 The existence at Community level of advisory committees with representatives from national social partner organisations.

However, this reasoning shows the entrepreneurial action of the Commission in providing a very extensive interpretation of the social acquis, deducing proactively some institutional IR requirements from EU law and soft law provisions that do not impose such conditions explicitly or in a binding way. Firstly, while Directives *may* be implemented by social partners at the national level, it should be recalled that these Directives do not state that they *must* be implemented by social partner agreement. Secondly, Articles 154–5 TFEU provide indeed a binding institutional infrastructure for the European social dialogue, but how far does it imply requirements for IR infrastructure at the national level? In the case of implementation of European collective agreements by Council Directive, national implementation can occur through national legislation. In that case the 'institutional acquis' of the European social dialogue does not imply the existence of national collective bargaining infrastructure (although implementation by agreements is allowed). In the case of 'voluntary implementation', a developed system of industrial relations at the national level is necessary to ensure implementation. The logical implication of Article 154 is then indeed that Member States need a system of industrial relations that allows for bipartite agreements (implementing the European ones). However, with reference to Article 154 TFEU, a declaration to the Amsterdam Treaty states that Member States have no obligation to apply these European voluntary agreements directly or to work out rules for their transposition or any obligation to amend national legislation in force to facilitate their implementation. Put differently, when introducing the social dialogue procedure into the Treaty, the MS wanted to make sure that this did not imply any obligations on them to adjust their national industrial relations systems. Arguing some years later that the EU10 must adapt their industrial relations systems to comply with the 'institutional acquis' of the European social dialogue seems a rather discretionary and maximalist interpretation by the Commission. Thirdly, regarding the role of the social partners in the employment strategy, except for a legal obligation for the Employment Committee to consult the European social partners, there is no binding legal requirement on the involvement of the social partners. The employment guidelines do include a strong rhetoric on the involvement of the national social partners. However, they are not binding. Moreover, given that participation of the social partners in the European employment strategy is problematic in several of the EU15, it does not seem fair to include this as a condition to join the EU. Finally, the required presence of national social partner organisations' representatives in Community-level advisory committees assumes indeed the existence of national social partners' organisations, but the Commission takes it a step further by deducing from such a requirement that the EU10 would need to establish a particular structure of collective bargaining. At the same time, in the absence of strong legally binding requirements, the Commission's discourse on the social dialogue as part of the social acquis can only function as an element of persuasive policy making rather than as a legally enforceable threat to condition accession to the EU.

### *IR as part of the social acquis: a persuasive discourse rather than sanctioning membership conditions*

To sum up, social dialogue, although routinely framed by the Commission as 'an integral part of the Community acquis,' is above all an unsanctioned normative discourse with which the Commission hopes to influence the framing of institution building in the EU10, rather than a stringent condition to join the EU. Requirements on IR infrastructure were not part of the high-profile political and economic criteria for EU membership; neither did they take a central place in the screening on the administrative acquis that focused on public authorities. Although Commission documents define social dialogue as part of the 'social acquis' and deduce from the latter some implications for IR at the national level, no systematic and thorough screening has taken place. When it came to assessing the readiness of the then candidate countries to join the European Union via the Commission's regular reports, only a few lines were devoted to the social dialogue, and while noting mainly advancement in relation to the legal acquis in the social field, remarks on the more problematic 'institutional acquis' were mainly limited to a repeated 'the bipartite dialogue should be improved'. In the end, the poor state of bipartite structures in the EU10 has not stopped them from joining the EU since, as argued earlier, there was only so much pressure that the Union could exercise over the national systems of industrial relations because at the end of the day there are only limited legal requirements. A full template is missing, the normative justifications for IR systems are not well established, and, last but not least, IR systems require the formation of the societal forces that can shape and give substance to an institutional framework that otherwise remains entirely void of any function.

Therefore, while the EU has developed a discourse on 'social dialogue as part of the social acquis' as a way to promote in a soft way IR infrastructure at the national level in the context of enlargement, it has at the same time taken initiatives to strengthen bottom-up the societal forces that constitute the living practice of IR. These are discussed in detail in the next section.

## Capacity-building for social dialogue in the EU10[11]

### *Providing an institutional framework and funding for a bottom-up process*

In its 1998 Communication on the European Social Dialogue, the European Commission outlined its three-pronged strategy to address the challenges of IR in the candidate countries; firstly, assistance for the social partners in the EU to develop links with and support the development of independent, representative trade union and employers' organisations in the candidate countries; secondly, support for the political and administrative bodies in the applicant countries to adapt the national legal frameworks to promote the development of the social dialogue structures; and thirdly, support to involve social partners from the applicant countries in the European social dialogue structures to help them learn about its underlying principles (European Commission 1998: 20–1). Aware that capacity-building is essentially a bottom-up process, the Commission stresses that the mechanisms to develop the organisational, financial and personnel capacities of social partner organisations should be driven by the social partners themselves (European Commission 2004: 9).

In fact, the European social partners have been very active in developing relationships with their counterparts in Central and Eastern Europe as early as the beginning of the 1990s, both in order to adapt their own internal organisational and governing structures and policy agendas to accommodate the new arrivals (Blavoukos and Pagoulatos 2008, Pérez-Solórzano Borragán 2003, 2004) and to inform the latter on European policy making and social dialogue in particular.

This has been challenging particularly when trying to identify the relevant partner organisation in CEE (Pérez-Solórzano Borragán 2004). The ETUC first created a trade union forum in 1990 as a setting for member organisations to meet with organisations from CEE and the Balkans. While organising round tables, conferences and training visits, the ETUC granted observer status for trade unions from CEE in 1994 and opened up full membership to trade unions from the candidate countries in 2000. Training visits have been essential instruments to socialise the Central and Eastern European social partners in 'the values of free enterprise, competition, wealth creation' (De Buck 2002), and training partners in the CEE were regarded as a key priority to ensure their reliability and readiness for accession.

Also UNICE (now BUSINESSEUROPE) prepared from the mid-1990s for enlargement, for instance, via exchange of information and experience on the pre-accession strategy in the Industrial Forum on Enlargement, or via the yearly Round Tables of Employers' and Industrial Organisations of EU Member States and candidate countries (UNICE 1999). The UNICE-BOSMIP programme, set up in 2003, became the employers' federation's tool to train business associations in the candidate countries through a series of seminars, relying also on the expertise of employers' organisations from the EU15.

Such capacity-building is not the prerogative of the European cross-sectoral federations. Increasingly, also the sectoral European social partners' organisations play a role in supporting social dialogue in the CEE, although this has particularly taken shape after accession, which corresponds with the more general gradual strengthening of the European sectoral social dialogue itself over the last years (see Chapter 4).

Moreover, capacity-building for social partners in the NMS also takes place independently from the European social partner organisations. Thus it can take the shape of tripartite initiatives between government, management and labour in a candidate country, or of bipartite twinning between social partners in old and new Member States – at either cross-sectoral or sectoral level – without interference of the European confederations.

Finally, it is important to note that management and labour can organise capacity-building either separately or as joint initiatives. In many capacity-building initiatives trade union organisations in the NMS only meet with trade unions from the old Member States; while employers' organisations have their separate initiatives. However, other capacity-building practices include joint meetings and initiatives of both management and labour.

Despite the variety of practices of capacity-building for IR in the NMS, there is a common underlying feature: namely, the strongly supporting role of the EU, and the European Commission in particular. Although the Commission argues that capacity-building should be driven by the social partners, hardly any of the initiatives would have seen the light without the support of the EU. Such support results from providing an institutional framework and technical assistance, and above all by financing the capacity-building initiatives. The cross-sectoral and sectoral European social dialogue committees obviously provide an important forum for exchange of experience and best practices amongst social partners from old and new Member States (see also Chapter 4). Moreover, several times a year, the Commission organises the Liaison Forum to bring together national social partners from the different sectors to discuss a particular topic of European policy and IR. For all this institutional infrastructure, the Commission functions as secretariat and provides technical assistance, and often plays a central role in setting the agenda.

Most importantly, the EU functions (by far) as the main source of financial support for capacity-building for IR in the NMS. Three funding instruments have been used for this, namely the PHARE programme,[12] the European Social Fund and the European Social Dialogue budget lines.

***Pre-accession support through PHARE***

The PHARE programme was originally created in 1989 to assist Poland and Hungary and gradually developed into one of the three pre-accession instruments financed by the EU to assist the applicant countries in their preparations to join the Union.[13] Before it developed into a fully-fledged pre-accession instrument in 1997, it was already occasionally used to support IR in the post-communist reform process in CEE. Some first initiatives in this sense were taken in 1993 (Weber 1997), but only very few social dialogue projects were submitted by the governments of the candidate countries. Moreover, they focused on securing financial support for government-sponsored tripartite bodies in which the autonomy of the social partners was questionable, while the social partners were hardly involved in the funding process (see Langewiesche 1995, 1997, Vaughan-Whitehead 2000). After the 1997 Luxembourg Council, the PHARE programme became a fully-fledged funding instrument to support the pre-accession priorities set out in the Accession Partnerships. Following the logic of the institutional acquis discourse outlined above, support for the social dialogue responds to one of the three PHARE objectives namely to strengthen public administrations and institutions to function effectively inside the European Union. These initiatives are part of the PHARE National Programmes and the use of twinning has been the main instrument. Twinning is a horizontal mechanism that involves the secondment of EU Member State experts in the implementation of the acquis to the candidate country (but also to new Member State, or potential candidate country) to facilitate the transposition, enforcement and implementation of EU legislation through the exchange of expertise and experience. The experts typically come from more than one member state and may be public servants or members of employers' organisations or trade unions. The projects last up to two years and are built around jointly agreed EU policy objectives.

Social dialogue capacity-building initiatives under PHARE include the elaboration of expert analysis of the strengths and weaknesses of the social dialogue structures in the candidate countries; good practice guides to encourage social partners at the national, regional, sector, company and branch levels to adapt best practice; the raising of public awareness of the social dialogue; support for the creation of new social dialogue mechanisms and wider discussions about health and safety; and support for capacity building to participate in other funding programmes. These have been implemented through workshops, conferences, specifically tailored training programmes and study visits. For example PHARE project SR 0006.01 set up to develop social dialogue in Slovakia twinned Dutch and British experts from governments, employers' organisations and trade unions with Slovakian colleagues. Focused on two pilot sectors, the chemicals industry and construction, the project aimed to reinforce social dialogue at national, sector and company level; increase knowledge of EU decision-making processes and of the implementation of EU Directives; improve capacity building of each party in the bipartite and the tripartite social dialogue; improve positions for employers' organisations and trade unions and the involvement of the works council. The project involved a start-up conference, a two-day training course on social partner organisations' membership and services led by employers' organisation and trade union experts from the Netherlands and UK, followed by the creation of a specialist subgroup to better communicate social dialogue and a two-week training cycle targeted at social partners involved in collective bargaining and social dialogue (Czíria 2003). Another typical PHARE twinning project worth €2 million of PHARE contributions was set up in 2002 with the aim to create an institutional structure for sectoral social dialogue in Hungary. This time the project was drafted by a Hungarian committee involving social partners and government representatives to respond to the Commission's repeated criticism of the weakness of social dialogue in the country. The twinning partners were the Hungarian government and the Danish Labour Market Authority.

***Capacity-building via ESF and social dialogue budget-lines***

In addition to PHARE, which has functioned as a pre-accession instrument and was managed by DG Enlargement, the main financial support for capacity building for IR is channelled through the European Social Fund (ESF) and the European Social Dialogue budget headings, both managed by DG Social Affairs. Like PHARE, also the ESF has a much wider remit than supporting social dialogue. The ESF promotes employment and working conditions throughout the EU. Unlike PHARE, the ESF applies to existing Member States, and is only available for regions facing problematic economic conditions. ESF support is thus channelled through national and/or regional authorities. However, the partnership principle and the involvement of the social partners have always been considered crucial to delivering the targets of all ESF-funded projects. Hence, developing the capacity of the social partners is a priority of the ESF, and a substantial amount of the 2007–13 ESF budget has been made available for capacity-building initiatives from the social partners in 'Convergence regions'. To give an example: in 2006 Latvia received funding for two initiatives; a project 'Strengthening the Capacity of the Free Trade Union Confederation of Latvia' allowing the trade unions to expand their activities outside Riga by explaining the importance of social dialogue and trying to attract new members; and 'Strengthening the Capacity of the Employer Confederation of Latvia' to develop innovative entrepreneurship in the country.

However, it is up to the government – in collaboration with its social partners – to take the initiative. Although the Commission has limited data available on the amount of ESF funding effectively used for capacity building, it is clear that to date the available money is strongly underused.[14] In six Central and Eastern European countries, around 1 per cent of the countries' allocated funds are used for capacity building, covering mostly projects related to methods, tools, logistics, training and awareness raising activities.[15]

Therefore, by far the most used channel to fund capacity-building initiatives is two budget lines provided under the European social dialogue; namely the budgets headings 'industrial relations and social dialogue' and 'information and training measures for workers' organisations'[16] (DG Employment Social Affairs and Inclusion 2011). Unlike the PHARE and ESF funding, these budget lines allow for action by the social partners independently of any government initiative. They are directly focused on social dialogue and IR issues, and do not depend on a broader scheme of governmental action. For that reason, they could also already be used before accession, for instance, by the European social partners providing activities for capacity building in the candidate countries.

The 'industrial relations and social dialogue' budget line provides grants to promote social dialogue at cross-industry and sectoral level. Each year around eighty projects are supported. The total funding available under this budget heading in 2010 was €16 million (European Commission 2011: 198). In any case, applicants need to provide a minimum contribution from their own resources of 5 per cent – 20 per cent of the total project (European Trade Union Institute 2010: 158–62). One of its key priorities are measures to strengthen the capacity of social partners to contribute to the European social dialogue with particular attention to New Member States and Candidate Countries through information and training seminars. Applicants can be European social partners, national or regional members of European social partners, European social partners dealing with activities related to European social dialogue, organisations linked to industrial relations, public authorities and international organisations active in the fields of social dialogue and/or industrial relations. In the period 2007–2010, twenty-three social partner-led capacity-building projects were financed under this budget line. Of these, twelve were led by European social partners, eight by social partners from the EU12 and three by EU15 social partners, covering a broad spectrum of sectors.[17] In addition, the International Training Centre of the International Labour Organisation (ILO) (Turin) and the ILO (Brussels) received funding to coordinate a number of social partner capacity-building projects in a variety of sectors. Most importantly, BUSINESSEUROPE and the ETUC have led/are leading four 'European Social Dialogue Integrated Programmes' and two 'ESD Resource centre' projects under this budget heading, which each include a major component on social partner capacity building. The integrated programmes (IP) aim to improve industrial relations at the national level and strengthen the interaction of national social partners in the NMS with the European social dialogue. They involve four types of initiatives: rounds of seminars in each country which assess the needs of national social partner organisations; the development of studies and seminars on the role of social partners in social and economic change; the creation of resource centres for trade unions and employers to provide (mainly online)[18] information; and the development of targeted training and mentoring to representatives from the new member federations. The first IP was launched in 2003 involving social partners in the Czech Republic, Lithuania, Hungary, Poland and Slovakia to prepare them to contribute to the European social dialogue. The 2004–06 integrated programme was extended to all MS while the 2006–08 round was extended to the EU15 as well as the Candidate Countries. The 2008–10 round developed a focus on South-East European countries without overlooking other Member States.

Finally, the budget line 'information and training measures for workers' organisations' is intended to finance information and training measures for workers' organisations, including representatives in the Candidate Countries. Between 2007 and 2010, seven projects were financed under this budget line, four of which were led by social partners from the EU12 from five different sectors.

***Problems with capacity building***

Firstly, there is a risk that candidate countries mention the completion of capacity-building projects in specific areas to help the closing of chapters in the accession negotiations even if the project had not been successful (Tulmets 2005: 672), or that initiatives remain without any longer-term effects. For example a 2002 PHARE project aimed to establish bipartite sectoral social dialogue committees in eighteen industries in Hungary proposed legislation to establish representativeness criteria for the social partners as well as co-determination. The legislation was halted in 2006 by the then President, László Sólyom who referred the draft laws on social dialogue to the Constitutional Court, which revoked the co-determination right of social partners (Berki and Neumann 2009).

Secondly, and more importantly, the irony of capacity-building is that it requires that the actors involved have sufficient resources to engage in it. The social partners in the NMS often lack enough resources to engage in capacity building, due to inadequate language skills, poor knowledge of EU policy, and above all lack of time and financial resources. The often poorly staffed organisations need to spend their time on national issues, and often do not have the extra resources to consider EU and transnational activities as priorities (even if that would strengthen their capacity). Social partners from the CEE, for instance, complained that they have to pay the money for travel to Brussels upfront, while being reimbursed only after meetings, which they can simply not afford.[19]

Thirdly, capacity building is at once too ad hoc and too bureaucratic. Twinning tends to happen rather ad hoc since the selection of partners from the Member States is not necessarily guided by rational criteria but framed by issues such as national affinity or successful pre-existing bilateral relations (Tulmets 2005: 665).

Thus the national model provided by the experts from the old Member State is not necessarily the best one for the newcomer, while there is no way to guarantee that capacity building takes place in a coherent way across countries and sectors.

At the same time, many social partners complain about the excessive bureaucratic nature of the EU funding sources. This is particularly the case for the ESF, which is so complicated hardly any social partners managed to engage in it. Moreover, the requirement for co-funding functions as a very strong restraint. The Commission is therefore proposing a revision of the ESF functioning, which should ease reimbursement procedures under €50,000, reduce to 5 per cent the co-financing rate for countries under programme assistance, and allow the Member States to delegate the financial management of programmes and projects to social partners.[20]

Fourthly, in the absence of a clear template, capacity-building and twinning initiatives often lead to very partial adoption of IR practices, either because of a deliberate choice by the adopting actors or due to their lack of resources. Tulmets, for instance, argues that the creation of new organisations or structures in the Candidate Countries and NMS tend to be a hybrid between those of the twinning partners in the old Member States and the organisational traditions and exiting capabilities in the NMS (Tulmets 2005: 671). An illustrative example of this dynamic is the collective agreements register set up in Slovenia in 2006 on the recommendation of a 2003 twinning project that brought together German and Slovenian partners to improve social dialogue in the country. The register only partially reproduces the system of registration in Germany due to capability restrictions.

More importantly, capacity-building initiatives may be set up with very different intentions. Trade unions, for instance, may aim at building up a full-ranged IR system at cross-sectoral, sectoral and company level, while employers' organisations may focus their efforts of capacity building on developing lobbying strategies and a decentralised IR system. Moreover, European employers have never been in favour of developing a strong industrial relations system at EU level, so it is difficult to identify their incentive to support industrial relations in new countries in order to save European social dialogue.

One can conclude that there remain strong limitations on the current capacity-building initiatives for IR in the NMS. As a result of the lack of resources of the social partners in the NMS and of the demanding bureaucratic procedures, there is a considerable underuse of the available EU funding devoted to capacity building. The total of around thirty capacity-building projects funded over the last four years is clearly not huge. This implies, for instance, that about half of the sectors in which there is European social dialogue, have not presented any capacity-building initiative. Moreover, in terms of impact, there is surely no guarantee that the ad hoc nature of capacity building and the different interests at stake will result in the sort of multi-level IR system (cross-sectoral, sectoral, company level) the EU would like the NMS to develop. Having said that, the capacity-building initiatives have clearly contributed to sharing of practices and to a better understanding of both EU policies and IR systems.

## Conclusion

This chapter has discussed the initiatives launched by the European Union to strengthen the European social dialogue in light of the challenges posed by the accession of the countries from Central and Eastern Europe. The social dialogue constitutes a particularly challenging case of policy transfer given the absence of commonly agreed normative principles about the desirability of IR as well as models of industrial relations systems to define the templates and benchmarking criteria that the acceding countries would be expected to incorporate and conform to. At the same time, IR are inherently autonomous and can only operate as far as the societal forces can provide the bottom-up dynamics for it, which explains the reluctance of public authority to intervene in the sphere of industrial relations.

The EU's intervention in this area has therefore been channelled through two approaches. On the one hand, the Commission has tried to persuade the candidate Countries of the importance of a developed IR system, by presenting social dialogue as part of the 'social acquis', although the legal basis for that is weak and a systematic screening in terms of conditionality has not emerged. On the other hand, the EU has supported capacity building via financial support. However, such capacity-building struggles with structural limitations and some ambiguity about the different interests of the actors involved in it. The picture of the state of IR in the NMS, in particular at sectoral level, illustrates that there is still a long way to go.

## Notes

1 The geographical remit of this chapter is concerned only with the new members from Central and Eastern Europe, thus not including Cyprus and Malta.
2 While there is a general tendency to a decrease in trade union membership across the EU, trade unions in Lithuania, Estonia, Slovakia, the Czech Republic and Poland have experienced the largest decline in membership since 2000 in percentage terms with trade union density in 2008 varying from 68.8 per cent in Sweden to 7.6 per cent in Estonia (European Commission 2011: 9).
3 The old Member States who joined the EU in several waves before 2004.
4 Hungary is the exception as the main tripartite forum is the National Interest Reconciliation Council while there is no legislation regulating social dialogue. (European Foundation for the Improvement of Living and Working Conditions, 2008: 27).
5 Corporatist theorists of the 1920s and 1930s got discredited by fascist abuse of it. Theoretical considerations of post-Second World War development of industrial relations were particularly made in the 1970s and 1980s, but even neo-corporatist writings, which came most close to making normative arguments, would claim 'defining corporatism in terms of its praxis' so that 'the concept is liberated from its employment in any particular ideology or system of ideas' (Schmitter 1979: 8). See Smismans 2002: 106.

6 Commission, Employment and Social Affairs, 'Promoting Social Dialogue in an Enlarged Europe' Conference, Ljubljana, 9–10 January 2004.
7 In order to evaluate the extent to which candidates meet the political criteria, the Commission not only provides a description of their various institutions (Parliament, Executive and Judiciary), but examines how the various rights and freedoms are exercised in practice. With regard to human rights, the Commission analyses the way in which the candidate countries respect and implement the provisions of the major human rights conventions, including in particular the European Convention for the Protection of Human Rights and Fundamental Freedoms. As regards respect for minority rights and the protection of minorities, the Commission devotes particular attention to the implementation of the various principles laid down in the Council of Europe Framework Convention for the Protection of National Minorities. Measures undertaken by the countries in order to fight against corruption are also examined.
8 The paragraph on administrative adjustment to implement European employment policy and the European Social Fund does not even mention the social partners.
9 DG for Employment and Social Affairs, special issue of the European Social Dialogue Newsletter 2000.
10 A number of Directives have provided an important legal framework for workers' consultation at the level of the enterprise, in particular in enterprises of a European dimension namely: 98/59/EC on collective redundancies; 2001/23/EC on transfers of undertakings; 89/391/EEC on safety and health at work; 94/45/EC on European Works Councils; 2001/86/EC supplementing the European company statute with respect to workers' participation; 2002/14/EC on informing and consulting employees.
11 Part of this assessment is based on observer participation by Stijn Smismans at the Social Partners Liaison Forum on Capacity-building which took place on 12 December 2011 in Brussels. Some data and findings result from statements by Commission officials and social partners' representatives at this meeting, as official documents are not available.
12 'PHARE' stands for 'Poland and Hungary: Assistance for Restructuring their Economies' but has gradually become a pre-accession instrument also for other countries.
13 Since 2007 EU funding for candidate countries is channelled through a single instrument, namely the Instrument for Pre-accession Assistance (IPA).
14 Statement by Commission official dealing with the ESF, at Liaison Forum meeting December 2011. A more comprehensive dataset is promised by 2014.
15 *Ibid.*
16 Each year around thirty projects are supported. The total funding available under this budget heading in 2010 was €16.4 million (European Commission 2011: 198).
17 Data provided by Commission official responsible for the budget heading, at Liaison Forum December 2011.
18 For ETUC see www.resourcecenter.etuc.org; for BUSINESSEUROPE see www.erc-online.eu.
19 Several statements by social partners' representatives on Liaison Forum meeting December 2012.
20 Statement by Commission official dealing with the ESF, at the Liaison Forum December 2011.

## References

Berki, E. and Neumann, L. (2009), *Constitutional Court Ruling Paves Way for New Social Dialogue Law*, European Industrial Relations Observatory on-line, www.eurofound.europa.eu/eiro/2009/10/articles/hu0910019i.htm, accessed 28 March 2012.

Blavoukos, S. and Pagoulatos, G. (2008), '"Enlargement Waves" and Interest Group

Participation in the EU Policy-Making System: Establishing a Framework of Analysis', *West European Politics* 31(6), 1147–65.

Council of the European Union (1995) Madrid European Council (15 and 16 December) Presidency Conclusions, DOC/95/9

Czíria, L. (2003), *Project Supports Social Dialogue*, European Industrial Relations Observatory on-line, www.eurofound.europa.eu/eiro/2003/07/inbrief/sk0307101n.htm, accessed 28 March 2012.

De Buck, P. (2002), Speech at the MGYOSZ Centennial General Assembly: UNICE, Budapest, 30 September.

DG Employment and Social Affairs (2000), *European Social Dialogue Newsletter*, special issue.

DG Employment, Social Affairs and Inclusion (2011), *Capacity Building*, http://ec.europa.eu/social/main.jsp?catId=481&langId=en, accessed 22 October 2011.

DG Enlargement (2006), *Twinning Brochure*, Brussels.

Dimitrova, A. (2002), 'Enlargement, Institution-building and the EU's Administrative Capacity Requirement', *West European Politics* 25(4), 171–90.

ETUC (1998), *European Union Enlargement: Involving Social Partners – Protecting the Welfare State*. Resolution adopted by the ETUC Executive Committee in their meeting held in Brussels, 15–16 December.

European Commission (1997), *Commission Information Note on the 'New Policy Guidelines for the PHARE Programme in the Framework of Pre-accession Assistance'*, Brussels, 24 March.

European Commission (1998), *Communication from the Commission on Adapting and Promoting the Social Dialogue at Community level*, COM(1998) 322 final, Brussels.

European Commission (2000), *Industrial Relations in Europe 2000*, Publications Office of the European Union, Luxembourg.

European Commission (2002), *Communication from the Commission 'The European Social Dialogue, a Force for Innovation and Change'. Proposal for a Council Decision Establishing a Tripartite Social Summit for Growth and Employment* COM(2002) 341 final, Brussels.

European Commission (2004), *Communication from the Commission on Partnership for Change in an Enlarged Europe – Enhancing the Contribution of European Social Dialogue*, COM(2004), 557 final, Brussels

European Commission (2005), *Guide to the Main Administrative Structures Required for Implementing the Acquis*, Informal working document for guidance only (updated May 2005).

European Commission (2008), *Industrial Relations in Europe 2008*, Publications Office of the European Union, Luxembourg.

European Commission (2011), *Industrial Relations in Europe 2010*, Publications Office of the European Union, Luxembourg.

European Commission, Employment and Social Affairs (2004), *'Promoting Social Dialogue in an Enlarged Europe', Conference*, Ljubljana, 9–10 January.

European Foundation for the Improving of Working and Living Conditions and European Commission (2004), *Industrial Relations Developments in Europe 2003*, Office for Official Publications of the European Communities, Luxembourg.

European Foundation for the Improvement of Living and Working Conditions (2008), *Capacity Building for Social Dialogue at Sectoral and Company Level in the New*

*Member States, Croatia and Turkey*, Dublin.
European Trade Union Institute (2010), *Trade Unions and Transnational Projects: A Guide to Managing European Training Projects*, Brussels.
Grosse, Tomasz G. (2010), 'Social Dialogue During Enlargement: The Case of Poland and Estonia', *Acta Politica*, 45, 112–35.
Karnite, T. (2006), *Unions Call for Renewed Social Dialogue*, European Industrial Relations Observatory on-line, www.eurofound.europa.eu/eiro/2005/12/feature/lv0512103f.htm, accessed 28 March 2012.
Langewiesche, R. (1995), 'The PHARE Programme and the Social Dimension 1990–1995 – an Overview', *Transfer* 1(3), 411–25.
Langewiesche, R. (1997), 'Phare Social Dialogue programmes – some Lessons from 18 Months of Experience – a Structural Reflection', *Transfer*, 3(2), 437–45.
Mailand, M. and Due, J. (2004), 'Social Dialogue in Central and Eastern Europe – Present State and Future Development', *European Journal of Industrial Relations* 10(2), 179–97.
Malovà, D. and Haughton, T. (2002), 'Making Institutions in Central and Eastern Europe, and the Impact of Europe', *West European Politics* 25(2), 101–20.
Meardi, G. (2007), 'More voice after more exit? Unstable Industrial Relations in Central Eastern Europe', *Industrial Relations Journal* 38(6), 503–23.
Neumann, L. (2007), 'European Labour Standards' Impacts on Accession Countries: The Hungarian Case', pp. 63–80 in Leisink, P., Steijn, B. and Veersma, U. (eds), *Industrial Relations in the New Europe: Enlargement, Integration and Reform*, Cheltenham: Edward Elgar.
Neumann, L. and Tóth, A. (2002), *Project seeks to strengthen autonomous social dialogue at sector level*, European Industrial Relations Observatory on-line, www.eurofound.europa.eu/eiro/2002/12/feature/hu0212106f.htm, accessed 28 March 2012.
Ost, D. (2011), 'Civil Society after "Post-communism"', pp. 163–77 in Liebert, U. and Trenz, H.J. (eds), *The New Politics of European Civil Society*, London and New York: Routledge.
Pérez-Solórzano Borragán, N. (2003), 'The Organisation of Business Interests in Central and Eastern European Countries for EU Representation', pp. 213–28 in Greenwood, J. (ed.), *The Challenge of Change in EU Business Associations*, Basingstoke: Palgrave Macmillan.
Pérez-Solórzano Borragán, N. (2004), 'EU Accession and Interest Politics in Central and Eastern Europe', *Perspectives on European Politics and Society* 5(2), 243–72.
Pérez-Solórzano Borragán, N. (2006), 'Postcommunist Interest Politics: A Research Agenda', *Perspectives on European Politics and Society* 7(2), 134–54.
Schmitter, P. (1979), 'Still the Century of Corporatism?', pp. 7–52 in Schmitter, P. and Lehmbruch, G. (eds), *Trends Toward Corporatist Intermediation*, London: Sage.
Sedelmeier, U. (2011), 'Europeanisation in New Member and Candidate States', *Living Reviews in European Governanc* 6(1), www.livingreviews.org/lreg-2011-1, accessed 28 October 2011.
Smallbone, D., Blackburn, R. and Hart, M. (2005), *Effective European Social Dialogue in an Enlarged Europe: Engaging Small Firm Managers and Workers in the European Social Dialogue*, UK Presidency Social Dialogue Event, London, 17 November.
Smismans, S. (2002), 'Institutional Balance as Interest Representation', pp. 89–108 in Joerges, C. and Dehousse, R. (eds), *Good Governance in Europe's Integrated Market*, Oxford: Oxford University Press.

Tulmets, E. (2005), 'The Management of New Forms of Governance by Former Accession Countries of the European Union: Institutional Twinning in Estonia and Hungary', *European Law Journal* 11(5), 657–74.

UEAMPME ENTER (2004), www.ueapme.com/enter/, accessed 28 October 2011.

UNICE (1999), European *Business Supports Enlargement of the European Union*. UNICE Statement in View of the Helsinki European Council, Brussels, 3 December.

UNICE (2000), *UNICE Position Paper on Enlargement*, Brussels, 2 October.

UNICE-BOSMIP (2004), *Enlargement. An Opportunity for Business*, Brussels.

Vaughan-Whitehead, D. (2000), 'Social Dialogue in EU Enlargement: Acquis and Responsibilities', *Transfer* 6(3), 387–98.

Vaughan-Whitehead, D. (2007), 'Work and Employment Conditions in the New EU Member States: A Different Reality?', pp. 41–62 in Leisink, P, Steijn, B. and Veersma, U. (eds), *Industrial Relations in the New Europe: Enlargement, Integration and Reform*, Cheltenham: Edward Elgar.

Weber, T. (1997), *Trends in the Development of Labour Markets and Labour Relations in Central and Eastern Europe*, European Industrial Relations Observatory on-line, www.eurofound.europa.eu/eiro/1997/09/feature/eu9709146f.htm, accessed 28 March 2012.

Weiss, Manfred (2004), 'Enlargement and Industrial Relations: Building a New Social Partnership', *International Journal of Comparative Labour Law and Industrial Relations* 20(1), 5–26.

Wiesenthal, H. (1996), 'Organized Interests in Contemporary East Central Europe: Theoretical Perspectives and Tentative Hypotheses', pp. 40–58 in Ágh, A. and Ilonszki G. (eds), *Parliaments and Organised Interest: The Second Steps*, Budapest: Hungarian Centre for Democracy Studies.

*Nicole Kerschen*

# 8

# The European Union as institutional model and policy context for industrial relations in France: new power games between the social partners and the State

The influence of European Social Dialogue and European Employment Strategy is not only perceptible in the new Member States of the European Union, it is very easy to prove that France is undergoing major changes in this respect.

From 2001–10, French social partners became essential actors of the employment policy. Previously, they acted under the strict control of the State, which asked them, for example, to create unemployment insurance by a national cross-industry agreement at the end of the 1950s. Progressively they extended their domain by organising pre-retirement measures for older workers and active measures for some categories of unemployed people in order to promote employability. This pattern changed with the beginning of the new millennium, when some trade unions and employer organisations made proposals in line with European employment guidelines on active measures for unemployed, asked for more autonomy in defining rules in this field and came into conflict with the Government. Relationships between social partners and the State had to be revised.

Progressively, French social partners, Government and Parliament put forward the European social dialogue model in order to transpose it into the French legislation. This has to be considered as a fundamental shift in the relationship between social partners and the Government, on the one hand, and between social partners and the Parliament on the other hand. New opportunities were also offered to French national social partners by European social partners, who started to negotiate autonomous framework agreements which had to be implemented by national social partners. The transposition of these framework agreements revitalised bargaining in France at national cross-sectoral level. At the same time, recommendations of the Council on the implementation of Member States' employment policies put pressure on the French Government especially regarding social partnership. Social partners had to be involved into National Action Plans; they made their own contribution; they acquired some power in the definition and implementation of the French employment policy.

This chapter aims to show the different aspects of this quasi-revolution in a country where the State has been omnipresent for more than two hundred years.

## Transposition of European social dialogue model into French legislation

Traditionally, the French State has determined key labour regulation through legislation and had some difficulties transferring power to social partners. At the same time, social partners were considered weak, highlighted especially by a relatively low rate of unionisation at only 8 per cent, one of the lowest of the Member States. This situation is progressively changing thanks to the cooperation of social partners, the Government and the Parliament.

## From the 'common position paper' to the legal reform on social dialogue (2001–08)

In 2001, French social partners – meaning trade union confederations considered by law as representative[1] and confederations of the employers at national level[2] – signed a *position commune*[3] (common position paper), in which they showed their willingness 'to create a new dynamic in order to complement the role of the legislation and the role of bargaining'. Confédération générale du travail (General Confederation of Labour) (CGT), the main trade union, did not sign this paper. Signatories asked for 'sufficient space', in which they could exercise full responsibility by defining, adapting and improving rules intended to govern the relationship between workers and employers. They suggested clarification of what falls under the competence of either the State or social partners.

They defined three domains:

- the domain of the legislator. According to the French Constitution, Parliament would be competent to define general principles intended to guarantee international treaties signed by France and the 'general interest of the Nation', for example minimum age of employment, maximum working time, protection of maternity rights, etc. These principles would be considered as belonging to the 'absolute social public order', which means that social partners could not depart from them.
- the shared domain of the legislator and social partners. Methods and practical details concerning the application of general principles defined by the legislator would be negotiated by social partners at the appropriate level. These agreements would be valid only if a majority of trade unions were not opposed to them.

- the domain of social partners. Social partners would be competent to improve rules belonging to the 'relative social public order' and to create new rights (Borenfreund and Souriac 2003).

Social partners also suggested that, on national cross-industry level, a procedure similar to European social dialogue of Articles 154 and 155 of the Treaty on the functioning of the EU (TFEU) (previously Articles 138 and 139 of the Treaty establishing the European Community (EC Treaty)) would apply. Before submitting proposals in the employment relations field, the Government would have to consult social partners on the content of the envisaged proposal. This dialogue might lead to negotiations between management and labour. If social partners manage to sign a collective agreement and the law needs to be changed in order to enable the application of this agreement, Government and Parliament would have to respect the balance of the agreement. If social partners refuse to start negotiations or if they fail to reach an agreement, the legislation would continue its course. This initiative from social partners is reminiscent of the initiative from European social partners at the beginning of the 1990s, which led to the modification of the EC Treaty.

In 2004, the Government committed itself, in a public statement, to consult social partners before drafting a proposal regarding labour law in order to ask whether they wanted to start national cross-industry negotiations. This commitment has been registered in the *exposé des motifs*[4] (statement of motives) of the bill concerning lifelong learning and social dialogue presented by the Government in 2004. It was considered as a contribution to the development of social democracy. But this statement raised objections from social partners for two main reasons. On the one hand, it was not in line with their common position paper from 2001; on the other hand, no legal measure guaranteed the autonomy of social partners.

During 2006, the Government asked experts to make proposals in order to undertake a major reform. A first report on the modernisation of the social dialogue analysed the European social dialogue model and some national models (Germany, USA, United Kingdom and the Netherlands) and made two proposals. On the one hand, a joint social agenda would be set up by the Government and social partners. On the other hand, a space for negotiation would be guaranteed to social partners by the Government before each legal proposal. This report also made proposals for the transposition of the collective agreements into legislation (Chertier 2006). It was complemented by a second report on social partners' representativeness and the financing of their organisations (Hadas-Lebel 2006). Social partners expressed their opinion through joint statement on 'how to strengthen social dialogue' from the Economic and Social Council, which had been consulted by the Government after the publishing of the previous reports (Conseil Economique et Social 2006). On the basis of these expert reports and the advice of the Economic and Social Council, the Government started a new reform of social dialogue.

## Creation of the social dialogue *à la française*

The law of 31 January 2007 on modernising social dialogue[5] introduced into the French Labour Code a preliminary chapter named 'Social Dialogue' containing three Articles (Articles L.1, L.2 and L.3).

Article L.1 stipulates that any reform proposed by the Government on individual and collective industrial relations, or employment and vocational training, should first be subject to dialogue with representatives of trade unions and employer organisations. This Article excludes reforms on social protection and tax policies, even if they have an indirect impact on labour, reforms at sectoral level and reforms initiated by the Parliament (but not by the Government). This compulsory procedure, named 'concertation' in French requires the Government to pass on to social partners policy documents on possible directions of action, which present 'diagnoses, objectives and main options'. Social partners will be able to indicate whether they intend to embark on negotiations and how much time they will need to reach an agreement. In the case of an emergency, the Government may act without a 'concertation', but it has to justify such a decision.

Article L.2 obliges the Government to consult the Commission Nationale de la négociation collective (National Collective Bargaining Commission), the Comité supérieur de l'emploi (Higher Employment Committee) and the Conseil national de la formation professionnelle tout au long de la vie (National Council for Lifelong Vocational Training) on the bill drawn up following the application of Article L.1.This procedure, which involves tripartite bodies, is called 'consultation' in French. As social partners are members of these bodies, they have the opportunity to check if the government's proposal is in line with the collective agreement.

In accordance with Article L.3, Government has to present an annual report to social partners on the possible directions of its policy in the field of individual and collective labour relations, employment and vocational training, as well as the timeframe to achieve its objectives. At this point, management and labour have to present a progress report on their ongoing negotiations and the timetable for the negotiations they intend to start during the current year. Last but not least, the Government has to inform the Parliament on the different procedures related to Articles L.1 and L.2. This procedure is called 'information'.

## First steps to implement the law on social dialogue

The Government applied Article L.1 for the first time in 2007, by inviting social partners to start negotiations on modernisation of the labour market. A national cross-industry agreement was signed on 21 January 2008 by all trade unions, except the main one (CGT). The aim of this agreement was, on the one hand, to make it easier for firms to hire employees, and on the other hand, to make labour contracts secure and to improve back to work measures. A new form of ending a labour contract was also created: *the breaking off by common consent*. This collective agreement contained measures which were immediately applicable, measures that needed changes by law and measures which needed further negotiations. The social partners reminded the Government that their agreement was based on a balance between rights and duties of both sides. The Government submitted a complementary bill to the Parliament, which was adopted into law on 25 June 2008. This collective agreement and the complementary law are considered in France as the expression of the 'flexicurity *à la française*'.

Article L.1 was applied for a second time, when social partners were asked by the Government to think about new conditions to revitalise social democracy. As in 2001, they agreed a 'common position paper' on representativeness of trade-unions,[6] which contained representative criteria like number of members and contributors, financial transparency, independence, respect of republican values, age, influence and audience. Audience has to be proved through the results of elections. It must be stressed that, regarding the representatives of employees, that this 'common position paper' has been signed by only the two main trade unions, the CGT and the Confédération française démocratique du travail (French Democratic Confederation of Labour) (CFDT). On the basis of this position, the Government drafted a bill, which specified representativeness criteria especially for trade-unions competent at national cross-industry level. The law was adopted on 20 August 2008.[7] Representative unions will be admitted on a list by the Ministry for Labour after the advice from an independent tripartite body, the Haut Conseil du dialogue social (High Council for Social Dialogue). Only representative trade unions at national cross-sectoral and sectoral level may enter into negotiations. In the future, collective agreements will only be valid if signatories represent at least 30 per cent of employees and if trade unions, which represent 50 per cent of those who voted, are not opposed to it. It must be mentioned that the weakest trade unions, who did not sign the 'common position paper', raised an objection to this reform.

Social partners started a new negotiation on vocational training and lifelong learning in 2008, after the Government applied for the third time Article L.1. A collective agreement was signed on 7 January 2009[8] and a law adopted by the Parliament on 24 November 2009 transposed it into the legislation.[9]

The achievement of these three major reforms on flexicurity, on social dialogue and the representativeness of social partners and on vocational training and lifelong learning proves that the law on social dialogue *à la française* is a success. But the enforcement of this law raised fundamental questions regarding the link between social democracy and political democracy.

It is also worth mentioning the annual meetings between the Government and social partners, under the leadership of the French President, during which the annual Social Agenda is set up according to Article L.3. The idea of a 'Social Agenda' reminds us of the 'Social Agenda for social policy' from the European Commission. But there is a difference between both Agendas, the French one is an annual Agenda, while the European one is a long-term Agenda, for example from 2006–10. Since 2008, the Government and the social partners agree, each year, on a list of reforms which have to be undertaken and implemented, methods that have to be used for each reform, especially bargaining, and the timeframe that has to be respected. Social Agenda 2008 was devoted to flexicurity, vocational training, representativeness of trade unions and the fight against poverty. Social Agenda 2009 integrated topics like implementation of social dialogue in very small undertakings, equality between women and men, complementary pensions. Social Agenda 2010 was focused on the social impact of the economic crisis, especially on employment, and on the reform on pensions. During the second half of 2010, trade unions vehemently opposed the reform on pensions, which the Government pushed through Parliament by brute force. This conflict between the Government and social partners seems to have had an impact on the drafting of the Social Agenda for 2011.

Indeed, social partners set up their own social agenda at the beginning of the year. Priority has been given to youth employment; concrete aspects of the vocational training law 2009; and the renegotiation of the unemployment insurance measures during the first half of 2011. The second half of 2011 included an in-depth assessment of the implementation of two major national cross-sectoral agreements. The preparation of new negotiations on the collective agreement 2008 on modernisation of the labour market is at stake. Social partners also want to measure the effect of the 2005 collective agreement on active ageing. For the first time in March 2011, social partners organised a meeting with the Senate, which is the Second Chamber of the French Parliament, in order to present their Social Agenda. This event fits into the debate raised from the origins of the law on social dialogue, that is to say the link between social democracy and representative democracy.

### Relationship between social partners and Parliament

Three different questions are under discussion: extension of social dialogue procedure to reform proposals made by Parliament (and not only by the Government), benefits provided by social dialogue and constraints imposed by collective agreements on the Parliament.

Parliament extended, on an experimental basis, Article L.1 to reforms proposed by both Chambers, the National Assembly and the Senate, on individual and collective industrial relations, employment and vocational training, which means that they both will have to inform social partners on their proposal and ask them whether they are willing to embark on bargaining. In case of emergency, the Parliament may act without prior concertation. In December 2009, the Senate, whose President is a former Ministry of Labour, convinced of the advantages of social dialogue, first took this kind of decision, followed in February 2010 by the National Assembly. Implementation will be assessed in September 2011 and perhaps Article L.1 will be changed. This debate takes place in the context of a revalorisation of the role of the French Parliament, which aims to promote a co-production of laws between the Government and Parliament.

In June 2010, Parliament published an advice on the extension of Article L.1, which questioned benefits of the compulsory procedure on social dialogue (Cherpion 2010). Does the experience prove that laws made under social dialogue procedure are of a better quality? The report expressed an opinion in favour of the social dialogue by developing the following arguments. First, the Government has to draw up in advance the paths of its reform. Secondly, compulsory social dialogue procedure asks social partners to meet more regularly. It also opens discussions between experts. But most important of all, a law legitimated by both social partners and Parliament would be less likely to be a subject of controversy.

Since the publishing of the 'common position paper' (2001), there is a heavy debate on the role of social partners in law making. Since 2007, even if the dialogue with social partners is compulsory, neither the Government nor Parliament consider that they are legally obliged to follow the outcome of negotiations between social partners. Experts argue that, according to the French Constitution, social partners are not competent to 'make law'. Some experts call for a reform of the Constitution, while others try to avoid it by proposing minor changes (Bernaud 2007). But it seems also that members of Parliament from all parties have some difficulties in considering the pre-eminence of social democracy over representative democracy.

## Revitalisation of national negotiations due to European social dialogue

In France, negotiations can be carried out at national, sectoral and company level, and although the traditional level is the sectoral level, the company level is becoming more and more important. Since the 1970s, some collective agreements, especially on employment, have been signed at national level. But European social dialogue promoted by the Maastricht and Amsterdam Treaties (1992 and 1997, respectively) provided new opportunities for the French negotiation on national cross-industry level.

French social partners obtained greater autonomy through the transposition of the European autonomous framework agreements signed by European social partners and through the resulting implementation of European frameworks of action.

### *Implementation of European autonomous framework agreements on telework, work-related stress, harassment and violence at work, inclusive labour markets*

Since the Lisbon European Council in 2000, European social partners contributed to the European Employment Strategy by negotiating framework agreements at European level, which they decided to implement 'in accordance with the procedures and practices specific to management and labour and the Member States', as specified under Article 155 of the Treaty on the Functioning of the EU. These agreements were named 'autonomous agreements' and as a result, they had to be implemented at national level by European social partners' members. European social partners encouraged and monitored negotiations. Between 2000–10, four autonomous framework agreements on telework (2002), work-related stress (2004), harassment and violence at work (2007), inclusive labour markets (2010) have been signed by European cross-industry social partners.

In order to implement these European framework agreements, French social partners chose a traditional tool belonging to the industrial relations system, namely the accord national interprofessionnel (national cross-industry agreement). The same tool has been used for the implementation of all European autonomous framework agreements. Five representative trade union confederations have signed national agreements, which have been extended to all firms and to all workers by a decree issued from the Ministry of Labour. Normally, the Ministry controls that rules set down in the agreement do not conflict with the law.

It is worth noting that, unlike Luxembourg, which in 2004 introduced into its legislation a new type of agreement, a 'cross-industry social dialogue agreement',[10] with the aim to ensure within the future implementation of European autonomous framework agreements, France did not create a new type of agreement. Moreover, the method adopted in France did not deviate from national regulatory traditions. Nevertheless, new topics entered the French legislation without passing through Parliament. This leads us to the question, what would happen if the rules set down in the cross-industry agreement conflicted with the common legislation? Would they take precedence over the common legislation? This would be consistent, because otherwise implementation of a European agreement by a Directive would be a safer way than implementation by national social partners.

The first framework agreement on telework (2002) was in line with the employment guidelines on modernisation of work organisation and forms of work, which belonged to Pillar III 'Encouraging adaptability of businesses and their employees' of European Employment Strategy (1998 to 2002): The Council recognised working conditions as the exclusive domain of the social partners and invited them to negotiate agreements at different levels (Kerschen and Roussel-Verret 2006). Collective agreements had to be implemented by 15 July 2005. French social partners had nearly met this deadline, because they implemented the European framework agreement by signing a national cross-industry agreement on 19 July 2005. The decree that extended the agreement to all workers and all undertakings was published on 30 May 2006.[11]

The second European framework agreement on work-related stress (2004) took place in the domain of health and safety at work and quality of employment. It has been part of the work programme 2003–05 of European social partners. French social partners implemented this autonomous framework agreement by a national cross-industry agreement, signed on 2 July 2008, some months before the end of the implementation period. It has been extended by decree on 23 April 2009[12] to all firms and all workers. This agreement accelerated social dialogue in

France where the topic on work-related stress had mostly been an expert issue. Social partners enriched the European framework agreement by adding provisions on the following issues: definition of stress, work organisation, reconciliation of family, private and working life, responsibility of the employers (European Social Partners 2008).

The third European framework agreement on harassment and violence at work (2007) has been part of the work programme 2006–08 of European social partners. It is complementary to the agreement on work-related stress. It has been implemented by French social partners by signing a national cross-industry agreement on 26 March 2010. This agreement has been extended by decree on 23 July 2010.[13]

By the beginning of 2011, French social partners had not yet started negotiations on the implementation of the fourth European framework agreement on inclusive labour markets (2010), which has been part of the working programme 2009–10 of European social partners. Moreover, this topic does not appear in the Social Agenda for 2011 set up by them. But it must be mentioned that the deadline for transposition could be met by the social partners by March 2013.

The transposition of European autonomous framework agreements into French legislation occurs under the control of the State. It includes neither alternative implementation methods or procedures for negotiations nor new power games between the social partners and the State, contrary to research results regarding other Member States of the EU (Larsen and Andersen 2007).

### *Implementation of frameworks of actions on lifelong learning and gender equality promoted by European social partners*

In line with their work programme 2003–05, European social partners established two frameworks of actions, one for the lifelong development of competencies and qualifications (2002) and one on gender equality (2005). These topics belonged to the shared domain of competence between Member States and social partners in the European Employment Strategy (Kerschen and Roussel-Verret 2006). Priorities were set up by both frameworks of actions.

French social partners signed a national cross-industry agreement on 5 December 2003 on the access of employees to lifelong learning.[14] It has been extended to all firms and to all workers by decree on 17 December 2004.[15] This agreement has also been at the basis of the Law of 4 May 2004 concerning vocational training and lifelong learning.

In the field of gender equality, French social partners signed a national cross-industry agreement on 1 March 2004,[16] i.e. prior to the establishment of the European framework of actions (2005). This agreement was extended to all firms and all workers by decree on 22 March 2005.[17] It took into account four priorities of the European framework of actions: addressing gender roles, promoting women in decision making, supporting work-life balance, tackling gender pay gap. It has been signed by five representative trade union confederations. In the law of 23 March 2006,[18] an objective concerning equal pay for women and men by

2010 has been set up. We would like to stress that an original provision of this law, designed to set quotas for women on company boards and electoral lists, has been withdrawn by the Constitutional Council, because it was deemed incompatible with the French Constitution.[19] In 2009, France changed its Constitution. From 1 January 2012, undertakings without a collective agreement or an action plan promoting professional equality between women and men are liable to sanctions by the State.

French social partners are increasingly using autonomous action. It seems obvious that European social dialogue has had an influence on revitalisation of collective bargaining at national cross-industry level. But in two domains – promotion of professional equality between women and men and of active ageing – expected results have not been realised at company level and the Government had to intervene in order to force social partners to act.

### Impact of the European Employment Strategy: contribution of French social partners in National Employment Action Plans

The first French National Employment Action Plan was drawn up in 1998 by the Government alone as a matter of urgency. Before submitting the action plan to the Commission, it did consult the social partners, who perceived this as 'a first awareness action', which could not give rise to substantial changes. In November of the same year, the Ministry for Labour and Employment established a new body, the Comité de dialogue social pour les affaires européennes et internationales[20] (Social Dialogue Committee on European and International Issues). This Social Dialogue Committee has a tripartite composition, bringing together representatives of the different ministries concerned, permanent members representing five trade union confederations considered by law as representative at the national level and permanent members representing employers at the national level. One of its three missions is to involve 'social partners in all stages of the procedure to coordinate employment policies instituted by the Luxembourg European Council of 21 November 1997'. In this context, social partners will 'make their contribution to the implementation of the guidelines'. This Committee has been very active since 1998,in two different and clearly distinguishable periods.

From 1999 to 2004, social partners played an increasing role in the drafting of national employment action plans in the framework of the European Employment Strategy. During this period, the Council asked France to involve social partners in major reforms, for example the implementation of European employment guidelines on active ageing. When the EU revised the Lisbon Strategy in 2005 by defining integrated guidelines on economic policies and employment, French social partners lost their new power and the Social Dialogue Committee on European and International Issues became a consultative body among others.

## The increasing power of social partners in the Social Dialogue Committee on European and International Issues (1999–2004)

In 1999, involvement of social partners in the coordinated employment strategy took the form of a consultation prior to the drafting of the action plan. In 2000, the Social Dialogue Committee became a 'forum of debate', in which social partners presented their contributions. The Government took them up, worked out 'the contribution from social partners' and drafted a separate chapter in the National Action Plan of 2000.

The real innovation occurred in 2001, when five working groups were set up under the auspices of the Social Dialogue Committee on topics defined in common: lifelong learning, active ageing, quality of employment and job insecurity, difficulties for firms in recruiting workers, and employment issues tackled at the local level. A broad consensus has been reached among social partners on the concept of quality of employment, which has been published in the National Action Plan of 2001 in a separate text box. It must be stressed that this concept differs from the European concept of quality of employment. On the one hand, it includes traditional elements of the French approach on quality like the open-ended and full-time labour contract and wages, and on the other hand, it refers to the European multi-dimensional concept addressing both job characteristics and the wider labour market issues like social dialogue, lifelong learning, health and safety at work, etc.[21] Moreover, a synthesis of contributions of social partners was drawn up by the Government, which took into account their contributions pillar by pillar. It has been published at the end of the National Action Plan in a separate section.

The work of social partners in 2002 has been devoted to the COPARSOC project,[22] an exchange of good practice among social partners on the European level. The object of COPARSOC consisted of two actions:

- dissemination and debate about the compendium of good practice produced by the European social partners;
- evaluation of the employment process and National Action Plans in an experimental European network of associated social partners.

French social partners adopted the COPARSOC method by establishing a working party at the Social Dialogue Committee to debate the choice of good practices that they wanted to incorporate into the National Action Plan. New topics like short contracts and job insecurity, gender equality, changes in multinational companies were submitted for discussion. This informal meeting led to 'the autonomous contribution from social partners', which gave priority to the debate on practices favourable to employment.

In the National Action Plan of 2003, the Government announced a major reform on social dialogue in response to several Council recommendations. The Council asked France 'to strengthen social partnership' (2000),[23] 'to involve social partners' (2001)[24] and 'to pursue efforts within the framework of social dialogue' (2002)[25] on topics like modernising work organisation, curbing older workers' early withdrawal from working life or promoting a comprehensive lifelong learning strategy. The Government wanted social partners to enter into negotiations on these topics. It also offered the social partners new forms of participation in drafting the National Action Plans in the future by creating working groups including representatives of the Administration, the public employment service and the social partners. The aim of this new process was to reach a shared diagnosis between stakeholders regarding labour market, employment and vocational training.

In 2004, the Government included social partners in the drafting of the National Action Plan. While the Administration compiled the different measures regarding the employment guidelines, social partners expressed their opinion on each guideline. As regards the writing of French action plans, the National Action Plan of 2004 appeared as the most complete document, in which different opinions of social partners regarding each employment guideline were reproduced in text boxes. The names of each trade union or employers' organisation were even mentioned. Unfortunately, it was also the last National Action Plan drafted by the Government together with social partners.

Even if social partners had a secondary responsibility in drawing up the National Action Plans – these Plans are the responsibility of the Member States – they had the opportunity to, at least, influence the debate on the national employment policy from 1999–2004. They also acquired more power through the Council's recommendations asking France to involve them into new approaches, like active ageing.

### Implementation of the Council recommendations on social partnership: the collective agreement on active ageing

French social partners undertook negotiations on active ageing in 2005 after being invited by the Government to do so. Active ageing is a difficult topic in France, however, for two main reasons: on the one hand, measures on early retirement have been widely used, in order to avoid redundancies during crisis periods, from the 1970s on; on the other hand, legal retirement age has been diminished from 65 to 60 in the 1980s. Therefore, the employment rate of people aged 55 to 64 was only 34.8 per cent in France in 2002.

Since 2000, the Council addressed French recommendations on this topic. One recommendation asked France to 'strengthen efforts to curb older workers' early withdrawal from working life by developing a more comprehensive approach towards active ageing involving the social partners'. During the discussions on the pension reform between the Government and social partners in 2003, social partners committed themselves to negotiate on employment of older workers at national cross-industry level. By doing so, they recognised the relationship between pensions and employment of older workers under the guidance of the Open Method of Coordination (OMC) on pensions. It was the first time that French social partners agreed to connect social security policy and employment policy.

In the national cross-industry agreement signed on 13 October 2005, social partners declared explicitly their willingness to contribute, in their domain of competence, to reach the Lisbon objective regarding an employment rate of people aged 55 to 64 years of 50 per cent by 2010. Therefore, they adopted a 'global approach' on active ageing based on main lines consistent with European employment guidelines (Willmann 2006). The Government integrated this agreement into a national action plan to develop seniors' employment (2006–10).[26] National cross-industry agreement on 5 December 2003 on the access of employees to lifelong learning and the law of 4 May 2004 concerning professional training and lifelong learning are also part of this action plan.

Implementation of this reform needed further negotiations at company level. An assessment showed weak results. Between 2002–09, employment rate of people aged 55 to 64 years raised only from 34.8 per cent to 38.9 per cent. Therefore, the Government took, on 20 May 2009, a decree to sanction firms, which would not be covered by a collective agreement or an action plan after 1 January 2010.[27]

## Social Dialogue Committee on European and International Issues, a consultative body among others (from 2005 onwards)

From 2005, under the revised Lisbon Strategy, the Government prepared a National Reform Programme based on the integrated guidelines on economic policies and employment. The Secrétariat Général des Affaires Européennes (General Secretariat of European Affairs), an Administration placed under the authority of the Prime Minister, coordinated the National Reform Programme on an interministerial basis. It consulted social partners by presenting the project to the Social Dialogue Committee. Some proposals, from social partners, which were accepted by the Government, were integrated into the National Reform Programme, while others became a separate contribution from the social partners. Moreover, each trade union and each employer's organisation might express its position, but those positions were not part of the National Reform Programme, even if they were transmitted by the Government to the Commission together with the National Reform Programme. No wonder that the French National Reform Programme 2005–07 did not mention the contribution of social partners.

The National Reform Programme 2008–10 devoted one section to the implication of social partners in major reforms linked to employment and vocational training. First, it presented the Government's reform on social dialogue *à la française* as a prerequisite. Secondly, collective agreements signed by social partners as a contribution to the European Employment Strategy and the revised Lisbon Strategy were listed: agreements on lifelong learning (2003), on gender equality (2005), on active ageing (2005), on diversity and against discrimination at work (2006), on modernisation of the employment market (2008). The contribution of the social partners in the fight against poverty and social exclusion has also been mentioned.

From 2006, France adopted the European approach on active inclusion in line with the OMC on social inclusion. Therefore, social partners became members of the Conseil national des politiques de lutte contre la pauvreté (French National Council against poverty and exclusion), in which nongovernmental organisations are also represented. Each National Reform Programme is submitted to this Council, which delivers public advice. Last but not least, the Secretariat General of European Affairs consulted also the Comité Economique, Social et Environnemental (French Economic, Social and Environmental Council), which is a consultative body including representatives of social partners and civil society.

Even if social partners are consulted through three different bodies – Social Dialogue Committee on European and International Issues, National Council against Poverty and Exclusion, and Economic, Social and Environmental Council – they no longer have the opportunity to commit themselves in the drawing up of the part of the National Reform Programme devoted to employment policy.

## Conclusion

At the end of this analysis, one has mixed feelings about the role played by the social partners in reforms on industrial relations, labour law and employment policy over the last ten years.

It is obvious that French social partners struggled in order to obtain more space in which they could exercise full responsibility. The creation of the social dialogue *à la française* marked an important step in this context. It became a success story when it was followed by several negotiations initiated by the Government through the Social Agenda. European social partners provided also new opportunities for French social partners, who started negotiations at national cross-industry level on new topics agreed on the European level, like telework, work-related stress, harassment and violence at work, lifelong learning and gender equality. Moreover, through the implementation of the European Employment Strategy, French social partners acquired an increasing power in employment policy until the EU decided to revise the Lisbon Strategy and to integrate the employment guidelines with the guidelines on economic policy. The National Reform Programme revived the responsibility of the State, especially regarding macro-economic constraints.

French social partners will have to face new challenges. The domain in which social dialogue procedure applies, excluding social protection reforms, is still limited. Moreover social partners did not succeed in obtaining a guarantee from the Government and Parliament that they would respect the balance of collective agreements which they would transpose into legislation. French social partners seem to have less power than European social partners, because they are not competent or not yet competent to make statute.

## Notes

1 CGT, CFDT, Confédération Générale du Travail – Force Ouvrière, or simply Force Ouvrière (General Confederation of Labour – Workers' Force) (CGT-FO), Confédération française des travailleurs chrétien's (French Confederation of Christian Workers) (CFTC), Confédération française de l'encadrement – Confédération générale des cadres (Confederation of Management – General Confederation of Executives) (CFE-CGC).
2 Mouvement des Entreprises de France (Movement of the French Enterprises (MEDEF), Confédération Générale des Petites et Moyennes Entreprises (General Confederation of Small and Medium-sized Enterprises and Real Employers) (CGPME), Union professionnelle artisanale (Professional Artisan Union) (UPA).
3 Common position paper, 16 July 2001 on the ways and the means to develop collective bargaining.
4 Law no 2004-391, 4 May 2004 on lifelong learning and social dialogue. JORF, 5 May 2004, p. 7983.
5 Law no. 2007-130, 31 January 2007 on modernising social dialogue. JORF, 1 February 2007.
6 Common position paper, 9 April 2008 on representativeness, development of social dialogue and financing of trade unions.
7 Law of 20 August 2008 on renovation of social democracy and reform of working time. JORF, 21 August 2008, p. 13064.
8 National cross-industry agreement, 7 January 2009 on development of lifelong learning and securing professional career.
9 Law of 24 November 2009 on orientation and lifelong learning. JORF, 25 November 2009, p. 20206.
10 Article L.165-1 Labour Code. This article has been introduced into the Luxembourg legislation by Law on 30 June 2004, Memorial A no. 119, 15 July 2004, p. 1782.
11 Decree of 30 May 2006 on extension of the national cross-industry agreement on telework. JORF, 9 June 2006, p. 8771.
12 Decree of 23 April 2009 on extension of the national cross-industry agreement on work-related stress. JORF, 6 May 2009, p. 7632.
13 Decree of 23 July 2010 on extension of the national cross-industry agreement on harassment and violence at work. JORF, 31 July 2010, p. 14192.
14 National cross-industry agreement of 5 December 2003 on the access of employees to lifelong learning, *Bulletin officiel* no. 2004/13.
15 Decree of 17 December 2004 on extension of the national cross-industry agreement on the access of employees to lifelong learning. JORF, 24 December 2004.
16 National cross-industry agreement, 1 March 2004 on diversity and professional equality of women and men. *Bulletin officiel*, no. 2004/18.
17 Decree of 22 March 2005 on extension of the national cross-industry agreement on diversity and professional equality of women and men. JORF, 5 May 2005.
18 Law of 23 March 2006 on equal pay for women and men. JORF, 24 March 2006.
19 Decision no. 2006-533 of 16 March 2006, JORF, 24 March 2006, p. 4446.
20 Decree no. 98-1080 of 30 November 1998 on creation of the Social Dialogue Committee on European and International Issues. JORF, 1 December 1998, p. 18096.
21 Council Decision of 22 July 2003 on guidelines for the employment policies of the Member States. OJEU 05/08/2003. Annex. *The Employment Guidelines* L. 197/17.
22 Contribution by the National Social Partners to the Luxembourg Process, Subsidy agreement VS/2001/0750 between the European Commission and the European Association for Territorial Excellence (EUREXTER).
23 Council Recommendation of 14 February 2000 on the implementation of Member States' employment policies, OJEC 25/02/2000 L. 52/36.
24 Council Recommendation of 19 January 2001 on the implementation of Member States'

employment policies, OJEC 24/01/2001 L. 22/32.

25 Council Recommendation of 18 February 2002 on the implementation of Member States' employment policies, OJEC 01/03/2002 L. 60/75.

26 It was presented to the Economic, Social and Environmental Committee on 6 May 2006 during the national Conference on seniors' employment.

27 Decree no. 2009-560, 20 May 2009 on the content and the validation of collective agreements and action plans in favour of the employment of older workers. JORF, 21 May 2009.

## References

Bernaud, V. (2007), 'Réforme du dialogue social: faut-il inviter le Conseil constitutionnel à la table des négociations?', *Droit Social* 2, 174.

Borenfreund, G. and Souriac, M.-A. (2003), 'Les rapports de la loi et de la convention collective: une mise en perspective', *Droit Social* 1, 72.

Cherpion, G. (2010), *Avis présenté au nom de la Commission des Affaires Sociales sur la Proposition de loi visant à étendre la modernisation du dialogue social aux propositions de loi (no. 2499) et la proposition de résolution tendant à réviser le Règlement de l'Assemblée Nationale (no. 2491)*, Assemblée Nationale no. 2571 and 2572, 2 June.

Chertier, D.-J. (2006), *Pour une modernisation du dialogue social*. Report to the Prime Minister, Paris, *La Documentation francaise*, www.ladocumentationfrancaise.fr/rapports-publics/064000351/index.shtml, accessed 16 April 2012.

Conseil Economique et Social (2006), *Consolider le dialogue social*, Avis Aurelli et Gautier adopted 29 November.

European Social Partners (2008), *Implementation of the European Autonomous Framework Agreement on Work-related Stress*, Report adopted at the Social Dialogue Committee, 18 June.

Hadas-Lebel, R. (2006), *Pour un dialogue social efficace et légitime: représentativité et financement des organisations professionnelles et syndicales*, Report to the Prime Minister, Paris, May, *La Documentation francaise*, www.ladocumentationfrancaise.fr/rapports-publics/064000364/index.shtml, accessed 16 April 2012.

Kerschen, N. (2005), 'The Social Partners in the European Employment Strategy: Specific Guidelines and National Action Plans for Employment', pp. 165–203 in De Schutter, O. and Deakin, S. (eds), *Social Rights and Market Forces: Is the Open Coordination of Employment and Social Policies the Future of Social Europe?* Brussels: Bruylant.

Kerschen, N. and Roussel-Verret, I. (2006), 'Stratégie européenne pour l'emploi et dialogue social. Vers la construction d'un modèle européen de relations professionnelles', Lien social et Politiques no. 56, *Le fédéralisme social. Les défis de la gouvernance à niveaux multiples.*

Larsen, Trine P. and Andersen, Soren Kaj (2007), 'A New Mode Of European Regulation? The Implementation of the Autonomous Framework Agreement on Telework in Five Countries', *European Journal of Industrial Relations* 13(2), 181–98.

Willmann, C. (2006), 'Promouvoir le "vieillissement actif": les modestes propositions des partenaires sociaux', *Droit Social* 2, 144.

# PART III

## The European Union as policy context for industrial relations

Peter Turnbull

# 9

# Labour and liberalisation: organised opposition to an 'open market' on the European waterfront

## Introduction

Economic liberalisation has long been the driving force of European integration, often to the detriment of working people. It is well established that market making (economic) policy in the European Union (EU) 'runs ahead' of market correcting (social) policy, creating pressure on the industrial relations system in Member States and compelling the social partners to adapt to more intense competition. In fact, in the eyes of many observers, liberalisation appears to have been 'an unstoppable tide for labour interests to contend with' (Greenwood 2003: 149), especially as the European Commission has become more adept at deploying different strategies to extend its scope for autonomous action beyond merely setting the agenda for market integration (Schmidt 2000). For example, the Commission might deliberately propose a far-reaching liberalisation of a particular economic sector that will coax, if not compel, the Council of Ministers into action in order to (collectively) define a 'lesser evil' (compromise) position that satisfies the (qualified) majority. Alternatively, the Commission might target particular Member States or leading firms who fail to comply with the rules and regulations of the open market in order to 'divide and conquer' any opposition to economic liberalisation. In Europe's ports, the former strategy was clearly manifest in a proposed Directive *On Market Access to Port Services*, widely referred to as 'Ports Package 1' (PP1) (Commission 2001b), that was narrowly rejected by the European Parliament in November 2003 following a concerted international campaign of industrial and political action by European port workers. A revised version of the Directive ('Ports Package 2' or PP2), was proposed by the Commission less than a year later (Commission 2004), only to be decisively rejected by the European Parliament. Once again, the Directive met with vehement opposition, which culminated in a mass demonstration outside the Parliament building in

January 2006 when almost 10,000 dockers confronted riot police in the streets of Strasbourg. While Members of the European Parliament (MEP) voted on the Directive, windows of the Parliament building were smashed and the surrounding streets were clouded with tear gas.

The failure of the Commission and the supporters of an open market for port services has deep historical roots, which are elaborated in the following section, but the opposition of organised labour proved more decisive, as the subsequent narrative clearly demonstrates. Chastened by the port workers' vehement opposition to the proposed Directives, and embarrassed by the votes in Parliament, the Directorate-General for Energy and Transport (DG TREN) now accepts that EU ports policy cannot be addressed through a 'one size fits all' ports directive (Barrot 2007, Commission 2007a). But as the mid-term review of the Lisbon strategy concluded, much of the transport sector is 'open only on paper' (Commission 2005: 8). Consequently, in the words of a senior official in the Commission's Maritime Transport Policy Unit, the ports still 'need more Europe',[1] otherwise 'it would be the wild west'.[2] The Commission therefore changed tack, from legislative intervention designed to force the different interest groups to define a 'lesser evil' form of liberalisation to open consultation with the social partners and other key stakeholders. But while the Commission's (2007b) latest strategy – an action plan developed on the back of an extensive consultation with stakeholders in 2006–07 – might appear to be more consensual, throughout this process DG TREN sought to identify differences and exploit divisions between the stakeholders. This 'divide-and-conquer' strategy has been thwarted by a new coalition of interests in the port transport industry, with organised labour once more playing a leading role.

In general, European-level union organisations 'possess extremely restricted capacity either to influence capital or the EU decision makers, or to communicate with the members whom they in theory represent' (Hyman 1999: 111). But several European industry federations, including the European Transport Workers' Federation (ETF), have become a real (supranational) force to be reckoned with in recent years (Bieler 2005). As the experience of European port workers clearly demonstrates, when local and national conflict is externalised and new transnational coalitions form, then labour and other interest groups are able to pool their resources in order to effect (or in this case resist) change. In this respect, the dockers' success in their campaigns against the supranational state is an object lesson for the wider European labour movement.

The general conditions under which trade unions are most likely to cooperate at a European level have been elaborated by Bieler (2005), as have various transnational strategies that organised labour might pursue (*ibid.*, see also Tarrow 2005). Initially, during the 'war on Europe's waterfront' against PP1, port workers fought a campaign of organised resistance, demonstrating that while EU politics may be institutional politics there is still room for grass-roots mobilisation (Turnbull 2006). During the campaign against PP2, however, the force of argument was co-joined to the argument of force, with greater emphasis on conventional forms of political action as well as building alliances with other stakeholders (Turnbull 2007). The coalition of interests that formed during this period continues to frame the ongoing debate on future European ports policy. Moreover, during the latest phase of consultation (2006–07), dockworkers expressly engaged with the 'struggle for ideas' (Bieler 2005: 465), seeking to 'recapture the ideological initiative' (Hyman 1999: 108) by reconnecting the Lisbon quadrilateral of economic, social, employment and environmental policy. Whether this will cure the Commission of its 'acute obsessive competitiveness disorder' (Hay 2007: 25) remains to be seen. Nonetheless, the contentious actions of European port workers, their national trade unions and both European and international federations clearly demonstrates the capacity of organised labour to resist economic liberalisation at the EU level.

## EU ports policy

Although the European peninsula 'is a maritime economy *par excellence*' (Commission 2006a: 11), ports have historically been the 'Cinderella' of the Community's Common Transport Policy (CTP) (Chlomoudis and Pallis 2002). In fact, maritime (and air) transport was initially deemed to fall outside the scope of the CTP, despite Articles 74–85 of the Treaty of Rome recognising transport as an area for Community action.[3] It was 1974 before the European Court of Justice confirmed the Community's policy-making authority in the maritime sector, which led to the creation of a Community Port Working Group to examine the impact of different institutional, ownership and management structures, as well as charging practices and port labour arrangements. European ports have always defended these differences, principally on the grounds of subsidiarity. Given that the Port Working Group drew its membership from the major European ports, it was hardly surprising that the Group should conclude that there was no need for a specific EU ports policy (PWG 1977). The Commission accepted this argument, or more precisely acknowledged the desire of Member States to retain their autonomy with respect to seaports (Carossino 1982).

Following the Treaty of Maastricht, however, transport policy was placed 'in the forefront of the moves towards the completion of the internal market' (Commission 1992: 4). The primary objective of the Commission in relation to ports was to establish 'transparency of accounts' to identify financial flows between various public bodies, port authorities, operators, and the users of port facilities and services. In theory, this would allow the Commission to distinguish investment projects of public interest that operate under non-discriminatory access and usage conditions (and thereby comply with EU competition rules) from public investment in facilities or services for dedicated use by particular users or customers (which thereby breach EU rules on state aid). Any such 'distortions' of the market could then be 'corrected' by Community action. To this end, the Commission published a Green Paper on seaports – the Community's first policy document to deal exclusively with ports – that sought to establish, *inter alia*, common criteria for infrastructure investment and charging principles for the use of that infrastructure

(Commission 1997). In short, the Commission determined that 'port infrastructure should be priced in such a way that users would bear the real costs of the port services and facilities they consume' (Commission 1997: 3).

The financing of port infrastructure and the 'user pays' principle proved to be the most contentious elements of the Green Paper, although it was now the ports themselves, via the European Sea Ports Organisation (ESPO)[4] and local politicians and MEPs, rather than Member States or government ministers in the Council, who took up the gauntlet of defending the vested interests and status quo of Europe's ports. In all its public policy pronouncements, ESPO expressed its commitment to 'systematic liberalisation', subject to 'the need for gradualism', but advocated competition and more systematic guidelines on state aid as the most effective mechanism to achieve this: 'Improving ports' performance is not, in ESPO's view, achieved by pan-European co-ordination of port development ... [it] is a responsibility of the ports and will come about through free and fair competition' (ESPO 1998: 1 and 4; see also ESPO 1996). This argument was reluctantly accepted by the Commission (Chlomoudis and Pallis 2002).

In the furore over how to establish a 'level playing field' with respect to port investment and charging, the proposals in the Green Paper for Community action 'in the form of developing a regulatory framework aiming at the more systematic liberalisation of the port services market' (Commission 1997: 4) were pushed to the stern. However, while private port operators expressed reservations on the questions of investment and charging, they strongly supported the liberalisation of port services, especially for cargo handling in southern Europe (FEPORT 1998). In particular, global port terminal operators and international shipping lines were keen to exploit increasing demand following China's entry into the World Trade Organisation. Market access would also allow them to integrate their schedules with inland transport and offer global logistics solutions to transnational corporations.

Transnational capital was therefore increasingly aligned against the *local* interests of Europe's public port authorities. Moreover, in the new millennium, transport was anchored in the Lisbon Agenda (Commission 2001a, 2006b) and Member States were not only committed to the further liberalisation of transport but in several cases (e.g. Greece, Italy and Spain) were frustrated by the 'complicity' of local port interests who defended what many politicians, port users and other commercial interests regarded as monopolistic and inefficient port services. These included the exclusive provision of port services by public authorities and in particular restrictions on the use of port labour, both in terms of 'exclusive supply' and 'restrictive work practices'. As the Commission had previously maintained:

> Port services have usually functioned in isolated frameworks protected by exclusive rights and/or legal or *de facto* monopolies of public or private nature ... port labour rigidities remain characteristic of the sector, mainly related to the registration of port workers and the existence of labour pools in a number of EU ports.[5] (Commission 1997: 19)

The Commission's response to these 'exclusive rights', 'labour rigidities' and labour pools was the proposed Directive *On Market Access to Port Services* (Commission 2001b), which included enforced competition (a minimum of two service providers for all port services) and the right to 'self handling' (to effect a deregulation of the labour market). The proposals on 'self-handling', defined as 'a situation in which a port user provides for itself one or more categories of port services' (Commission 2001b: 28), were originally put to the Commission by the European Community Shipowners' Association (ECSA) and the European Shippers' Council (ESC) in 1998 (*Fairplay* 26 July 2001). When combined with 'the right to employ personnel of his own choice to carry out the service' (Commission 2001b: 29), the principle of 'self-handling' would allow shipping lines to employ seafarers to load or unload cargo (instead of registered/recognised dock workers). This option was particularly attractive to short-sea shipping lines as their vessels spend a larger proportion of time in port.[6]

For their part, ESPO and the Federation of European Private Port Operators (FEPORT)[7] expressed 'substantial concerns' about some of the concrete measures in the Commission's proposal, although not with the general principles of liberalisation embedded in the Directive. More importantly, they were able to secure amendments acceptable to their members at the conciliation committee established under the EU's co-decision procedure (Verhoeven 2003). That left organised labour as the principal opponent of PP1, frustrated by what they regarded as a rather perfunctory period of consultation prior to the publication of the Directive and aggrieved by the Commission's subsequent failure to appreciate the adverse social consequences of self-handling. While the Commission expected strong objections from European port unions, they did not anticipate organised opposition on the scale that the Directive invoked.

## From conflict (PP1) to coalitions (PP2)[8]

Although the Commission frequently acts as an 'agent' for the interests of globalising capital (Greenwood 2003, Tarrow 2005), thereby providing EU-based transnationals 'with economic space and other kinds of comparative advantage' (Böröcz and Sarker 2005: 159), it should not be assumed that while capital is capable of transcending space, labour is necessarily confined to place. Certainly, both the structures and the strategies of organised labour appear unequal to the challenge of European integration (Martin and Ross 2000). But as Tarrow (2005) demonstrates, there is a course that labour can navigate through the waves of globalisation and liberalisation (depicted as a movement from the top left-hand corner to the bottom right-hand corner in Figure 9.1) and in a European context the existence of supranational governance institutions, with jurisdiction coterminous with the scope of the capital-labour struggle in question, can provide an ideal opportunity for workers in their struggles against trans-national capital. By utilising the theoretical framework depicted in Figure 9.1, it can be demonstrated how dockworkers were able to exploit the political opportunity structures of the EU to decisive effect.

Following Tarrow (2005), the course of action initially involved the *global framing* of their interests by rank-and-file dock workers (i.e. recognising that their terms and conditions of employment were seriously threatened by PP1) and then both *internalising* these issues (effecting a migration of international pressures and conflicts into domestic politics) and *diffusing* their claims and forms of contention from one Member State to another (see Figure 9.1). During the war on Europe's waterfront (2001–03), coordinated 'educational stop-work meetings' were used to debate PP1 in the workplace ('global framing') and port unions lobbied their national governments and organised local strike action against the Directive ('internalisation').[9] Diffusion was facilitated by well-established relational networks of union activists within specific port ranges (e.g. the 'northern range' from Le Havre to Hamburg, the Baltic and Mediterranean), as well as (non-relational) electronic networks (e.g. www.havenarbeiders.be and www.havenforum.nl) and 'brokerage' undertaken by intermediaries who were able to effect a rapprochement between 'rival' union organisations at the national and international levels.[10] These (horizontal) labour networks cut across, and interconnected, the various levels of the (vertical) union hierarchy. In doing so, they not only facilitated the kind of 'internal social dialogue' that European unions desperately need to initiate if they are to engage rank-and-file members (Hyman 1999), but they also helped to ensure more effective 'union articulation' (i.e. stronger inter-relationships between the workplace, national and international levels of organisation). Consequently, European dock workers were able to bridge 'the horizontal spatial divide between political cultures and the vertical gap between levels of the international system' (Tarrow 2005: 127).

Crucially, the *scale shift* was marked by a change in both the number and level of coordinated contentious actions. These actions – which included the first ever pan-European dock strikes, mass demonstrations in the streets of Barcelona,

**Figure 9.1 Transnational activism**

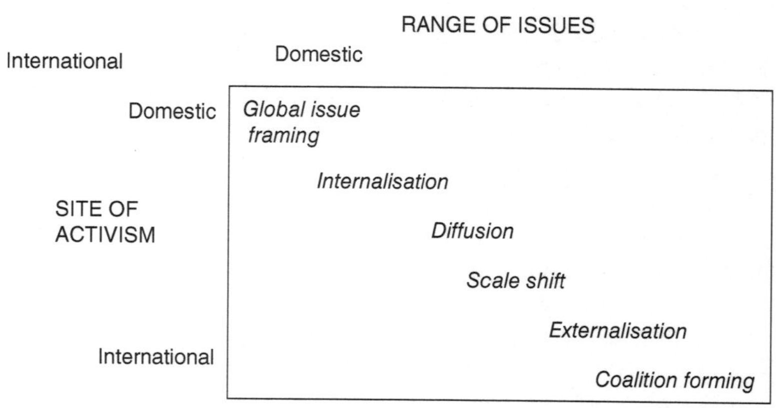

Brussels, Rotterdam and Strasbourg, and coordinated trans-national action targeting specific shipping lines whose managers sought to pre-empt the provisions for self-handling in the Directive – involved a very different focal point for union action, as well as different actors, objects and even new identities. Embedded identities were still very much in evidence and were loudly, and proudly, articulated – the rallying cry of Belgian dockers, for example, was 'Handen af van de Havenarbeid *wet Major*!'[11] – but many dockers now recognised that, as 'European port workers', their future livelihood depended on their ability to *externalise* their conflict (i.e. project their domestic claims to international institutions and foreign actors) (see Figure 9.1).

Even with the alignment of forces set against them – international shipping lines, shippers, ESPO, FEPORT, the Commission and Council – the dockers' campaign against PP1 was sufficient to scupper the Directive, although the vote in Parliament was very close (229 to 209, with 19 abstentions). More importantly, in the context of a political opportunity structure that favours conventional as opposed to unconventional action, and domestic as opposed to international forms of contention (Marks and McAdam 1999), dockworkers had added unconventional international action to their repertoire and demonstrated the nerve, and capacity, to say 'NO'. In similar situations, most European unions have lost their nerve (Hyman 2005), which in turn dilutes any (conventional) strategy of institutional engagement, invariably leading to dependence and co-option on the part of national and especially international union organisations (Tarrow 2005). Moreover, having deployed the 'argument of force' to decisive effect, dock workers found that other interests were now more willing to take on board the force of their argument in subsequent encounters – but not, it seemed, the Commission.

Just before she left office, Loyola de Palacio, the Transport and Energy Commissioner and a former minister in the conservative Spanish government, announced a second Directive *On Access to the Port Services Market* (Commission 2004). Thus, not for the first time, a departing Commissioner fired a parting shot across the bows of an interest they had come to dislike, with no small degree of consequence for the interest(s) concerned (Greenwood 2003). Following the failure of the Spanish government to fully liberalise its own port services market in the face of militant opposition by dock workers (Turnbull and Wass 2007), it was clear that de Palacio was seeking to 'upload' a policy of liberalisation (PP1) to the European level that could then be 'downloaded' to the domestic level (Turnbull 2006). But with PP2, the Commission seriously miscalculated the interests and intentions of the industry's principal stakeholders. For labour, this created an organising space for *coalition forming* with other stakeholders (see Figure 9.1).

While the headlines in the industry press went overboard when they declared that 'Everyone hates it' (*Lloyd's List* 25 January 2005), it was evident from the outset that PP2 did not have the broad base of support enjoyed by its predecessor. Indeed, the underlying doctrine and key objectives of the second Ports Package were the same as those of the first (Commission 2004), but several Member States (e.g. Germany, the Netherlands and the United Kingdom) objected to the Directive on numerous counts of policy and process (e.g. authorisations for new port service providers and compensation for outgoing service providers) (see, for example, Deloitte 2005; Department of Transport 2005). More importantly, ESPO (2004, 2005b) and FEPORT (2005) echoed these concerns and raised objections to the proposed concession periods for port investors as well as a range of other technical issues in the Directive. An impact assessment undertaken by ESPO concluded that PP2 would 'have virtually no positive impact on the European seaports sector but might, on the contrary, lead to a negative investment climate in ports, more bureaucracy, legal uncertainty and even create additional hindrances to market access' (ESPO 2006: 5). Even the Commission's own economic evaluation concluded that the potential impact of the Directive on transport charges was small (ECORYS/ Trademco 2005).

Both public ports and private employers called for a host of amendments to PP2, but more telling was their decision to no longer insist on the inclusion of self-handling in the proposed Directive. Both ESPO and FEPORT, for 'reasons of proportionality and subsidiarity', determined that this issue was best set out at local or national level (ESPO 2005a, 2005b, FEPORT 2005), although both organisations also expressed their desire 'to avoid unnecessary social unrest' (FEPORT 2005: 9) which 'could create an unstable climate for potential investors' (ESPO 2004: 2) and impose direct costs on service providers and users that 'seem to go unnoticed by the European legislative authorities' (FEPORT 2005: 9). Even the ship-owners (ECSA) were prepared to see self-handling excluded from the second Ports Package, despite championing this issue during the war on Europe's waterfront. This diminished, but did not eradicate, much of the hostility between capital and labour.

In addition to ESPO, FEPORT and ECSA, it seemed that the supranational institutions of the EU – minus the Commission – were prepared to heed the warnings of organised labour on the deleterious social consequences of PP2 (e.g. CoR 2005, EESC 2005). When the Transport Committee of the Parliament met in November 2005, more than 300 amendments had been tabled by MEPs. Voting at this crucial Committee stage 'descended into farce' (*Lloyd's List* 23 November 2005) when MEPs first voted narrowly against rejecting the Directive outright by twenty-six votes to twenty-two, with one abstention; then adopted various compromise amendments; but finally rejected the Directive as amended by twenty-four votes to twenty-three. To confuse the issue still further, in the final vote of the day MEPs passed a motion to send the Directive to the plenary of the European Parliament in January 2006 without any amendments. Consequently, several 'allies' of organised labour, most notably ESPO, joined them in calling for the Directive to be rejected outright by Parliament. The Parliament duly obliged by 532 votes to 120 (with twenty-five abstentions).[12]

Throughout the campaign against PP2, organised labour was concerned 'to keep the support of our allies'[13] and therefore deployed more 'measured' forms of industrial and political action against the supranational state and global capital (Turnbull 2007). Port unions were under no illusion that these 'allies' had come to them because of their new-found interest in sinking the Directive, as well as their desire to avoid further costly disruption to the transport system and global supply chains. As Tarrow (2005) notes, coalitions often form in the face of a common threat, and this was certainly how the Commission was now perceived by a large(r) section of European port interests. However, a temporary alignment of interests is not the same as a more enduring alliance. For 'event coalitions' to form, objectively common organisational interests and framing are necessary but not sufficient – organisational representatives must also calculate a benefit from pooled resources, be able to commit credibly to delivering promised resources, and develop mechanisms to resolve the inevitable tensions that arise among coalition parties (Levi and Murphy 2006). For the port coalition to endure beyond a specific event (i.e. the vote in the European Parliament) required a degree of institutionalisation and most crucially in this instance an 'opportunity spiral' triggered by the action and reaction of external agencies and alliance partners (Tarrow 2005).

At the initiative of ESPO, the major stakeholders held a series of 'non-meetings' throughout 2005. A similar 'non-meeting' was held in December 2002 during the war on Europe's waterfront when the unions asked other stakeholders to sign a joint declaration against 'self-handling', which they flatly refused. In contrast, when they met to discuss PP2, the social 'partners' and other stakeholders found they shared rather more common ground, most notably on the question of self-handling. Crucially, Parliament's rejection of PP2 did not signal the demise of the new coalition, which continued to meet on an informal basis, knowing that the demise of the Directive was simply the ebb in a tide of liberalisation. When the Commission used the occasion of ESPO's Annual General Meeting in Stockholm (June 2006) to launch a new phase of consultation on future EU ports policy, other stakeholders, and in particular the ETF, expressed concerns about the 'close working relationship' between the Seaports Organisation and DG TREN, raising doubts about the stability of the new 'coalition' of port interests. But this did not prevent stakeholders agreeing that, at the forthcoming workshops organised by the Commission to debate and develop future EU ports policy, 'the more heterogeneous will be the opinions expressed by stakeholders, the more likely it is that the European Commission will produce legislative acts',[14] which is something they were all keen to avoid.

More importantly, as ESPO moved closer to the Commission, there was an opportunity for the ETF to enter informal discussions with FEPORT on a future European social dialogue. Historically, ESPO had always opposed social dialogue – officially on the grounds that it is a business organisation whose members are not major employers of dock labour in many EU Member States – which left ports as the only transport mode without a European Sector Social Dialogue Committee. Just prior to the launch of the Commission's consultation process, FEPORT's members determined to engage in social dialogue with the ETF. By the end of the consultation period, ESPO and other stakeholders, including ECSA, were pressing to be on board the social dialogue. Thus, while the Commission was hoping to exploit divisions within the industry, the consultation process brought interest groups closer together, enabling the sector to 'heal ... from the Ports Package trauma' (ESPO 2007: 93). This is not to gainsay that conflict and divisions have been eradicated – far from it – rather to highlight how the industry has 'take[n] its own future in hand' (Barrot 2007: 2).

## Alliances and divisions on the future EU ports policy

The Commission's attempt to divide port interests during the consultation phase (2006–07) was evident from the outset. When organising the port policy workshops to debate different areas of future EU ports policy,[15] the Commission invited the principal stakeholders but asked their representatives to speak in a personal capacity, to 'express their own views' rather than 'read pre-written papers'.[16] This raised concerns about the status of any statements made, or opinions offered, by stakeholders, which was compounded by the fact that workshop participants were asked to respond to questions set out by the Commission in a 'non-paper' prepared for each workshop. Leaving aside the fact that the non-papers (in English only) were distributed less than two weeks before the relevant workshop, giving most interest groups very little time for internal debate, these papers did 'not represent any official position of the Commission', nor did they 'constitute any commitment by the Commission'.[17]

More telling, however, was the Commission's open disappointment that the workshops did not generate more 'heated discussion', despite repeated calls for participants to 'be provocative'.[18] At one workshop, the European Shippers' Council (ESC) was congratulated for 'ruffling a few feathers', which in the words of one member of the DG TREN team was 'exactly what we want'.[19] But more typical was the prolonged silence in the room at the Hamburg Workshop – to the point of embarrassment – when the Commission called for an open debate on port tariffs. Immediately after the Workshop, when talking in private, several stakeholders were adamant that they were not prepared to debate their differences in front of the Commission, especially on a topic as sensitive as pricing and handling charges.[20] On several occasions the Commission invited participants to 'take issue' with other stakeholders, but these requests were politely declined. Even when speakers were critical of port services or charges, they generally refrained from 'naming and shaming' the port(s) in question. Only the shippers (ESC at Naples; see also ESC 2007) and short-sea shipping lines (Grimaldi at Hamburg and Lisbon) were prepared to proffer public condemnation of specific ports.

Instead, what emerged from the workshops was a broad consensus on a range of policy issues that were subsequently reflected in the Communication from the Commission *On European Ports Policy* (Commission 2007b) (e.g. Community guidelines on state aid and the application of environmental legislation to port development projects). By any measure, the Communication falls well short of the proposed Directives *On Market Access to Port Services*. This was a direct result of participation in the consultative workshops, which not only connected different (previously opposed) interests in the port transport industry but forced them to modify their policy position so that it could be publicly justified as promoting collective well-being (see Neyer 2003). As a result, 'self-handling', the most contentious proposal of PP1 and PP2, was quickly dropped from the agenda.[21] For most international shipping lines, the cost savings that might be derived from self-handling are simply too small compared to the risks of further disruption to their own operations and global supply chains (OSC 2005). Consequently, at the Valencia Workshop devoted to labour issues, the General Secretary of ECSA declared that 'the words "self handling" have been deleted from our word processor'.[22] Community action on self-handling was dealt a further blow by the announcement of a Sector Social Dialogue Committee for the ports, as employment-related matters will now be the responsibility of the social partners. Both management (FEPORT) and labour (ETF and IDC) are determined to settle such matters at the port or national level and thereby avoid any Community action.

Underlying the industrial and political strategy of port worker trade unions and their international federations is an engagement with ideas. In particular, organised labour in the (port) transport sector has challenged the neo-liberal fixation with price or cost competition and what it means to be competitive in a global industry. For example, while the Commission simply equates 'more competition' (a 'good thing') with open access to the market and more competitors (e.g. a requirement for at least two providers of every port service), European port unions have identified at least four 'levels' and two different 'forms' of competition. The levels of competition include: (i) between port ranges (e.g. 'northern range' ports compete for central and east European trade with Mediterranean ports); (ii) within port ranges (e.g. between the ports of Le Havre, Antwerp, Rotterdam and Hamburg in the northern range); (iii) within individual Member States; and (iv) within the same port. The two different 'forms' of competition are simply price (cost) and non-price (service) factors. Given the sheer density of European ports, most with overlapping hinterlands, the selection of a particular port of call from within a group of intra-regional alternatives is more often determined by 'site' (i.e. the provision of facilities and the efficiency of port services) rather than 'situation' (i.e. relative location or 'intermediacy'). As a result, the key criteria for shipping lines when selecting ports of call are speed of vessel turnaround, handling/productivity rates, berth availability/capacity, operational flexibility, working hours and labour relations. More intense price competition in this context might actually undermine the ability of port operators to meet customer requirements. For example, given the relatively high proportion of labour costs in total operating costs, price competition is often translated into work intensification and downward pressure on wages and other terms and conditions of employment, which might then lead to the de-motivation of port workers (and lower productivity) and conflict between the social partners (and disruption to ports services) (ETF 2007a, IDC 2007).

The ETF's critique of neo-liberalism and the Commission's approach to competition and market access in the port transport industry is just one component of the unions' attempt to reconnect the Lisbon quadrilateral of economic, social, employment and environmental policy, especially as the Common Transport Policy is now focused primarily on competitiveness – faster, cheaper and more efficient transport – often to the detriment of social sustainability (ETF 2007b). In the 'struggle for ideas' over the Common Transport Policy and a future European ports policy, the ETF has launched a new initiative to develop a Trade Union Vision On Sustainable Transport (TRUST). As an example of how ideologies can be used to highlight conflicts in the world economy (see Bieler 2005), consider the construction of ever larger container vessels that now ply the dominant east–west trade routes between the 'global triad' of Europe, North America and South East Asia. The Commission (2007b) simply accepts this development as an outcome of globalisation and technological development, which in turn demands the construction of much larger container terminals with suitable road and rail links, as well as the dredging of deeper port access channels, often to the detriment of the natural environment and employment (e.g. when new automated terminals are constructed). The TRUST, in contrast, views mega-shipbuilding as a major factor driving world trade (i.e. as a cause and not simply an outcome of globalisation), leading to further consolidation in the international shipping industry which gives the major carriers even greater bargaining power vis-à-vis ports around the world (see also IDC 2007). This power is often used to demand public investment in port infrastructure (e.g. dredging deeper access channels or reclaiming land for mega-terminals). As Janelle and Beuthe (1997: 200) note, transnational transport and logistics:

> acts as a catalyst for reduced restrictions on international trade, promotes new technologies and markets them on a global basis, seeks both national and international policy measures to support expanded transport investments, *and often discourages regulatory measures to internalize the negative social and environmental costs associated with transport activities.* [Emphasis added]

The instability of globalisation, mega-shipbuilding and competitive (over) investment in European port facilities has been dramatically exposed by the global financial crisis, which hit world trade and Europe's maritime industries especially hard. Thus, while the TRUST initially focused on social sustainability, transport unions increasingly emphasise the importance of economically sustainable (green) jobs and the consequent need to build a sustainable environment. This creates opportunities to build alliances with both community and environmental groups in the city-port regions of the EU. The 'commitment' of port unions and their international federations to European social dialogue was in fact driven primarily by a desire to preclude Community intervention and retain local and national control over employment-related port policy. Any Community action in relation to the environment, certainly beyond the stated intention to clarify the application of existing environmental legislation to any future port development (Commission 2007b), will no doubt create another 'opportunity spiral' for organised labour and other stakeholders in European ports to contend with. Such developments do not yet constitute a new form of 'community unionism', but they certainly offer the potential for new social movements in the maritime regions of the EU and an opportunity for the opponents of neo-liberalism to re-embed markets in a legitimate social purpose.

## Conclusion

Immediately prior to the consultation with industry stakeholders in 2006–07, members of the Maritime Transport Policy Unit in DG TREN argued that European ports needed common policies to replace the 'proliferation of policies and systems now in place'[23]. By identifying and creating divisions between the stakeholders, DG TREN sought to establish grounds for the liberalisation of the port services market and the deregulation of the waterfront labour market. Initially, these policies were resisted primarily, if not exclusively, by organised labour, breaking the traditional pattern whereby 'Unions' engagement with the EU has largely abdicated contentious politics' (Hyman 2005: 35). This abdication no doubt accounts for the predominantly 'top-down' focus of much research on the impact of the EU on industrial relations in different Member States and different economic sectors. In the case of European ports, in contrast, the opposing force – from the 'bottom up' – proved equally decisive in shaping the contemporary pattern of industrial relations in general and EU port policy in particular.

After demonstrating 'power in movement' (Tarrow 1998) during the campaign against PP1, European port unions were consequently able to force other stakeholders to address their concerns during the debate on PP2. The failure of the Commission to redress these concerns, as well as the objections of other stakeholders, led to the creation of an unlikely alliance between labour and important business interests, resulting in a resounding defeat for PP2 in the European Parliament. Through this new alliance of interests, the port transport industry has been able to steer its own course through the latest consultation phase. In particular, the social partners have come to appreciate that 'deliberative institutions' (e.g. 'non-meetings', sector social dialogue, and the Commission's port policy workshops) provided them with strategic capacities they would otherwise not enjoy.

These developments are not without their dangers for organised labour, especially at the international level where the comitology of the EU 'is as far removed from the capacities and inclinations of the typical local movement constituency as are the seats in these supranational organizations' (della Porta and Kriesi 1999: 20). But the 'new international unionism', certainly on the European waterfront but also evident in other sectors (e.g. Bieler 2005; Fairbrother and Hammer 2005) is a 'layered' and 'networked' form of organisation with its campaigns rooted in the day-to-day realities of workers' lives. For port workers, this reality is increasingly driven by, or certainly threatened by, European policy developments. As opportunities unfolded, European port unions moved beyond 'surface conflict' with (global) capital and the supranational state over the terms of any (neo-liberal) reforms – they are now in a position to influence the agenda of EU ports policy and present an alternative understanding of competitiveness. Moreover, unlike the opponents of the Services Directive (Hay 2007), port workers have challenged the economic advantages of product market liberalisation and not simply the social costs of labour market deregulation. While this is unlikely to cure the Commission of its obsession with cost/price competition in the industry, it has diverted the course of Community action and represents an important steer for the labour movement as a whole: by expanding the (industrial and political) range of issues and (geographically) extending the sites of contention, trade unions and their members can engage with social regulation at the European level to ensure the defence of social policy at the national and local levels.

## Notes

1 Interview notes, October 2006.
2 Fotis Karamitsos, Maritime Director, DG TREN, quoted in *Lloyd's List*, 29 April 2005.
3 Article 84(2) stated that 'The Council may, acting by unanimity, decide whether and to what extent and by what procedure appropriate provisions may be laid down for sea and air transport'.
4 ESPO represents public port authorities while its sister organisation, the Federation of European Private Port Operators (FEPORT) represents private terminal operators. Both organisations were created in the early 1990s (post-Maastricht) following the greater emphasis on ports policy in the CTP.
5 In many ports, operators only employ a 'core' workforce for highly skilled tasks (e.g. crane driving) which they supplement on a daily basis from a labour pool to accommodate fluctuating labour demand as vessels come and go.
6 For example, seafarers could be deployed to lash or unlash cars and trucks on roll-on/roll-off vessels and/or to remove or fasten container twist-locks on feeder services, instead of employing more expensive local dock workers while the ship's crew 'stand idle'.
7 See note 4.
8 Empirical data presented in this and subsequent sections is drawn from a long-term research project on EU ports policy, based on interviews with the principal stakeholders, case studies of major European ports, and participation at the workshops organised by the Commission (2006–07) to debate and develop future EU ports policy.
9 Such action persuaded both the Belgian and Swedish governments to oppose the Directive in the Council.
10 Acrimonious relationships prevailed between rival port unions in several Member States, most notably France, Spain and Sweden, and at the international level a grassroots federation, the International Dockworkers' Council (IDC), had emerged from the long-running dispute in the port of Liverpool in the late 1990s to rival the International Transport Workers' Federation (ITF) and its European organisation (ETF).
11 Literally, 'Hands off the national port law' (the *wet Major*) which defines 'dock work' and the 'port zone' and restricts such work to 'recognised dockworkers'.
12 The Socialist (PES), Liberal (ALDE), Green, Left-wing (GUE/DEM) and UEN groups voted against the Directive. Not even half the Conservatives (PPE/DE) voted in favour.
13 Interview with Frank Leys, ITF Dockers' Secretary, November 2005.
14 As these were 'non-meetings', no official minutes were recorded. However, the ETF produced 'Briefing Notes' for its affiliates, which is the source of this quote. During a subsequent interview with one of the major business organisations, the stakeholders' position was explained to the author in no uncertain terms: 'We agreed not to wash our dirty laundry in front of

the Commission' (interview notes, February 2007).

15 Six workshops were held at the ports of Antwerp (Port Authorities and Port Services, November 2006), Hamburg (Port Financing, January 2007), Lisbon (Sustainable Development of Port Capacity and Environmental Issues, February 2007), Valencia (Labour Issues and Technical-Nautical Services, March 2007), Naples (Hinterland Connections, April 2007) and Tallinn (Competition/Cooperation with Neighbouring non-EU Ports and Promoting the Image of Ports, May 2007).

16 This request was made in all the Commission documents that accompanied the six workshops.

17 This statement was repeated in all the non-papers.

18 Naples Workshop, meeting notes. There are no official meeting notes from the workshops. The reference is to the author's own transcript of the workshop.

19 Naples Workshop, meeting notes.

20 Hamburg Workshop, meeting notes.

21 This issue featured in the Commission's first draft of the agenda for the Valencia Workshop, but was subsequently excluded from the non-paper.

22 Meeting notes.

23 Interview notes, October 2006.

## References


Barrot, J. (2007), Keynote speech, 'European Port Policy', presented at the ESPO Annual Conference, Algeciras, Spain, 1 June.

Bieler, A. (2005), 'European Integration and the Transnational Restructuring of Social Relations: The Emergence of Labour as a Regional Actor?', *Journal of Common Market Studies* 43(3), 461–84.

Böröcz, J. and Sarker, M. (2005), 'What is the EU?', *International Sociology* 20(2), 153–73.

Carossino, A. (1982), *Report Drawn up on Behalf of the Committee of Transport on the Role of Ports in the Common Transport Policy*, Document 1-844/82, European Parliament Working Documents.

Chlomoudis, C.I. and Pallis, A.A. (2002), *European Union Port Policy: The Movement Towards a Long-Term Strategy*, Cheltenham: Edward Elgar.

Commission (1992), *The Future Development of the Common Transport Policy: A Global Approach to the Construction of a Community Framework for Sustainable Mobility*, COM(92) 494 final, Brussels: Commission of the European Communities.

Commission (1997), *Green Paper on Sea Ports and Maritime Infrastructure*, COM(97) 678 final, Brussels: Commission of the European Communities.

Commission (2001a), *European Transport Policy for 2010: Time to Decide*, COM(2001) 370, Brussels: Commission of the European Communities.

Commission (2001b), *Proposal for a Directive of the European Parliament and of the Council On Market Access to Port Services*, COM(2001) 35 final, Brussels: Commission of the European Communities.

Commission (2004), *Proposal for a Directive of the European Parliament and of the Council On Market Access to Port Services*, COM(2004) 654 final, Brussels: Commission of the European Communities.

Commission (2005), *Working Together for Growth and Jobs: A New Start for the Lisbon Strategy*, COM(2005) 24 final, Brussels: Commission of the European Communities.

Commission (2006a), *Communication from the Commission to the Council and the European Parliament on Keep Europe Moving – Sustainable Mobility for our Continent. Mid-term Review of the European Commission's 2001 Transport White Paper*, COM(2006) 314 final, Brussels: Commission of the European Communities.

Commission (2006b), *Green Paper – Towards a Future Maritime Policy for the Union: European Vision for the Oceans and Seas*, COM(2006) 275 final, Brussels: Commission of the European Communities.

Commission (2007a), *Accompanying Document to 'Communication on a European Port Policy': Full Impact Assessment*, 2007/TREN/004, Brussels: Commission of the European Communities.

Commission (2007b), *Communication on a European Ports Policy*, COM(2007) 616 final, Brussels: Commission of the European Communities.

CoR (2005), 'Opinion of the Committee of the Regions on the Proposal for a Directive of the European Parliament and Council *On Market Access to Port Services*', Brussels: Committee of the Regions.

della Porta, D. and Kriesi, H. (1999), 'Social Movements in a Globalizing World: An Introduction', pp. 3–22 in della Porta, D., Kriesi, H., and Rucht, D. (eds), *Social Movements in a Globalizing World*, London: Macmillan.

Deloitte (2005), *Impact Assessment Port Services Directive: the Netherlands*, Utrecht: Deloitte Consultancy BV.

Department of Transport (2005), *EC Directive on Market Access to Port Services: Briefing for UK Members of the European Parliament Economic and Social Committee of the Regions*, London: HMSO.

ECORYS/Trademco (2005), *Complementary Economic Evaluation Study on the Commission Proposal for a Directive* On Market Access to Port Services, Framework Contract No. TREN/A1/17-2003/Lot 1, Rotterdam/Athens: ECORYS/Trademco.

EESC (2005), 'Opinion of the European Economic and Social Committee on the Proposal for a Directive of the European Parliament and Council *On Market Access to Port Services*', Brussels: European Economic and Social Committee.

ESC (2007), *Position Paper on a EU Ports Policy*, Brussels: European Shippers' Council.

ESPO (1996), *Report of an Enquiry into the Current Situation in the Major Community Sea-Ports*, Fact Finding Report, Brussels: European Sea Ports Organisation.

ESPO (1998), 'Response to the Green Paper on Sea Ports and Maritime Infrastructure', Brussels: European Sea Ports Organisation.

ESPO (2004), '*Directive Proposal on Market Access to Port Services* – Initial Response of ESPO', Brussels: European Sea Ports Organisation.

ESPO (2005a), 'Market Access to Port Services: European Parliament – TRAN Committee – Public Hearing 14 June', Statement by Giuliano Gallanti, Chairman of ESPO, Brussels: European Sea Ports Organisation.

ESPO (2005b), 'Market Access to Port Services: Paper adopted by ESPO General Assembly', Brussels: European Sea Ports Organisation.

ESPO (2006), *Annual Report 2005–2006*, Brussels: European Sea Ports Organisation.

ESPO (2007), *Annual Report 2006–2007*, Brussels: European Sea Ports Organisation.

ETF (2007a), *Contribution of the ETF to the European Commission's Consultation on a Future Port Policy for the Union*, Brussels: European Transport Workers' Federation.

ETF (2007b), 'Lisbon Strategy and Transport Workers', TRUST Discussion Paper,

Brussels: European Transport Workers' Federation.
Fairbrother, P. and Hammer, N. (2005), 'Global Unions: Past Efforts and Future Prospects', *Relations Industrielles* 60(3), 405–31.
FEPORT (1998), 'Position of FEPORT on the Commission's *Green Paper on Sea Ports and Maritime Infrastructure*', Brussels: Federation of European Private Port Operators.
FEPORT (2005), 'Position Paper on the Proposed Directive *On Market Access to Port Services*', Brussels: Federation of European Private Port Operators.
Greenwood, J. (2003), *Interest Representation in the European Union*, Houndmills: Palgrave Macmillan.
Hay, C. (2007), 'Keynote Article: What Doesn't Kill You Can Only Make You Stronger: The Doha Development Round, the Services Directive and the EU's Conception of Competitiveness', *Journal of Common Market Studies* 45(Annual Review), pp. 25–43.
Hyman, R. (1999), 'Imagined Solidarities: Can Trade Unions Resist Globalization?', pp. 94–115 in Leisink, P. (ed), *Globalization and Labour Relations*, Cheltenham: Edward Elgar.
Hyman, R. (2005), 'Trade Unions and the Politics of the European Social Model', *Economic & Industrial Democracy* 26(1), 9–40.
IDC (2007), *Position Paper on a European Ports Policy*, Barcelona: International Dockworkers' Council.
Janelle, D. and Michel Beuthe, M. (1997), 'Globalization and Research Issues in Transport', *Journal of Transport Geography* 5(3), 199–206.
Levi, M. and Murphy, G.H. (2006), 'Coalitions of Contention: The Case of the WTO Protests in Seattle', *Political Studies* 54(4), 651–70.
Marks, G. and McAdam, D. (1999), 'On the Relationship of Political Opportunities to the Form of Collective Action: The Case of the European Union', pp. 97–111 in della Porta, D., Kriesi, H. and Rucht, D. (eds), *Social Movements in a Globalizing World*, London: Macmillan.
Martin, A. and Ross, G. (2000), 'European Integration and the Europeanization of Labor', pp. 120–49 in Gordon, M.E and Turner, L. (eds), *Transnational Cooperation Among Labor Unions*, Ithaca, NY: ILR Press.
Neyer, J. (2003), 'Discourse and Order in the EU: A Deliberative Approach to Multi-Level Governance', *Journal of Common Market Studies* 41(4), 687–706.
OSC (2005), *The Proposed Directive on Port Services and Container Terminal Operations in Northern Europe*, London: Ocean Shipping Consultants.
PWG (1977), *Report of an Enquiry into the Current Situation in the Major Community Seaports*, Brussels: Port Working Group of the Commission of the European Communities.
Schmidt, S.K. (2000), 'Only an Agenda Setter? The European Commission's Power Over the Council of Ministers', *European Union Politics* 1(1), 37–61.
Tarrow, S. (1998), *Power in Movement: Social Movements and Contentious Politics*, Cambridge: Cambridge University Press.
Tarrow, S. (2005), *The New Transnational Activism*, Cambridge: Cambridge University Press.
Turnbull, P. (2006), 'The War on Europe's Waterfront – Repertoires of Power in the Port Transport Industry', *British Journal of Industrial Relations* 44(2), 305–26.
Turnbull, P. (2007), 'Dockers *versus* the Directives – Battling Port Policy on the

European Waterfront', pp. 120–49 in Bronfenbrenner, K. (ed), *Global Unions and Global Companies*, Ithaca, NY: Cornell University Press.

Turnbull, P. and Wass, V. (2007), 'Defending Dock Workers – Globalization and Industrial Relations in the World's Ports', *Industrial Relations* 46(3), 582–612.

Verhoeven, P. (2003), 'Editorial', *ESPO News*, 9(10), 1–2.

*Nick Parsons*

# 10

# The European Union and posted workers: industrial relations disputes framed by European policy

## Introduction

A posted worker is a worker who, for a limited period of time, carries out his or her work in a Member State of the European Union (EU) other than the State in which he or she normally works. The Commission estimated that there were one million posted workers in 2005, constituting 0.4 per cent of the EU's working-age population, although precise up-to-date data is unavailable (European Commission 2007). Posted workers are common in the construction industry, but are also important in transport, telecommunications, entertainment, repairs, maintenance and servicing industries. They can be posted to another Member State either by a contract between a user company and a company for which they work directly or through a temporary work agency operating transnationally. User companies employ posted workers to access skills that are in short supply or not available on their own labour markets and/or to access labour at a cheaper rate than would be possible if they recruited workers from their own country. Although the 2008 financial crisis may have put a brake on this development in the short to medium term, in particular through its impact on the construction sector, it seems highly likely that in the longer term the phenomenon of posted workers will increase in importance. All other things being equal, the 2004 and 2007 enlargements to the east could be expected to increase the number of workers posted from the newer Member States to high-wage economies in EU15 countries. Indeed, many newer Member States have seen a rapid increase in the number of temporary work agencies operating on their territory (Eurofound 2008), although figures are unavailable for how many of these operate across borders.

Despite attempts to balance the freedom to provide cross-border services against the risk of social dumping through the undermining of local labour conditions through the 1996 Posting of Workers Directive (PWD), the issue has become a controversial one, with calls for a reform of the Directive following some contentious interpretations of it by the European Court of Justice (ECJ) and some high-profile disputes over the use of such workers, particularly in Sweden and the United Kingdom.

This chapter begins by outlining the legislation applicable to posted workers and the European Court of Justice (ECJ) interpretation of that legislation before examining how this European policy context has affected industrial relations in the UK and Sweden. An explanation then follows of the outcomes of UK disputes over posted workers followed by a discussion of the wider implications of both the Swedish and UK disputes before conclusions are drawn.

## EU policy on posted workers

In order to offer the posted worker protection, the Directive requires Member States to ensure that undertakings guarantee the minimum standards of employment conditions that prevail in the host country to any posted worker where these have been decided by law and/or, for certain activities, mainly in the construction industry, universally applicable collective agreement (Article 3(1)). In the absence of a system of declaring collective agreements to be universally applicable, Member States may base themselves on collective agreements which are generally applicable to all similar undertakings and/or those concluded by the most representative employer and labour organisations at national level. The terms and conditions covered notably include pay and working time.

This Directive has been interpreted by the ECJ in the light of Article 56 of the Treaty on the Functioning of the EU (TFEU). This states that 'restrictions on freedom to provide services within the Community shall be prohibited in respect of nationals of Member States who are established in a State of the Community other than that of the person for whom the services are intended'. Not only is discrimination on the grounds of nationality in the provision of services contrary to EU law, but any restriction, even if it applies indiscriminately to domestic and foreign service providers, is to be eliminated if it prevents, hampers or makes less attractive the provision of services within a Member State by companies established in another Member State. As a result many ECJ rulings have dismantled national administrative barriers to the freedom to provide services, such as the need for work permits or prior authorisation for posted workers, and the need for bank guarantees, establishments and payments to employer funds for bad weather payments, etc. in the host country for service providers (Parsons 2009). More controversially, however, the ECJ has also ruled on the wages applicable to posted workers, and the validity of collective agreements and collective action to enforce them.

## The Laval, Lindsey and South Hook Disputes

In 2004, Laval un Partneri, a Latvian construction company, posted workers from Latvia to work on a contract to refurbish a school and build an annexe in Vaxholm, a suburb of Stockholm. The workers were paid just under two-thirds of the rate stipulated in the construction industry collective agreement, signed between the Byggnads construction union and the Swedish Construction Federation. Byggnads began talks with Laval in June 2004, to persuade them to sign up to the industry agreement, but in September 2004, the company announced that it had signed an agreement with the Latvian Building Workers' Union and therefore did not need to sign one with the Swedish union. Following further deadlock in talks, Byggnads began a blockade of the building site on 2 November, which continued throughout the following month (Woolfson and Sommers 2006: 53–5).

Laval applied to the Swedish Labour Court to get the blockade declared illegal, but the Court supported the union, declaring in its interim finding: 'actions like this … cannot be seen as going against good labour market practices' (cited in *ibid.*: 56). Nevertheless, the Swedish Labour Court also decided to seek a preliminary opinion from the ECJ before making a final ruling on the case. On 18 December 2007, the ECJ ruled that, in the absence of a collective agreement declared to be universally applicable, it is illegal for a trade union to blockade a building site in order to force a provider of services established in another Member State to enter into negotiations with it on the rates of pay for posted workers and to sign a collective agreement with more favourable conditions than those resulting from the relevant legislative provisions (in this case Swedish legislation providing minimum conditions for posted workers through the implementation of the PWD). This is considered an unjustified restriction on the freedom to provide services as it would make it less attractive, or more difficult, for the service provider to carry out work in the host Member State. The ECJ emphasised that the PWD does not impose an obligation on foreign service providers to respect working standards beyond the minima set out in the Directive. Collective action, such as that in this case, may be legal if it serves the overriding public interest, such as protecting workers' jobs and conditions of employment, and is proportional to that interest. This was not, however, considered to be the case in the Laval dispute.

The Lindsey oil refinery dispute broke out in similar circumstances to the Laval dispute. Following tenders from host country and foreign firms, part of a £200m contract for building works was given to IREM, an Italian company, to expand the French company Total's oil refinery in Lindsey within the UK. IREM shipped in one hundred of its permanent Italian and Portuguese workers, with some 300 more to follow. This led to a wildcat strike by hundreds of workers joined by local unemployed construction workers and engineers, in protest at what they saw as discrimination against local workers, claiming that they had been excluded from applying for the jobs and that local pay rates were being undercut by the posted workers. This was denied by both Total and IREM, but by 4 February, twenty-two other sites in the UK were affected with an estimated 6,000 workers taking part in (illegal under UK law) sympathy strike action, mainly in refineries and power stations (*The Economist* 2009). The dispute ended when talks brokered by the government-funded independent arbitrator ACAS (Advisory, Conciliation and Arbitration Service) led to Total agreeing to employ 102 British workers on the project with no loss of employment for the posted workers. However, ACAS found no evidence to support the claims that posted workers were being used to undercut the local workforce (Grice 2009). However, just as the strikers voted on 5 February to return to work four days later, another dispute erupted when construction workers demonstrated outside the London offices of Alstom over the French company's decision to subcontract the equipping of the new Staythorpe power station in Nottinghamshire to foreign subcontractors, and continued their action with demonstrations at the worksite. In March, at another Alstom site on the Isle of Grain in Kent, it was announced that the wages for foreign workers would be raised from £10 to £14 per hour, the nationally agreed rate, after the Unite and GMB unions claimed they had been given a copy of a Polish worker's contract with a subcontractor brought in by Alstom, showing the lower rate, and threatened a national strike ballot (BBC 2009d).

A fresh wildcat strike broke out at the South Hook liquefied natural gas terminal near Milford Haven in West Wales on 19 May 2009 as workers claimed that a Dutch subcontractor, Hertel, had broken an agreement to offer jobs to local workers by bringing in Polish workers. The walkout by 200 workers at South Hook was accompanied, once again, by sympathy action with an estimated 2,500 workers walking out at refineries in North Killingholme, Lincolnshire, and 250 at Aberthawe power station in South Wales. As at Lindsey, the subcontractor claimed that foreign workers were sourced due to a local skills shortage. However, on 21 May, just two days after the start of the stoppage, Hertel announced that it was going to withdraw forty non-UK workers and replace them with UK nationals (Sturcke 2009b, BBC 2009e).

## Reactions to the disputes: two competing visions of Europe

In both the British and Swedish cases, reactions to the presence of posted workers were very similar, with unions arguing for a reform of the PWD to prevent what they saw as the threat of social dumping and employers arguing for the freedom to provide services across borders in conformity with Article 56 TFEU. The main difference was the position taken by the respective governments.

Thus, in June 2004, a few days after the Laval dispute broke out, the Latvian deputy foreign minister expressed concern at 'outright discrimination on the basis of citizenship' (cited in Woolfson and Sommers 2006: 55), while the Byggnads union was accused of xenophobia and protectionist behaviour by the conservative opposition and employers' federations (*ibid.*). The Swedish government, on the other hand, maintained a 'neutral' position, although the Prime Minister, Göran Persson, was quoted as saying that the Swedish union had a 'right to take retaliatory measures' to ensure 'the survival of collective agreements' (*ibid.*). In the British case, government reactions were somewhat different, with Prime Minister Gordon Brown declaring the strikes to be 'not defensible' (BBC 2009b), while Lord (Peter) Mandelson, the Business Secretary and former EU Commissioner for Trade, accused the protestors of xenophobia and protectionism (Sturcke 2009a). However, the UK Government was split over the issue, with the Health Secretary, Alan Johnson, arguing that ECJ judgments had 'distorted' the intentions of the PWD by allowing undercutting and that, 'If workers are being brought across here on worse terms and conditions to actually get jobs in front of British workers ... that would be wrong and I can understand the anger about that' (Sparrow 2009). Echoing Latvian protests in the Laval dispute, the Italian Foreign Minister, Franco Frattini, was quoted by the *Wall Street Journal* as labelling the protests 'indefensible' (*Wall Street Journal* 2009).

Not surprisingly, employers also took the line that industrial action in both cases was protectionist. Thus, in a press release on 18 December 2009, the Swedish Confederation of Enterprise welcomed the ECJ's judgment in the Laval case:

> The judgement is clear, and it safeguards free movement as one of the four basic pillars of the Union ... The judgement means increased legal security for foreign companies that wish to come here and carry out work. The judgement is therefore an important, welcome contribution to increased mobility over borders for companies. (Svenskt Näringsliv 2009)

While direct quotes about the Lindsey dispute from employers' organisations are difficult to find, the BBC claims that the CBI, the British employers' organisation, 'backed Total' (BBC 2009c). At the European level, BUSINESSEUROPE confined itself to supporting ECJ rulings in the Laval and Viking cases, arguing that they 'will contribute to a better functioning of the internal market'. In consequence, there is 'no need for a revision of the Posting of Workers Directive' (BUSINESSEUROPE 2008).

In both the Laval and Lindsey cases, however, this is precisely what the unions were arguing for. The position of the Swedish Building Workers union and the Unite and GMB unions in Britain was summed up by the European Trade Union Confederation (ETUC) General Secretary John Monks in the following statement:

> it is apparent that, while we support strongly the free movement of labour, we need clearer and stronger traffic rules in the European Union which guarantee equal treatment of workers regardless of nationality, and that collective agreements are fully respected by employers. Some employers are undercutting such collective agreements and workers' anger should be directed at them and not at the migrant workers. ETUC is calling for a revised Posting of Workers Directive and a social progress protocol attached to the European Treaties to counter recent adverse decisions of the European Court of Justice which permit employers to ignore established agreements and, in effect, give them a license to undercut wages and conditions. (ETUC 2009)

The 'social progress protocol' would overturn the balance between economic freedoms and fundamental social rights so that in case of a conflict between the two, the former rather than the latter would have to be justified. Without such justification, fundamental social rights would have priority over economic freedoms and competition rules (Monks 2009). The problem here is that Treaty revisions would be necessary for this to take place, and this would require the agreement of all twenty-seven Member States. This is unlikely given the conflict of interests between the new Member States that can benefit from the economic freedoms to raise their standards of living and the old Member States that wish to preserve highly developed industrial relations and welfare systems.

In their potentially more achievable calls for a revision of the Posting of Workers Directive, the unions are supported by socialist Members of the European Parliament (MEPs). Poul Nyrop Rasmusssen, the president of the Party of European Socialists, argued that, 'The European Commission has done nothing to stop freedom of movement of workers from being exploited to drive down wages, despite repeated warnings. Now they are seeing the results', and further argued that the Commission's 'right-wing' attitude was undermining support for the free movement of workers (Brunsden 2009).

The European Commission, however, sided with the employers. In a statement in response to the strikes in the UK, Vladimir Spidla (2009), the Commissioner for Employment and Social Affairs, stated that:

> Free movement of workers, people and services are core values of the European Union … This openness has contributed to economic growth and to the rich diversity of our communities. Experience has clearly shown us that it is not by erecting barriers now and trying to restrict the internal market that we will protect ourselves from the crisis. Erecting barriers will not create jobs …
>
> The [PW] directive is an essential instrument to ensure the balance between protection of workers and economic freedoms and to avoid unfair competition …

Nevertheless, the Commissioner announced a 'series of projects and studies to better understand the impact of the directive on the ground and the consequences of the European Court judgements … On the basis of this analysis, we will be better equipped to consider whether a revision is necessary.' (*Ibid.*)

The far right in Britain sought to make political capital out of the disputes in the run-up to the 4 June European Parliament elections, arguing that the problem lies not in EU rules but in EU membership. Thus, for the UK Independence Party (UKIP) (2009), 'The only way we can run our economy, run our country, the way we want to is by leaving the European Union and being free and independent once again. British jobs for British workers will only happen when Britain is run by and for Britons'. Likewise, the British National Party (BNP) (2009) argued that, 'The only way our workers can be protected is by withdrawing from the EU and adopting an unashamedly protectionist industrial policy.'

## Explaining outcomes

Despite the condemnation of the strike action in both cases as 'xenophobic' and despite the opposition of the UK government in the Lindsey case and the ECJ in the Laval case, trade unions were not outright losers in the disputes. Indeed, the final settlement in the Lindsey case was seen as a victory for unions representing British workers, securing 102 jobs and a commitment from the Engineering Construction Industry Association (ECIA) to guidelines for the use of subcontracted labour. These stipulate that companies should give consideration to local labour when employing workers on such contracts (Moylan 2009). Given that construction in the energy sector is the only area of construction that is expected to withstand the current economic crisis this may be seen as an important step even if the guidelines have no legal status.

Even in the Laval case, the work in Vaxholm ultimately went to Swedish workers after Laval filed for bankruptcy, unable to withstand the economic impact of the Swedish workers' blockade. Although the ECJ judgment has made such action more difficult in the future for Swedish unions, both Byggnads and the ETUC were able to claim victory in that, despite the right to strike not being an area of EU competence, the ECJ ruling recognised it as a fundamental legal right (ETUC 2007).

In the Swedish case, worker solidarity, as seen in the scale of sympathy action, and government support for the action can be seen as explanations for this partial victory. Such solidarity can be explained by a belief in the 'Swedish model' and a desire to protect it from social dumping – a belief shared not only by the trade unions but also by the social democratic government – and the general acceptance of the Swedish population to sustain this labour market and social model despite the high tax burden that it carries. Collective bargaining and high wage levels are central to this model, hence the perceived threat to it when foreign service providers are seen to circumvent Swedish collective agreements.

Such considerations were not present in the Lindsey or South Hook cases, however, where the labour market model is a deregulated, free market one, where the government has nothing but praise for the free movement of services and labour, and where social solidarity in the form of sympathy strikes is illegal. In addition, wildcat strikes, such as those at Lindsey and elsewhere, are also illegal under British law. It would, then, have been relatively easy for the employers to go to court to get the strikes declared illegal and to obtain an injunction to remove protesters from around the entrance to the plants. Some explanation is therefore needed as to why Total gave in with apparent ease to the demands of 'British jobs for British workers'.

In the case of Lindsey, one explanation could be the scale of the dispute, with sympathy action hitting more than twenty sites around the country. Not only was there a risk of a potential disruption of power supplies, which was a matter of concern for both employers and government, but taking the legal route risked escalating the dispute and damaging Total's public image. It would also, for the government, have been a public relations disaster following Gordon Brown's talk, at the 2007 Labour Party Conference, of 'British jobs for British workers', although the government could, as it did throughout the dispute, have claimed neutrality. On the other hand, a long drawn-out war of attrition would not have been in Total's interest. Firstly, given the nature of the project, delays in construction are far more costly than hiring extra workers to bring about a speedy end to the dispute.[1] Secondly, many of the protestors were unemployed, and therefore would have had nothing to lose in a prolonged dispute. In this sense, one may wonder whether the Lindsey and South Hook disputes points to a new phenomenon of worker-unemployed solidarity to defend sectional-national interests, and what the consequences of this may be.

Before turning to this question, however, one other explanation for employer acquiescence to the demands of the strikers needs to be explored. As mentioned above, the strikes were illegal under UK law, and have been since the Thatcher reforms of industrial relations made wildcat and secondary action as well as mass picketing illegal in the 1980s. Taking legal action to end the action could have risked jeopardising this settlement. The Laval judgment of the ECJ may have declared the action of the Swedish unions illegal in this particular case, but it did, as argued above, recognise the right to strike as a fundamental right, and this included the secondary action taken by Swedish electricians, etc. who refused to supply the Vaxholm site. If the case went all the way to the ECJ, therefore, the employers may have won due to the ECJ's view of overriding public interest and proportionality, but the incongruence between UK and EU law regarding the right to strike would not have escaped comment. As EU law takes precedence over national law, the risk would therefore be that the Thatcher reforms of the 1980s would be undone, something British employers would be dead set against.

As for the New Labour government in power at the time, any extension of the right to strike in the UK would not have been welcome. In a period of recession and spiralling unemployment, memories of the impact of industrial action during the 1978/79 Winter of Discontent resurfaced. A repeat of the widespread strikes that led to the exclusion of Labour from office for the next eighteen years was something to be avoided and any extension of the right to strike would not help achieve this end. On the other hand, Brown had promised 'British jobs for British workers' and it was in the interests of the government to see a swift end to the dispute to avoid stoking up nationalist feelings that could see the far right make substantial gains, particularly in the forthcoming European Parliament elections.

The interests of employers and the then New Labour government thus coincided during the Lindsey dispute. Indeed, employers gave in to government pressure to resolve the dispute quickly for reasons of energy security.[2] Officials from Downing Street, the Department for Business, Enterprise and Regulatory Reform and from the Energy and Climate Change departments were all involved in talks over the dispute with energy firms (BBC 2009a). A further consideration for both employers and the state may well have been to end the dispute quickly in order to divert attention away from any reform of the PWD in order to continue to benefit from the advantages offered by Britain's decentralised collective bargaining system.

## Wider implications

As the substantive content of minimum standards in the terms and conditions of employment is not fixed in the PWD, but is related to minimum standards in the host country, it is supposed to offer protection, not only to posted workers, but also to host country labour forces, which may fear being undercut by cheaper labour, while respecting the freedom to provide services across national borders.

The issue of posted workers is thus part of a wider debate about the consequences of the internal market for labour which stretches back to the mid-1980s, when Jacques Delors promoted the idea of 'social Europe' in order to allay fears of social dumping in the build-up to the Single European Act (SEA). While the PWD was supposed to address such concerns, the Laval and recent UK disputes have reignited the debate. The problem in both Sweden and the UK is that the collective bargaining systems are either highly decentralised, as in the UK, or voluntary, as in Sweden. The terms and conditions of posted workers are therefore not necessarily subject to collective agreements but only have to comply with minimum legal provisions – the 1999 Posted Workers Act in Sweden and minimum wage legislation in the UK. As collective agreements improve upon these provisions, the PWD does not protect workforces from social dumping in those Member States without centralised bargaining arrangements. Such threats are reinforced by ECJ rulings that transform the provision of Article 3(1) of the PWD from a list of minima to an exhaustive list as any further restrictions placed upon companies posting workers are seen as restrictions on the freedom to provide services under Article 49 of the EC Treaty.[3]

Thus, rulings such as those in the Laval case pose a serious challenge to national systems of collective bargaining and social dialogue despite recognition by the Commission of their importance for development and for the protection of workers. Those Member States with decentralised systems of collective bargaining are most vulnerable here, but it can also affect those with centralised bargaining systems as the decentralisation of collective bargaining is a common feature of all EU industrial relations systems. Indeed, even where bargaining has remained centralised, flexibility is offered to individual companies through 'opt out' clauses (Parsons and Pochet 2008), undermining the very notion of universal application. Challenges to collective agreements on these grounds cannot be discounted (see, for example, the Portugaia Construcoes case),[4] undermining the ability of the social partners to conclude and enforce agreements in order to set the terms and conditions of employment in companies or sectors, thereby opening the door to competition on the basis of cheap labour. The effect has been to move from a 'non-discrimination approach' to a 'market access approach' to the treatment of service providers and posted workers in which the freedom to provide services takes precedence over the principle of equal treatment of all workers within a given territory (Barnard 2008). This is basically what the UK unions were complaining about when arguing that their workers were being excluded from jobs. The employers' response has been to argue that the skills required for the construction projects in the UK are simply not available locally, and recourse to posted workers is therefore both necessary and inevitable.[5] A 'varieties of capitalism' approach (Hall and Soskice 2001) may give some credence to such arguments. In the course of the paradigm shift in UK economic governance that began in the 1980s under the Thatcher governments, training became employer-led, focused on the needs of the company. At the same time, there was a shift away from manufacturing towards the service industries, particularly in the financial sector. As a result, the number of apprenticeships in manufacturing declined, as did the number of jobs available and the availability of skilled workers to fill them. In combination with EU provisions on the free movement of labour, this has reduced the perceived need for a highly skilled British workforce capable of undertaking construction work of a complex nature. This, coupled with the decentralised nature of British industrial relations and collective bargaining that is part and parcel of the deregulated Anglo-Saxon model, results in negative externalities for British construction workers, but these are not just a function of wage undercutting and social dumping.

The Lindsey and Laval disputes, though, were responses to such fears, and these have been exacerbated by enlargement which has given rise to an 'old versus new' Member State tension within the EU. The current economic crisis may, however, redefine the boundaries of such tensions. As mentioned above, one of the notable aspects of the Lindsey dispute was the solidarity shown between workers and the unemployed in their fight for 'British jobs for British workers'. In the current economic situation, with the ranks of the unemployed swelling across the EU, similar calls have been heard in countries such as Romania, the Czech Republic and Poland (Euractiv 2009a, 2009b, 2009c), while other Member States, such as France and Germany have been granting aid to industry to preserve employment. Although increasingly constrained by ECJ activism, social policy is still under the formal aegis of national governments, and they will bear the brunt of popular disaffection caused by the rise in unemployment due to the current economic crisis. As the fear of unemployment grows, it is likely that governments will face increasing pressure to protect the employment of their citizens or face the wrath of the electorate and risk a rise of the far right as such issues are hijacked by them. In this context, the presence of posted workers perceived as threatening local employment and undercutting local wages and conditions through unfair competition may enhance disaffection for the European project as a whole.

The problem here is one of the distribution of competences in a system of multi-level governance, and this is a second source of tension that disputes over posted workers reveal. As a spillover from economic integration, EU competence is encroaching upon what was previously the prerogative of nation states – labour market and social policies and laws. As the Laval case demonstrates, the risk is that national social models are undermined as national legislation must conform to the four fundamental (market) freedoms at the heart of European construction. In addition, this encroachment does not always take place through any process of negotiation and exchange involving political actors at either the national or EU levels, but, as in the case of the treatment of posted workers, through ECJ jurisprudence, or 'judge-made law' (Scharpf 2009). Due to its impact on national social models, this also reinforces notions of a democratic deficit at the heart of Europe, and potentially plays into the hands of Eurosceptic parties.

The 2009 European Parliament elections provide no firm evidence of this, although a small but significant rise in support for anti-EU parties can be seen. The issue of posted workers was still a controversial one shortly before polling on 4 June 2009, with the far right aiming to make political capital out of it. For Britain as a whole, the BNP and UKIP vote was stable, with the BNP increasing its share by 1.3 per cent to 6.2 per cent, and the UKIP share rising by 0.3 per cent to 16.5 per cent. In the Yorkshire and Humber constituency in which Lindsey oil refinery is located, both parties did better than the national average, with UKIP securing 17.4 per cent of the vote (a rise of 2.9 per cent compared to 2004) and the BNP 9.8 per cent (a rise of 1.8 per cent) (UK Parliament 2009). The BNP also won one of its two seats in the constituency, the first time it had ever had any MEPs elected. At the local authority level, it appears that local issues had a bearing on the results. In North Lincolnshire, the BNP gained 8.3 per cent, slightly less than at constituency level but a slight increase on the 8 per cent won in 2004. The real change, however, was in the UKIP vote which rose to 21.4 per cent from 17.4 per cent in 2004. In this area, UKIP came second to the Conservative Party (30 per cent) and pushed the Labour Party into third position by some 5 percentage points (UK Parliament 2004: 30, UK Parliament 2009: 42). Thus, in the area around the Lindsey refinery, nearly one in three voters opted for parties explicitly calling for the withdrawal of the UK from the EU. The combined total for these parties was within 0.5 per cent of the (largely Eurosceptic) Conservative Party, which polled the most votes.

## Conclusion

The issue of posted workers clearly encapsulates what Scharpf (1998) calls 'asymmetric integration'. Service providers are able to operate across borders and bring their own workforces with them, and this right that takes precedence over the rights of trade unions to negotiate and take action to enforce collective agreements governing the terms and conditions of employment of such workers when these agreements are not universally applicable. Even where collective bargaining systems are centralised, ECJ rulings do not offer blanket protection against social dumping to unions and collective agreements.

In allowing posted workers to benefit from lower wages and levels of social protection than their colleagues from the host country, ECJ rulings are at odds with the principles of equal treatment and equal pay for work of equal value. It is also questionable whether such judgments uphold the principle of fair competition. It could be argued that by allowing foreign service providers not to comply with collective agreements and public policy provisions in force in a particular worksite, they present a competitive disadvantage to service providers in the host country who do have to comply with them. As far as collective action is concerned, ECJ judgments have severely curtailed the ability of trade unions to defend host nation workforces against the threat of such undercutting. Were the use of posted workers as a cheap alternative to local labour to increase, this could threaten national social models and standards of living and working. It is therefore arguable that an overriding public interest is at stake at the Member State level.

The Temporary Agency Work (TAW) Directive, adopted in December 2008, could create another set of inequalities in that those sent to user undertakings by temporary work agencies in the same Member State would benefit from the principle of equal treatment from day one of their assignment whereas those sent by a temporary work agency from another Member State may only benefit from the protections listed in Article 3 of the Posting of Workers Directive. All of the above inequalities could be seen as a form of discrimination along the lines of nationality (of the worker or of the temporary work agency). In a context of economic crisis, such perceptions may well fuel nationalist sentiments.

Fearing precisely this eventuality, in both the Laval and UK disputes, protestors and their union officials were at pains to point out that the actions taken were not of a xenophobic nature, but were aimed at securing fair access to employment. A reform of the PWD appears necessary to secure this. The PWD should be reviewed with a view to bringing it into line with the TAW Directive, with the general principle being non-discrimination from day one of the assignment. The terms and conditions of employment should be governed by the legislation or collective agreement – national, sectoral or company – in force at the place of work unless these are inferior to terms and conditions of employment in the worker's home country. Not only would this ensure fair competition for employment and combat the threat of social dumping, but it would also contribute to the aim of the EU to promote improvements and an upwards harmonisation of living and working conditions across the Union, as stated in Article 151 TFEU. Neglect of this aim in the name of pursuing short-term competitiveness based upon low labour costs in a context of rising unemployment risks not only seeing a real take-off of the much-feared 'race to the bottom'. It could also ignite a real disillusionment with the course of European integration from which the only beneficiaries will be Eurosceptic nationalist parties. Essentially, this is an unintended consequence of the differentiated impact of EU hard law on different varieties of capitalism, all of which pleads for either a more flexible implementation of hard law, or the use of soft law in social policy in order that the different institutional configurations and social models present in the varieties of European capitalism can be accommodated and preserved.

Whether such a reform would have been sufficient to head off the UK disputes is, however, open to question. A national industry agreement covers all construction workers in Britain, including posted workers, but this was not sufficient to prevent perceptions of unfair treatment on the part of the British workforce. Ultimately, these disputes were a result not only of perceptions of the PWD and its interpretation by the ECJ. They were also a result of the trajectory of British capitalism since the 1980s, particularly in terms of its impact upon the skills base of British workers. That the latter managed to secure victory in their disputes suggests that the State and employers were willing to cede some employment opportunities in order to maintain wider institutional and labour market arrangements that they find beneficial but which, in the context of the free movement of labour and the freedom to provide services, impose negative externalities on British workers. Further disputes over contracts to construct coal-fired power stations cannot be ruled out. Lindsey and South Hook may be a harbinger of precisely what the New Labour government sought to avoid – a period of conflictual industrial relations that will serve the Eurosceptic (far) right.

## Notes

1 Interview with ECIA officials, 13 November 2009.
2 Interview with ECIA officials, 13 November 2009.
3 In 2008 the ECJ ruled that Luxembourg had contravened EC Treaty Article 49 and failed to properly implement the PWD in requiring a non-Luxembourg employer to comply with 'public order' legislation, applicable to all companies established in Luxembourg. This was deemed excessive for the protection of posted workers and imposed an additional burden for undertakings established in another Member State which went beyond the Directive's requirements and dissuaded them from providing services. For details see Case 319/06 Commission v Luxembourg.
4 In Case 164/99 Portugaia Construcoes, the ECJ ruled, on 24 January 2002, that if in concluding a collective agreement specific to one undertaking, a domestic employer can pay wages lower than the minimum wage laid down in a collective agreement declared to be generally applicable, whilst an employer established in another Member State cannot do so, this would constitute an unjustified restriction on the freedom to provide services.
5 The ECIA claims that there will be a shortage of between 30,000 and 35,000 engineering construction workers by 2013. Interview with ECIA officials, 13 November 2009.

## References

Barnard, C. (2008), *Employment Rights, Free Movement Under the EC Treaty and the Services Directive*, Mitchell Working Paper Series 5/2008, Edinburgh: Europa Institute.

BBC (2009a), 'Mandelson warns on protectionism', *BBC News*, 31 January, http://news.bbc.co.uk/1/hi/uk/7863047.stm, accessed 21 May 2009.

BBC (2009b), 'Brown criticises worker walkouts', *BBC News*, 1 February, http://news.bbc.co.uk/1/hi/scotland/tayside_and_central/7860001.stm, accessed 21 May 2009.

BBC (2009c), 'Foreign labour row "deal reached"', *BBC News*, 4 February, http://news.bbc.co.uk/1/hi/uk/7868777.stm, accessed 2 March 2009.

BBC (2009d), 'Polish workers' pay is increased', *BBC News*, 13 March, http://news.bbc.co.uk/1/hi/england/kent/7942585.stm, accessed 25 March 2009.

BBC (2009e), 'Gas workers end wildcat walkout', *BBC News*, 21 May, http://news.bbc.co.uk/1/hi/wales/8060255.stm, accessed 21 May 2009.

British National Party (2009), 'New British Jobs for British Workers Protests Shake Pro-EU Parties', 20 May, http://bnp.org.uk/2009/05/new-widcat-strikes-prove-betrayal-of-british-workers-by-membership-in-the-eu, accessed 22 May 2009.
Brunsden, J. (2009), 'UK strikes reignite dispute over posted workers', *European Voice*, 2 February 2009, www.europeanvoice.com/article/2009/01/uk-strikes-reignite-dispute-over-posted-workers/63811.aspx, accessed 2 March 2009.
BUSINESSEUROPE (2008), *No Need for Revision of Posting of Workers Directive after ECJ Rulings*, Position Paper, 7 October.
*The Economist* (2009), 'Discontents, wintry and otherwise', 5 February, www.economist.com/world/britain/displaystory.cfm?story_id=13061705, accessed 2 March 2009.
ETUC (2007), *Press Statement Viking and Laval Cases*, www/etuc.org/a/3666, accessed 25 August 2010.
ETUC (2009), *ETUC Comments on the Dispute Regarding Lindsey Oil Refinery in the UK*, www.etuc.org/a/5795, accessed 31 March 2009.
Euractive (2009a), 'Prague criticised for moving to send home foreign workers', 11 February, www.euractiv.com/en/socialeurope/prague-criticised-moving-send-home-foreign-workers/article–179339, accessed 31 March 2009.
Euractive (2009b), 'Job market nationalism on the rise as crisis bites', 17 February, www.euractiv.com/en/socialeurope/job-market-nationalism-rise-crisis-bites/article–179501, accessed 31 March 2009.
Euractive (2009c), 'Poland frets over foreign workers as economy slows', 17 March, www.euractiv.com/en/socialeurope/poland-frets-foreign-workers-economy-slows/article-180346, accessed 31 March 2009.
Eurofound (2008), *Temporary Agency Work and Collective Bargaining in the EU*, Dublin: European Foundation for the Improvement of Living and Working Conditions.
European Commission (2007), *Posting of Workers in the Framework of the Provision of Services: Maximising its Benefits and Potential While Guaranteeing the Protection of Workers*, Communication from the Commission, Brussels.
Grice, A. (2009), 'Foreign workers "did not undercut locals"', *Independent*, 16 February, www.independent.co.uk/news/uk/politics/foreign-workers-did-not-undercut-locals-1622992.html, accessed 2 March 2009.
Hall, P. and Soskice, D. (eds) (2001), *Varieties of Capitalism: The Institutional Foundations of Comparative Advantage*, Oxford: Oxford University Press.
Monks, J. (2009), 'European Court of Justice (ECJ) and Social Europe: a divorce based on irreconcilable differences?', *Social Europe* 4, www.social-europe.eu/2009/04/european-court-of-justice-ecj-a-divorce-based-on-irreconcilable-differences/, accessed 15 April 2009.
Moylan (2009), 'The refinery dispute's lasting legacy', *BBC News*, 5 February, http://news.bbc.co.uk/1/hi/business/7872932.stm, accessed 21 May 2009.
Parsons, N. (2009), *Labour Market Issues in the EEA: Posted Workers and the Freedom to Provide Services*, Briefing for the European Parliament Committee on Foreign Affairs, Brussels: TEPSA.
Parsons, N. and Pochet, P. (2008), 'Wages and Collective Bargaining', pp. 341–58 in Dyson, K. (ed.), *The Euro at Ten: Europeanization, Power and Convergence*, Oxford: Oxford University Press.
Scharpf, F. (1998), 'Negative and Positive Integration in the Political Economy of European Welfare States', pp. 157–77 in Rhodes, M. and Mény, Y. (eds), *The Future*

*of European Welfare: A New Social Contract?*, London: Macmillan.

Scharpf, F. (2009), 'Interview – "The only solution is to refuse to comply with ECJ rulings"', *Social Europe* 4, www.social-europe.eu/2009/04/interview-the-only-solution-is-to-refuse-to-comply-with-ecj-rulings/, accessed 15 April 2009.

Sparrow, A. (2009), 'Ministers to look at "distorted" EU employment law', *Guardian*, 1 February, www.guardian.co.uk/world/2009/feb/01/eu-law, accessed 2 March 2009.

Spidla, V. (2009), *Statement in Response to the Strikes in the UK*, http://ec.europa.eu/social/main.jsp?langId=mt&catId=89&newsId=450&furtherNews=yes, accessed 31 March 2009.

Sturcke, J. (2009a), 'Anti-foreign labour strikes bed in as talks continue', *Guardian*, 3 February, www.guardian.co.uk/politics/2009/feb/03/widlcat-strikes-foreign-labour-talks, accessed 2 March 2009.

Sturcke, J. (2009b), 'Contract workers continue wildcat strikes over hiring practices', *Guardian*, 20 May, www.guardian.co.uk/world /2009/may/20/contract-workers-widlcat-strikes, accessed 21 May 2009.

Svenskt Näringsliv (2009), *A Welcome Judgement and a Victory for Laval*, Press release, 18 December, http://svensktnaringsliv.se/english/pressreleases/article41228.ece, accessed 2 March 2009.

UK Parliament (2004), *European Parliament Elections 2004*, House of Commons Research Paper 04/50, London: House of Commons Library.

UK Parliament (2009), *European Parliament Elections 2009*, House of Commons Research Paper 09/53, London: House of Commons Library.

UKIP (2009), *Foreign Workers – It's all about EU Laws*, www.ukip.org/content/latest-news/906-foreign-workers--it's-all-about-eu-laws, accessed 22 May 2009.

Wall Street Journal (2009), *UK Refinery Workers End Strike*, 5 February, http://online.wsj.com/article/SB123383306620951857.html, accessed 2 March 2003.

Woolfson, C. and Sommers, J. (2006), 'Labour Mobility in Construction: European Implications of the Laval un Partneri Dispute with Swedish Labour', *European Journal of Industrial Relations* 12(1), 49–68.

*Janine Goetschy*

# 11

## The Lisbon Strategy, industrial relations and Social Europe: an assessment of theoretical frameworks and policy developments

The aim of this chapter is twofold. First, the chapter argues that to improve our understanding of Social Europe better use could be made of a mix of theories from different disciplinary fields (political science, sociology, law, industrial relations). In particular, the chapter defends the idea that in such an endeavour, industrial relations theories in the past have been insufficiently mobilised or mobilised mostly in a rather narrow manner by analysts of Social Europe and they have to catch up. Industrial relations theories especially need not to be forgotten, but they need to open themselves up to consider a variety of policy fields close to them (employment, social protection, economic, education policies), and related theoretical developments such as the varieties of capitalism and Europeanisation theories. Such an academic endeavour is more than necessary given that the practices of social and political actors have significantly changed in recent years and tended to be much less fragmented. Academics still tend to live in their segmented disciplinary routines, whereas decision making has embarked on more global, integrated and 'encompassing' trajectories. This was evident within the Lisbon Strategy (2000–10) and the subsequent project 'Europe 2020', but also with the 2008 and 2010 crisis management devices (at European Union (EU) and world level). Second, with these theoretical and disciplinary 'overtures' in mind, the chapter intends to give an account of the main changes that the Lisbon Strategy, and the two financial and economic crises in 2008 and 2010, have caused for Social Europe, its industrial relations, and its employment and social protection policies – in particular their content, regulatory modes and decision-making arenas.

## Theoretical developments in the 2000s

### *The theoretical toolkit for the study of Social Europe: industrial relations, varieties of capitalism, Europeanisation approaches*

The question of how useful classical industrial relations theories are for understanding the substance of Social Europe and its evolving character is often overlooked. Specialists have often been more eager to analyse Social Europe as a form of public policy from a political science perspective rather than from an industrial relations perspective.

Dunlop's systems model (Dunlop 1958) sees the industrial relations system as being composed of actors (unions, employers, employee representatives, governments, etc.), operating in given economic, technological, political and ideological contexts – with the aim being to reach both substantive and procedural rules in the field of labour relations. The model remains relevant as long as it takes stock of the successive improvements it has been subject to over time.

Dunlop's fairly 'simple, broad and systemic' approach helps to tackle current challenges of industrial relations and Social Europe, such as the search for

- a combined analysis of the variety of 'procedures' and 'arenas' producing EU labour, employment and social protection rules – be it European institutions or European social partners;
- a more integrated analysis of the content of different 'policy fields' (between industrial relations and other domains such as social protection or economic policy);
- more porous frontiers between the study of 'hard and soft law' (and even HRM devices);
- grasping Social Europe developments in rapidly evolving global contexts.

The study of industrial relations was more often considered in 'political economy' terms where political economy regimes and industrial relations regimes were closely linked. This was clearly the case with the famous neo-corporatist schools (Lehmbruch and Schmitter 1982, Crouch 1993), and even more so with the more contemporary theories around the varieties of capitalism in which labour relations, employment and social protection policies are reckoned to constitute crucial parts of each type of capitalism beside product, financial markets and education policies (Hall and Soskice 2001, Amable 2003, Streeck and Thelen 2005).

Those theories attribute a major role to the evolutionary character of the state linked to the continuous transformation of capitalism, resulting in return in the re-shaping of interest groups as well as changes in the nature and forms of social compromises, social conflicts and collective bargaining structures.

The advantages of the varieties of capitalism approach are multifold. The approach tries to grasp the internal complementarities and dynamics at play within a given type of capitalism across various policy fields (economic, employment, social, education, etc) and various institutions. It is not trapped in the narrow view of a single neo-liberal model and provides us with alternative models not limited either to the Rhineland model. Particularly relevant in a period of 'globalisation', the approach manages to give an account of the internal functioning of very different socio-economic systems in various geographic areas in the world, but also of the variety of socio-economic sub-systems at play within the EU itself. Its methodology further facilitates the comparison of those various types of capitalism.

Amable (2003) identified five types of capitalisms: Anglo-Saxon, social-democratic, Asiatic, European continental, Mediterranean to which a sixth type has been added – East European – by Rodrigues (2009). Prior to the 2008 and 2010 crises, most authors argued that the market-oriented Anglo-Saxon system and the social-democratic system were the most capable of adjusting themselves in a period of economic liberalisation and globalisation (in contrast to the European continental system, for example). But now, after the crises, the varieties of capitalism issue needs to be discussed in a renewed manner to allow for a clearer understanding of the diversity of Member State crisis management answers at both national and EU level. What has been happening during those recent periods to Member State typical features of their varieties of capitalism, i.e. the internal adjustments and mutual functionalities between policy fields and policy institutions? Previously, Streeck and Thelen (2005) had been trying (though essentially on a monographic basis) to assess the importance of internal changes at play in a given type of capitalism. They have been identifying five different patterns of institutional reshaping – displacement, layering, shift, conversion, exhaustion – reflecting changes of varying degrees of importance induced by economic liberalisation policies since the 1980s (from marginal changes to drastic ones). How are the 2008 and 2010 crises affecting their typology? Thelen (2009) reckoned that in periods of social and economic transformation, when it comes to thinking about institutional change, approaches that put the emphasis on power-distributional features of institutions and their historical legacy (i.e. historical institutionalism) present more advantages than approaches which stress the mutual coordinating functions of institutions (i.e. the variety of capitalism approach).

To summarise, we observe that innovative linkages among industrial relations, political science and political economy have essentially been set up at two moments i.e. in the 1970s with the wave of neo-corporatist theories and the 2000s with the wave of the variety of capitalism theories. As to the inter-relations between industrial relations and law, their study has been steadier over time; and we are witnessing presently a particularly fruitful period for sociology of law issues. Since the late 1980s, industrial relations have also been enriched by a wealth of other sociological study fields, be it sociology of professions, gender issues, immigration, or employment. Such inter-disciplinary linkages and cross-fertilisation meant progress for the study of both national and EU-level industrial relations and social developments.

Further, beside industrial relations (understood in its broad sense), the study of Social Europe has also started to draw benefits from political science developments, especially multi-level governance and Europeanisation theories (Hooghe and Marks 2001, Delanty and Rumford 2005, Marginson and Sisson 2006). Both theories are considered necessary to analyse EU public policies as resulting from 'to and fro' movements between the national level and the EU level in a vertical and horizontal manner (for a detailed presentation see Featherstone and Radaelli 2003). They argue that what need to be studied are the processes of institutional, strategic and normative adjustments and interactions which find their origin both at the EU and national levels.

Apart from encouraging a complementary use of intergovernmental, functionalist and cognitive theories on EU integration (previously often mobilised in an antagonistic manner), the two sets of theories (multi-level governance and Europeanisation) have themselves led to cross-fertilisation among disciplines, especially sociology and political science. The theories foster the study of formal and informal rules, of private and public entities. They consider that European integration is redesigning the opportunity structure for economic, political and social actors at the national and EU levels and put the emphasis on the adjustment deals between actors at various levels, insisting on ongoing dynamics, which are all crucial points also for the study of industrial relations. Being of an ongoing dynamic nature, Europeanisation approaches leave the future open and reject any determinism, be it from the EU to the national level, or the other way round.

## The European Social Model – a seminal 'integrated' concept: why has there been so much talk about it from the 1990s onwards?

To discuss the issue of the European social model is important, not only because there has been much debate within the EU level about it from the 1990s onwards, but also because it represented a conceptual attempt to 'integrate' industrial relations, employment, social policies and public services within a single framework. At the EU level, the concept of the European Social Model has been slowly replacing the previous concept of 'the European social dimension' which itself was inaugurated during the period of preparation of the internal market project at the end of the 1980s. This shift from the EU social dimension towards a 'European Social Model' concept had been taking place in a triple context.

First, the European Social Model concept took shape as a result of a progressive 'bottom up' Europeanisation process with the EU-level social agenda and procedures tending to resemble the national ones and trying to form thus a slightly more coherent set-up. This occurred in three ways: with the Maastricht social agreement (1992), EU regulatory modes were supposed to look increasingly like the national ones with legal and collective bargaining processes being more intertwined (Goetschy 2005); furthermore, national level employment priorities were entered into the EU agenda from the Amsterdam Treaty onwards; finally, with the Lisbon Strategy (2000), numerous other national sovereignty issues – social (pensions, health care, social inclusion), education/training and other industrial relations issues – were taken on board at the EU level and considered in a more closely interlinked manner with economic policies.

Second, it was considered that the European Social Model could be a useful political referent for carrying out reforms. EU institutions such as the Commission and the Council increasingly use the term 'European Social Model' within the frame of a political trade-off: in other words, the modernisation of the 'European Social Model' was increasingly invoked by 'institutional entrepreneurs of change' in order to safeguard some fundamentals; and it became an EU-level political referent used to legitimise fairly tough employment and social policy reforms at national level (Jepsen and Serrano 2006).

Third, with increasing globalisation during the 2000s the concept of European Social Model developed to its optimum level. On the one side, it was meant to spell out the EU's economic and social specificities and to set the limits of what the EU was likely to accept from globalisation developments, and on the other hand, it was meant to be a feature of EU's normative power (and normative ambitions) in the world.

Most authors have identified the following ingredients for describing the European Social Model (taking into account employment, social protection, industrial relations and public service policies): organised labour and employer organisations; developed collective bargaining structures; tripartite social dialogue structures; a set of advanced social rights; a regulatory state and public funding; elaborate social protection systems and redistribution policies; access to public services of quality (education and training, transports, etc ) (see Jepsen and Serrano 2006 for an outline of the various definitions of the European Social Model).

To sum up, one can say that despite the many shortcomings of such a 'catch-all' concept, it has proved useful from an academic and practitioner point of view for the following reasons:

- be it at national or European level, such a model enabled reflection on the workings of the entire set of economic and social institutions and the policy crossovers between economic governance, industrial relations, social protection, employment, public services; it encouraged multidisciplinary approaches;
- it furthermore enabled reflection upon the variety of forms it takes at national level and national coherence (Ebbinghaus and Hassel 1999);
- it enabled fruitful comparisons between the socio-economic systems of the EU, their common features, and those of other geographic areas in the world;
- being both a political referent and a heuristic tool, it also enabled researchers and practitioners to pool their ideas and facilitated transfers of knowledge between these two worlds.

It appears that by the turn of the 2000s, academic debate dealt with the European economic and social policies in a more global manner, following the European Social Model approach and even more so with the variety of capitalism approach which integrated not only employment, social protection, industrial relations and education/ training policies, but also economic policies (macro-economic, competition, industrial, regional) and even financial systems. The basic assumption was that there existed a very special mix of European economic and social policies combining social cohesion with fairly high economic performance which was organised differently in the various Member States.

The political economy design of the Lisbon Strategy (2000–10) relying on policy coordination, a better balance between policy objectives (economic versus social), new types of governance principles and interactions between the national and EU level, was largely inspired by the intellectual developments described above. The inter-relations between theoretical developments and the empirical reality of EU policy making have proven to be rather close during the 2000s, at least in the field of economic and social EU policies, with the Lisbon Strategy seeking legitimacy from academic experts both at an *ex ante* and *ex post* stage. Increasing globalisation, the 2008 and 2010 crises and the Europe 2020 project will require a renewal in the way we think about varieties of capitalism and the European Social Model in the area of both EU internal and external policy.

## Social Europe developments from the Lisbon strategy (2000–10) to EU 2020

The Lisbon strategy and the following Europe 2020 project (EU 2020) have been inaugurating new avenues for Social Europe. In light of these new avenues, two questions will be addressed in each of the following sections: a) Where did the originality of the Lisbon Strategy reside with regard to Social Europe? If the Lisbon Strategy entailed novel possibilities for Social Europe developments, it also presented certain risks and generated new difficulties for the functioning of Social Europe; and b) Further, how does the EU 2020 take into account both the experience of Lisbon Strategy (2000–10) and the new situation linked to the two economic and financial crises of 2008 and 2010?

### *An enlarged EU agenda: shelter or spring ball vis-à-vis globalisation or both?*

First, the Lisbon Strategy and its various Open Methods of Coordination (OMCs) have led to a substantial enlargement of the EU employment and social agenda on matters of national priority such as employment levels, labour market reforms, social inclusion and social protection reforms (pensions, health care). Previously, Social Europe had been dealing with matters which did not interfere too much with contentious national level debates. The increasing pressure for national labour market and social protection reforms in a context of globalisation (Cohen-Tanugi 2008), led to a substantial and incremental broadening of the EU employment and social agenda within the respect of the subsidiarity and sharing of competences. Despite such a transfer of national priorities into the EU agenda in practice, the legal bases for the various social OMCs of the Lisbon Strategy have not been developed as much as could have been expected in the Lisbon Treaty (2007) (such legal bases existed for the broad economic policy guidelines since 1992 and for employment since 1997). In the Lisbon Treaty, OMCs are mentioned in a brief manner with regard to social policies, industry, research and development, and environment. With regard to education and training policies which are at the heart of the Lisbon Strategy (2000–10) and EU 2020, no OMC principle is mentioned per se (although 'in practice' there exists a very active education and lifelong learning OMC process). The social competences within the Lisbon Treaty (2007) have remained largely untouched – except for the Charter of Fundamental Rights which constitutes a major step forward also for social rights.

It is easy to be enticed by the promise of broadening of the EU social agenda through the Lisbon Strategy, but the policy content of EU spearhead paradigms (such as flexicurity; new skills; active inclusion and non-discrimination; gender equality; sustainable pensions and health care systems; specific employment measures for the elderly and the young; the fight against child poverty; improvement of education systems and increasing of education levels, etc.), remained fairly general and minimal, and their implementation often ambiguous and highly diversified. Some authors, who are especially critical of Social Europe, considered that they were being coerced into propagating 'restrictive' social protection and employment reforms at national level.

The two crises in 2008 and 2010 have borne important consequences for Social Europe and the EU 2020 content. The reactions of governments, social partners and enterprises vis-à-vis the 2008 crisis through their substantial recovery plans, job-saving employment policies and social protection cushioning measures have influenced EU 2020 objectives (see European Commission 2010). To put urgent national policies on the EU agenda is considered more necessary than ever in EU 2020 with an important stress on employment, inclusion and social protection policies (they also appear now on the G20 agenda). In terms of employment policy, more traditional issues such as the fight against youth unemployment, long-term unemployment of specific groups (the low qualified, immigrants) are again central, although more 'innovative' devices around flexicurity and transitional labour markets remain also high on the EU agenda. The crisis measures (adopted by companies, governments, social partners) around job sheltering and drawing benefits from internal labour markets have been identified as fully legitimate by the vast majority of actors although emphasis tends to be put on their transitory character.

Of a more novel vein, in EU 2020, employment policies are now more closely linked to sustainable development with the hope of more 'green' job creation. They are also more closely linked with the knowledge-based society calling for a more anticipatory and prospective view of the labour market development of skills, closer links between education/training institutions and the skills of tomorrow – implying reforms in education/training institutions, in their curricula and the pedagogy around 'learning to learn'. The question of the 'quality of jobs' keeps a fairly low profile and is subordinate to the discourse on flexicurity – supposed to aim at a less unequal labour market between insiders and outsiders, to fight unemployment and to increase employment rates. However, in most countries numerous difficulties are linked to the flexicurity experiments, which are scattered and fragmented – neither being part of a coherent industrial relation framework where they would be closely linked with the collective bargaining system, nor being part of a deeply enough revised conception of social security rights. Besides, the financial difficulties to make such 'flexibility linked social security innovations' are far from being minor, especially given the high level of public deficits.

In terms of social protection, with the 2008 crisis, the fight against social exclusion and the search of social cohesion have come to the forefront in EU 2020 with the recognition of the need of cushioning measures for the most vulnerable. Both priorities, the cushioning orientation, caring for the most deprived on the one hand, and the need for medium-term social protection structural reforms on the other, rank very high in EU 2020 and are somehow at odds with each other.

With the 2010 Greek crisis, it became even more obvious that EU member states (the PIIGS[1] but also the other countries with high public debts and deficits) were expected to carry through rapid structural reforms – in terms of social protection, employment policies, public sector – in order to reduce public deficits in a significant manner and thus to try to restore lost confidence on behalf of financial markets. During this new phase, it is likely that some of the cushioning measures from the first period as well as the employment 'buffer' function fulfilled by the state and employers through job sheltering will lose ground.

### *The OMC under fire from the hard versus soft law debates: perspectives for the hybridisation approach*

The new forms of governance and cooperation devices (i.e. the variety of open methods of coordination) introduced by the Lisbon strategy and spread across numerous policy fields, inaugurated a new regulatory path for Social Europe (Falkner 2006, Goetschy 2007, 2009, Cochoy and Goetschy 2009, Zeitlin, Pochet and Magnusson 2005). The OMC is now added to previous regulatory methods, the Community legislative method, the contractual method (social partner collective agreements) and structural fund procedures. It led to the following interrogations both among politicians and academics. Is there a risk that the traditionally dominant community method will be slowly eroded by more inter-governmental methods (the latter rendering ambitious treaty reforms redundant)? Alternatively, will a subtle mechanism of hybridisation between the various regulatory tools occur? Another possible scenario sees the variety of regulatory methods work alongside one another, without interfering much with each other. If the Lisbon Strategy did not exclude compulsory devices in the employment and social fields, it marked its preference for the OMC of a softer nature; and a similar strategic position was adopted by the successive Commission social agendas (2000–05; 2006–10; 2008 renewed social agenda).

Since the mid-1990s, there has been some endeavour to reflect upon the potential hybridisation and complementarities between hard and soft law devices especially at EU level, although empirical evidence is not abundant – it exists, for instance, on gender policy (Rubery 2002, *Haar 2009*), employment policies (Kilpatrick 2006, Haar 2009) and social inclusion (Behning 2003) – and these efforts remain fairly scarce compared to the two other dominant trends. The first trend reflected a genuine fascination for soft law approaches essentially on behalf of political scientists (at least at first sight). The trend was represented by several European networks and research projects on new governance and the OMC (Sixth FPC and national projects). These approaches provided highly valuable insights into soft governance tools and outcomes, but have generally not been keen on linking them to the existing stock of hard law processes and outcomes in each specific policy field. The second trend was found among a majority of EU lawyers: they have been rather prompt in denigrating soft devices and dismissing them with the argument that they are detrimental to hard law developments (Natali 2009).

Adopting a more open perspective, authors in favour of hybridisation (such as Trubek and Trubek (2005), Velutti (2009) have provided us with some useful reflections on sociology of law. They draw attention to the dangers of compartmentalisation between hard and soft law, arguing for a less artificial divide between the two and for examining instead their potential complementarities. Indeed hybridisation theory presents several advantages. It shows that legal rules are not a static and insulated body but subject to changes over time and permeable to economic and political evolutions at national, EU and world level. It stresses the importance of socialisation processes which precede the making of laws and influence the quality of their implementation. It highlights the fact that conflicting social issues can be 'moderated' by soft tools at a first stage before becoming hard law in a later stage. Hybridisation between hard law and new governance can improve the quality of EU law-making and thus render it more legitimate. Useful complementarities can be displayed for example between the Charter of fundamental rights and an OMC guaranteeing its implementation, or between EU framework directives and more concrete implementation devices through an OMC process. Moreover, the hybridisation process between new governance and law can take place in different sequences: from EU hard to national soft law, from EU soft law to national hard law (member states might, for example, implement EU soft policies of the European Employment Strategy through national hard law measures), or from EU soft laws to national soft laws.

What has been the impact of the 2008 crisis for the various EU regulatory methods? It has prompted some hard law developments at EU and national level, and rendered the access to EU financial resources easier. It has contributed to speeding up the adoption of two directives (concomitant to the European Parliament elections in 2009, another favourable condition): the directive on temporary agency work in 2008; the revised directive on European Work Councils in 2009. It led in 2008 to the adaption and reform of both the European Globalisation Adjustment Fund (higher EU-level amounts granted; lowering of the threshold of the number of dismissed workers; prolongation of the period for financial help; exceptions to the rules if local economy severely hit) and the European Social Fund (no need for national co-financing for 2009 and 2010) in the face of urgent financial needs resulting from the crisis.

***What kind of policy coordination and policy hierarchies?***

The Lisbon strategy inaugurated the issue of policy coordination (at the EU and national levels) and the virtuous circles that are supposed to emerge from mutual coordination policy effects. The newly broadened employment and social policy agenda has been linked closely with other policy fields (economic, environmental, education and training, research and development) so as to reap benefits from policy coordination both at the EU and national levels. This development was meant to take place against the backdrop of a more traditional fragmented and piecemeal Social Europe lacking a coherent project. The risk of such interweaving and of the concomitant upgrading of both economic and employment/social issues remains, of course, the development of a hierarchy of policies where economic matters continue to override employment matters, the latter tending to having precedence over social issues (such as social inclusion) (Ashiagbor 2005). Such a trend became even more obvious with the 2005 Lisbon Strategy reform under the banner of simplification, redefinition of priorities and reduction of the number of integrated guidelines. Moreover, the Lisbon Strategy had to acknowledge and be in line with 'framing policies' such as the Growth and Stability Pact and the EU Monetary Policy.

With the 2008 crisis, the attempts to re-regulate financial markets in cooperation with other international organisations, the launching of EU-level and national-level recovery plans, the re-interpretation of the Growth and Stability Pact and of State aids have changed the macro-economic frames of the Lisbon Strategy: EU 2020 has been planning a more timely coordination of its ten 2010 guidelines with the other macro-economic processes. With the 2010 Greek crisis, the insufficiencies of EU economic governance have come to the fore more than ever before in EU history, and the regulatory and financial steps undertaken towards more economic governance have been extensive (see the 9 May 2010 EU rescue plan and the June 2010 European Council) through a painful (and ongoing) process with yet many uncertain dimensions and implications for the Eurozone and the twenty-seven Member State banking, economic and employment systems.

With 'EU economic governance' becoming a key element for the fate of Europe in 2010, the feared hierarchy of policy fields (with economy dominating) is of course very likely to remain in place and even to be reinforced; but beside being a necessity for the mere Eurozone survival, the new economic governance devices also represent new potentials for EU 2020. Thus, the EU 2020 content illustrates that to the old contradictions and hierarchies among policy objectives, new ones have been added such as: How to foster growth and higher consumption with a low carbon economy? How to recover growth requiring long-term public investment and to reduce the public debt? (Rodrigues 2009). With both crises (2008 and 2010), answering these questions, which are central to EU 2020, has become even more difficult.

### *The centrality of New Public Management Tools: measuring mechanisms as policy tools*

As shown through the Lisbon Strategy, the EU beside defining common paradigms in the employment and social fields, also intended to be a pioneer through the promotion and diffusion of New Public Management (NPM) tools (benchmarking, objectives to reach within a given calendar, development of indicators, regular assessments of policy implementation and impact, comparisons among Member States, peer reviewing, diffusion of best practices) in order to improve the efficiency of public policy-making and reduce its costs. Such tools help to enhance its reflexive capacity and auto-corrective mechanisms. Moreover, they can contribute to EU measures from a rolling agenda perspective with a longer time scale than before, a trend which should facilitate in-depth reforms. This approach is also reflected in the logic of changing EU presidencies and their 'rolling agenda' which puts a single Presidency's work into a partly pre-defined agenda. Such an evaluation culture has further inspired the EU social dialogue itself.

The dynamics of such NPM tools – which are not as coercive as some EU legal measures – were supposed to reside in the mutual learning capacities between Members States on the basis of the comparison of their respective results, and in the 'naming and shaming' of Member State's achievements. Since the early 2000s, the degree to which 'naming and shaming' should be used has itself been subject to EU and national-level political debate: it was watered down in the 2005 Lisbon Strategy reform. However, as some researchers (Bruno 2007) demonstrate, 'benchmarking' is a distant piloting tool which is far from neutral and which is highly ambiguous as it often mixes scientific judgements with political choices in a confusing way.

With the 2008 crisis and 2010 Greek crisis NPM tools will remain central in EU 2020 and processes. Some quarters plead for more constraining OMCs in concomitance to more stringent economic governance with the hope to reinforce thus the voice of the EU in the world. Ironically, the pressure of financial markets through their rating agencies which have been pushing for substantial reforms in EU economic governance seem also to be constituting a stronger trigger for hurrying national social reforms than OMC processes have ever been beforehand!

### *Toward more 'politicised' EU employment and social policies or both?*

What about the evolution of the role of EU-level social and political stakeholders with the Lisbon Strategy? The various OMCs have meant, first of all, an increased formal role for the European Council of Head of States, national governments and numerous expert committees. If the setting up of a yearly Spring Council on the Lisbon Strategy has on the one hand granted higher political profile to employment and social protection issues on the EU agenda, the development of expert committees within the NPM design has on the other hand given a more elite-driven touch to public policy-making – the latter indeed offering a specific way to channel and solve increasing Member State conflicts and diversity due among others to enlargement (Wendler 2004). By 'expert-driven committees' one must distinguish two types: on the one hand, those representing Member State interests such as the Employment Committee in charge of the European Employment Strategy, and the Social Protection Committee dealing with the OMCs on social inclusion, pensions, health care – both bodies being support committees of the Council of Employment and Social Affairs and comprising top-level civil servants, and on the other hand, the numerous expert and advisory committees comprising more specifically experts, academics and practitioners. The 2005 Lisbon Strategy reform was intended to better involve national governments in the process and to improve their political 'appropriation' of the Lisbon Strategy.

If one view has the growing role of the European Council leading to an increase in the 'politicisation' of EU matters, the other view has the important role of expert committees added to NPM tools meaning their relative 'de-politicisation'. Assessments of the research community have essentially put the emphasis on the second feature.

In the present crisis management situation and with the Lisbon Treaty institutional reforms favouring more EU centrality, 'politicisation' trends are likely to take over – though financial, economic and budgetary issues tend to be highly technically prone matters and thus imply a mix of both political and top level civil servant expertise.

As to the role of the Commission, it has become more complex since the 2000s: it has played a permanent initiating and steering function in the various OMCs (either on a Treaty basis or on an ad hoc basis), but also a slightly less active role in legislative initiatives compared to the past (see Haar 2009). Quality of implementation and 'less regulation' have also been general key contemporary concepts. The Commission has further pushed for the development of an autonomous dialogue among the EU social partners and encouraged them to draw up their own multi-annual programs (2003–05; 2006–08; 2009–10). It has also promoted social responsibility among private actors through Corporate Social Responsibility, essentially large enterprises.

As to the European Parliament, which had gained a co-decision role in social matters in the Amsterdam Treaty (1997), its role is limited to information and consultation as to the Lisbon Strategy and in OMC processes given that they are of an inter-governmental nature. The European Parliament had to confront two developments during the same period which weakened its role, i.e. the concurrent co-regulator role of social partners stemming from the Maastricht Treaty (1992) and their rather weak involvement in the Lisbon Strategy and various OMC processes.

The role of social partners – even if they have been regularly solicited to take part in the various OMCs (either on a Treaty basis or on an ad hoc basis) and in the Tripartite Summit previous to the yearly Lisbon Strategy EU spring council (this tripartite summit has now become an official institution within the Lisbon Treaty) – has been less emblematic in the 2000s than during the previous period of the post-Maastricht social agreement (1992) when many hopes were placed as to their social role for invigorating Social Europe (Smismans 2006).

Their involvement in the various OMCs has been unequal (more important in the European Employment Strategy than in the other OMCs) depending on the quality of the social dialogue in the various Member States: in general though most assessments reckon that their role in the Lisbon Strategy was insufficient (Natali and de la Porte 2009).

To conclude, it appears that on the one hand strong politicisation processes have been set up with the Lisbon Strategy, while on the other hand elite driven dynamics have also been heavily developing. These two powerful mechanisms are likely to remain permanent features of EU 2020, and to become even stronger with increasing globalisation, the Lisbon Treaty implementation and the ongoing crisis. Academic research concerning those two trends has often been a bit one-sided, opposing them, rather than trying to understand in which ways their respective political rationales relate to each other.

## Conclusion

This chapter has given an account of Social Europe and industrial relations major transformations with the Lisbon Strategy and with the 2008 and 2010 crises. Never have the inter-relations between theoretical developments and the empirical reality of EU policy-making been so close in the field of Social Europe than during the 2000s. On the one hand, the Lisbon Strategy governance philosophy called for academic expertise. Experimentalism, regular policy evaluation and reflexivity exercises were inherent features of the Lisbon Strategy in its very design which explains why so numerous academic research projects were carried out. On the other hand, since the late 1990s academic knowledge has been favouring more integrated (such as the varieties of capitalisms) and/or more inter-disciplinary approaches, ready to carry out encompassing analyses of the Lisbon Strategy project. Such proximity of interests between the policy-maker community and the academic community renewed both policy making and research: on the one hand, it helped policy makers to develop 'evidence-based policy making' and on the other academics to enlarge their research repertoire.

With two major financial, economic and employment crises (2008 and 2010) with worldwide systemic implications, the theoretical approaches described here are bound to be renewed or at least revisited. The Europe 2020 project (i.e. the follow-up of the Lisbon Strategy) and its ten Integrated Guidelines have obtained the European Council approval (June 2010 Council). Compared to the Lisbon Strategy 2000–10, the policy content of the EU 2020 project has been broadened largely as a consequence of the 2008 crisis. Among its five quantified key targets the fight against poverty, education and environmental issues has found a place beside employment and research and development matters. Financial regulation, a better coordination of the EU 2020 process with the GSP (Growth and Stability Pact), and the external dimension of the EU were already novel issues in EU 2020 in March 2010. But the April 2010 Greek crisis was going to lead to a major breakthrough in EU economic governance which will bear huge consequences for EU 2020, the future of the Eurozone, the world banking system and the EU altogether. The bulk of crisis management devices following the 2008 crisis have already exerted important consequences for national and EU-level industrial relations and Social Europe (see European Commission 2011).

Crisis management, the EU 2020 project and ongoing globalisation will continue to transform the shape of Social Europe and industrial relations in the coming decade, but the Lisbon Strategy has definitely exerted a decisive and lasting impact on Social Europe meta-features. On the academic front, this calls for mobilising imaginative and encompassing theoretical approaches based on innovative fieldwork studies.

## Notes

1 PIIGS is Portugal, Ireland, Italy, Greece and Spain.

## References

Amable, B. (2003), *The Diversity of Modern Capitalism*, Oxford: Oxford University Press.

Ashiagbor, D. (2005), *The European Employment Strategy: Labour Market Regulation and New Governance*, Oxford: Oxford University Press.

Behning, U. (2003), 'Implementing the "New Open Method of Coordination" in the Field of Social Inclusion', *Transfer* 9(4), 737–42.

Bruno, I. (2007), 'Déchiffrer l'Europe compétitive. Etude du benchmarking comme technique de coordination intergouvernementale dans le cadre de la stratégie de Lisbonne', unpublished Ph.D. thesis, Institut d'Etudes Politiques, Paris.

Cochoy, F. and Goetschy, J. (2009), 'La construction de l'Europe sociale: créativité institutionnelle communautaire et réalités nationales', *Sociologie du travail* 4/2009 (special issue on Social Europe), 447–60.

Cohen-Tanugi, L. (2008), *Euroworld 2015: A European Strategy for Globalization*, Final Report of the Europe and Globalisation Mission, chaired by Laurent Cohen-Tanugi, Paris: Centre d'Analyse Strategique.

Crouch, C. (1993), *Industrial Relations and European State Traditions*, Oxford: Clarendon Press.

Delanty, G. and Rumford, C. (2005), *Rethinking Europe, Social Theory and the Implications of Europeanization*, London: Routledge.

Dunlop, J.T. (1958), *Industrial Relations Systems*, New York: Holt and Co.

Ebbinghaus, B. and Hassel, A. (1999), *Striking Deals: Concertation in the Reform of Continental European Welfare States*, MPIfG Discussion Paper 99/3, Cologne.

European Commission (2010), *Europe 2020: A Strategy for Smart, Sustainable and Inclusive Growth*, COM (final).

European Commission (2011), *Industrial Relations in Europe 2010*, Brussels.

European Council (2010), *Presidency Conclusions*, 17 June.

Falkner, G. (2006), 'Forms of Governance in European Union Social Policy: Continuity

and/or Change?', *International Social Security Review* 59(2), 77–103.
Featherstone, K. and Radaelli, C.M. (eds) (2003), *The Politics of Europeanization*, Oxford: Oxford University Press.
Goetschy, J. (2005), 'The European Social Dialogue in the 1990s: Institutional Innovations and Paradigms', *Transfer* 11(3), 409–23.
Goetschy, J. (2007), 'The Implications of the Lisbon Strategy for the Future of Social Europe : "on the road" or "new age"?', *International Journal of Comparative Labour Law and Industrial Relations*, Winter, 499–524.
Goetschy, J. (2009), 'The Lisbon Strategy and Social Europe: Two Closely Linked Destinies', in Rodrigues, M.J. (ed), *Europe, Globalization and the Lisbon Agenda*, Edward Elgar, Cheltenham.
Haar, B.P. ter. (2009), 'The growing potential integration capacity of the Acquis of the European Social Model', *European Integration online Papers (EIoP)*, 13, Art. 26, http://eiop.or.at/eiop/texte/2009-026a.htm.
Hall, P.A. and Soskice, D. (2001), *Varieties of Capitalism: The Institutional Foundations of Comparative Advantage*, Oxford: Oxford University Press.
Hooghe, L. and Marks, G. (2001), *Multi-Level Governance and European Integration*, London: Rowman and Littlefield.
Jepsen, M. and Serrano, A. (eds) (2006), *Unwrapping the European Social Model*, London: Polity Press.
Kilpatrick, C. (2006), 'New EU Employment Governance and Constitutionalism', pp. 121–52 in de Búrca, G. and Scott, J. (eds), *New Governance and Constitutionalism in the EU and the US*, Oxford: Hart.
Lehmbruch, G. and Schmitter, P. (1982), *Patterns of Corporatist Policy-making*, London: Sage.
Marginson, P. and Sisson, K. (2006), *European Integration and Industrial Relations: Multi-Governance in the Making*, Basingstoke: Palgrave Macmillan.
Natali, D. (2009), 'The Lisbon Strategy a Decade on: A Critical Review of a Multi-disciplinary Literature', *Transfer* 15(1), 111–37.
Natali, D. and de La Porte, C. (2009), 'Participation through the Lisbon Strategy: Comparing the European Employment Strategy and Pensions OMC', *Transfer* 15(1), 71–91.
Rodrigues, M.J. (ed.) (2009), *Europe, Globalization and the Lisbon Agenda*, Cheltenham: Edward Elgar.
Rubery, J. (2002), 'Gender Mainstreaming and Gender Equality in the EU: The Impact of the EU Employment Strategy', *Industrial Relations Journa* 33(5), 500–19.
Smismans, S. (ed.) (2006), *Civil Society and Legitimate European Governance*, Cheltenham: Edward Elgar.
Streeck, W. and Thelen, K. (eds) (2005), *Beyond Continuity: Institutional Change in Advanced Political Economies*, Oxford: Oxford University Press.
Thelen, K. (2009), 'Institutional Change in Advanced Political Economies', *British Journal of Industrial Relations* 47(3), 471–98.
Trubek, D. and Trubek, L. (2005), 'Hard and Soft Law in the Construction of Social Europe: The Role of the Open Method of Co-ordination', *European Law Journal* 11(3), 343–64.
Velutti, S. (2010), *New Governance and the European Employment Strategy*, London: Routledge.
Wendler, F. (2004), 'The Paradoxical Effects of Institutional Change for the Legitimacy

of European Governance: The Case of EU Social Policy', *Eiop – European integration online papers* 8(7).
Zeitlin, J., Pochet, P. and Magnusson, L. (eds) (2005), *The Open Method of Coordination in Action*, Peter Lang: Brussels.

Maarten Keune

# 12

# Flexicurity: a new impulse for social dialogue in Europe?

## Introduction

For many years, the project of European integration has faced difficulties related to its emphasis on negative integration, i.e. the construction of the Single Market, and the limited development of positive integration, i.e. the development of common European social and labour market policies to shape the conditions under which markets operate (Scharpf 2002, Keune 2012). The weak social dimension causes legitimacy problems for the European Union (EU) in that it weakens the acceptance of the profound integration in the economic area and strengthens the image of the EU as a technocratic project. Also, in developing its social dimension, the EU faces the problem of how to strike a balance between further European integration in the social field and the deep-rooted and legitimate national diversity concerning the labour market and the welfare state (Zeitlin 2005). Different approaches have been developed to address these problems including a limited expansion of the social competences of the EU, the discourse about the European Social Model, the support from the EU for European social dialogue and the introduction of the Open Method of Coordination (OMC) concerning a wide range of social policy issues (Sabel and Zeitlin 2010; Keune 2012; Weiss 2010).

More recently, the concept of flexicurity was adopted first by the European Commission and then by other European actors, to address these same issues. The flexicurity discourse argues not only for increased market governance and labour market flexibility, but also for a strengthening of the security of workers and their families. What is more, it claims that there are positive interlinkages between the market and the welfare state and between economic and social policy. Flexicurity is also explicitly presented as a way to overcome the differences of interest between capital and labour and as a consensus-building concept that can provide a positive impulse to (European) social dialogue and collective bargaining.

In this chapter, the rise of this concept and the extent to which it has indeed been able to create bridges between capital and labour will be discussed. The structure of the chapter is as follows. In the first section, we discuss the emergence of the flexicurity concept at the EU level. Secondly, we discuss the prospect for flexicurity to become a driver for a revival of the European social dialogue, then we discuss the prospect for flexicurity in national-level social dialogue. The final section finishes the chapter by drawing together the conclusions.

## The concept of flexicurity and its adoption by the EU

European countries have developed extensive bodies of labour market and welfare regulations since the late nineteenth century, albeit with strong diversity between (groups of) countries. For a long period, i.e. until the late 1970s, these regulations predominantly had protective and security-enhancing objectives. Labour market regulations were to protect workers from the excesses of capitalism and the uncertainties of the market, and to redress, to some extent, the power imbalances between workers and employers (Davies and Freedland 1993, Crouch 2008). Also, the welfare state aimed to reduce the dependency of citizens on the market for their well-being by providing protection against risks related to poverty, illness, disability, old age and others (Esping-Andersen 1990).

As of the late 1970s, this trend was gradually reversed. In the context of the accelerating globalisation of the economy, an ideational shift towards neoliberalism and monetarism took place. In the new dominant discourse supply side economics started to replace demand side economics, the market replaced the State as the core mode of governance, and enterprises were argued to need high levels of flexibility to adjust to and compete in the global market. With the neo-classical market as the ultimate inspiration, the State increasingly became a 'competition state' (Jessop 2002) to which social progress is subordinated to and dependent on economic success. Labour market reform started to focus on the adjustment of labour supply to the requirements of the market, deregulation and labour market flexibility, and an increasing reliance on the market for employment creation. At the same time, welfare state reform focused on strengthening its productive rather than its protective function, on increasing labour market participation of the inactive and on reducing their dependency on the welfare state (Serrano Pascual 2009, Hudson and Kühner 2009). Hence, the dependency of the individual on the market as well as the power of capital was strengthened, while protection against the uncertainties the market creates was weakened.

In recent years, attempts have been made to reconcile the two trends, that is, to develop approaches towards labour market and welfare regulations that foster labour market flexibility on the one hand and on the other hand provide protection and security to individuals. Increasingly, it is argued that there are close links between competitiveness, innovation and productivity improvements on the one hand and social progress on the other. This argument is at the heart of the

EU discourse on the European Social Model that was initiated by Delors in the late 1980s. This ambiguous and polysemous discourse is used to provide a social identity and legitimacy to the EU, to depoliticise European integration, and to be inclusive as to different interests and ideologies (Serrano Pascual 2009). It argues that economic and social progress go hand in hand and are not contradictory to each other, and that both are at the core of European integration.

Within this context, flexicurity entered the European debate in the early 2000s. Flexicurity is generally defined as 'a policy strategy that attempts, synchronically and in a deliberate way, to enhance the flexibility of labour markets, work organisation and labour relations on the one hand, and to enhance security – employment and social security – notably for weaker groups in and outside the labour market, on the other hand' (Wilthagen and Tros, 2004: 169). It aims to reconcile the strong demand for further flexibilisation of the labour market, stemming from competitive concerns, with an equally strong demand for protection of employees and to produce so-called 'win-win strategies' that cater to the needs of both employers and employees.

The flexicurity approach presents a view of the labour market as the interplay of a number of different types of flexibility and security (Wilthagen and Tros 2004).[1] It argues that it is the combined effect of these different types of flexibility and security that determines the functioning and performance of the labour market. It also aims to overcome the traditional contraposition of labour market flexibility and security and argues that instead of being contradictory they can be mutually reinforcing (see, for example, Wilthagen and Tros 2004, Wilthagen 2005).

The concept of flexicurity was first employed in the mid-1990s in the Netherlands, in the context of the preparation of the Dutch Flexibility and Security Act and the Act concerning the Allocation of Workers via Intermediaries. These two acts aimed to inject additional flexibility into the labour market by relaxing dismissal protection, in particular for fixed-term contracts, and the rules to start a temporary work agency on the one hand, while generating a higher level of security for employees in flexible jobs on the other. They were a typical product of the Dutch Polder Model as well as the 'purple' (labour-liberal) coalition government of the 1990s, aiming to reconcile the interests of employers and workers, strengthening both competitiveness and protection.

Subsequently, Danish academics discovered that the labour market system that had historically developed in Denmark could be considered a flexicurity model as well, albeit different from the Dutch one. The Danish flexicurity model is presented as a system that encompasses the entire labour market and that consists of three, mutually reinforcing institutions: (i) flexible standard employment, resulting from low employment protection; (ii) extensive unemployment benefits providing income security to the unemployed; and (iii) active labour market policies aimed at skill upgrading and activation of the unemployed (Madsen 2006). What the models share is that, in both cases, the importance of social dialogue as a means to devise and legitimise flexicurity policies is underlined. The two countries have become the major examples of flexicurity cases.

The flexicurity discourse claims to not promote one specific labour market model but rather an open approach that can have manifold empirical manifestations through different combinations of flexibility and security. Indeed, Denmark and the Netherlands represent quite different models, both in terms of substance and of scope. And it is argued that in principle many more positive combinations between flexibility and security are possible. This illustrates the ambiguity of the flexicurity concept: there is no single flexicurity model and very different models and strategies can be subsumed under the term 'flexicurity' (Burroni and Keune 2011). Also, it does not prioritise different types of flexibility or security over others or specify how much flexibility or security is adequate (*ibid.*).

A number of commentators claim that this lack of specification of the flexicurity approach is an advantage and maybe even a must. For example, Rogowski argues that flexicurity needs to remain an aspiration rather than being identified with a concrete policy, and that 'for the success of flexicurity policies it seems crucial that the definition of the term flexicurity remains vague so that it can be used to address a range of sometimes contradictory policy goals' (Rogowski 2008: 86). In this conception, flexicurity takes on the role of a beacon that guides policy makers in the right direction by inspiring them to take a holistic approach, to explore interlinkages between policy fields and to aim for balanced strategies and outcomes.

However, the ambiguity of the concept also means that it is hard to recognise a 'true' flexicurity programme since we lack the parameters to effectively make the respective judgement. Instead of flexicurity guiding political actors, there is a danger that the interpretation of what is flexicurity and what it is not will become the focus of political struggle, with political actors trying to impose their views and using the flexicurity concept as a means of justifying traditional political positions. Also, instead of appealing to a broad range of actors, the concept may prove empty and meaningless.

### *The EU and flexicurity*

As mentioned before, the European Commission has been the main agent promoting flexicurity as a reform concept for European labour markets and as a core subject for social dialogue and collective bargaining. For the Commission, flexicurity represents a powerful discursive tool strengthening its (soft) regulatory capacity towards the Member States. Also, it is compatible in a number of ways with the Commission's roles and discourse in the area of economic, social and employment policy (Keune and Jepsen 2007) which are:

i The role of the Commission as disseminator of knowledge and 'best practices'. One of the main objectives of the European Employment Strategy is that of policy learning and dissemination of 'best practices' through the OMC. The two countries in the EU with the best labour market performance (at least in terms of the employment rate, the key indicator of success for the Commission) are also the two main national cases associated with the flexicurity concept, i.e. the Netherlands and Denmark.

ii The Commission's role as a broker between economic interests, i.e. between capital and labour and between different political and/or national constituencies. The flexicurity concept fits this role since it is explicitly forwarded as a win-win concept that can overcome the contradictions between diverging interests, without imposing a one best way solution.

iii The Commission's discourse on the European Social Model emphasises the idea that economic and social progress should go hand in hand as well as the idea of social policy as a productive factor. Flexicurity is easily fitted into this discourse and in fact can be presented as a concise illustration of these views.

The Commission has used its agenda-setting power to put flexicurity at the top of the European agenda and in particular at the core of the European Employment Strategy. Most importantly, in June 2007 the Commission issued a Communication entitled *Towards Common Principles of Flexicurity: More and Better Jobs Through Flexibility and Security* (CEC 2007). The document outlines the Commission's vision on labour market reform through flexicurity, organised around four so-called 'flexicurity components': flexible and reliable contractual arrangements, comprehensive lifelong learning strategies, effective active labour market policies and modern social security systems. It argues that national reform strategies should include these four components, but that there are different 'pathways towards flexicurity', depending on specific national labour market and welfare problems and institutional configurations. Through such strategies labour markets should be further flexibilised but at the same time security for workers should be enhanced. Additionally, it argues that flexicurity policies should be balanced and cater to the need of workers and employers, and notes the crucial importance of social dialogue for integrated flexicurity policies.

In December 2007 the Council adopted Common Principles of Flexicurity, a slightly modified version of the Communication, cementing the position of flexicurity as a core European approach. And it has remained at the heart of the European agenda ever since, as demonstrated by its prominent presence in the more recent EU 2020 strategy (CEC 2010) and the Commission's plans for a new flexicurity communication in 2012.

Given the ambiguous nature of flexicurity, however, it remains open to debate to what extent the EU's version of flexicurity indeed represents a 'neutral' or 'balanced' vision on labour market and social policy, and if it gives equal weight to positive and negative integration. Opinions on this question differ but a range of authors have argued that the European version of flexicurity emphasises the need for market-based reforms, increased labour market flexibility and activation, but that it is underdeveloped where security for workers is concerned (Serrano Pascual 2009, Vielle and Bonvin 2008, Keune and Jepsen 2007). This suggests that it is likely to appeal more to employers than to trade unions. In the following sections we will discuss if this is the case.

## Flexicurity and European social dialogue

As mentioned above, the flexicurity discourse supposes close links between flexicurity and social dialogue: social dialogue is argued to be a precondition for broad, comprehensive flexicurity strategies, while flexicurity is supposed to offer new impulses to social dialogue. In this section we will discuss to what extent this is the case where European social dialogue is concerned, whereas the next section turns to national-level social dialogue.

The European 'social partners' (i.e. European-level trade unions and employers' organisations) are involved in processes of consultation, concertation and social dialogue. Also, they received the competence to become, in principle, co-regulators of the European labour market. They have the right to negotiate framework agreements and then jointly request the Commission to start a process to convert these agreements into Directives such that they become formally incorporated into European law. Additionally, they can make so-called autonomous framework agreements, the enforcement of which is their own responsibility and which depends on their national member organisations.

However, their role as co-regulators of the labour market has been limited: to date only eight framework agreements have been signed and only four of those were converted into Directives (three new Directives and one revision). This should come as no surprise considering that whereas the European Trade Union Confederation (ETUC) supports the further development of European-level labour market regulations, the basic position of the main employers' organisation BUSINESSEUROPE is that there is no further need for such regulations and that European integration should centre on economic integration. Also, the employers have alternative channels to influence European policies and are not limited to European Social Dialogue in this respect. Trade unions have fewer options at the European level and are more dependent on Social Dialogue. They do not however have a sufficiently strong power position to muscle reluctant employers into concluding framework agreements.

An additional explanatory factor here is the changing role of the European Commission. While the more social democratically oriented Commissions of the 1990s would to some extent use the 'threat of a Directive' to overcome the employers' position and to ensure a more productive social dialogue, in recent years, the more liberal Commission has left the conclusion of agreements entirely to the social partners themselves. As a result, the European social partners do not play the role of co-regulators that is in principle open to them and the influence of business on European policies is much greater than that of labour.

To what extent can the recent debate on flexicurity provide new impulses to this social dialogue? Here first of all it should be reminded that in the past the European social partners have made a number of agreements that could be interpreted to follow the flexicurity philosophy. This is particularly the case for the framework agreements on part-time employment and fixed-term employment of the late 1990s, both converted into Directives. Although they do not represent comprehensive labour market strategies, they do, much like the Dutch flexicurity approach, aim to reconcile the need for flexible contracts with the need for security of workers. Hence, it could be argued that the European social partners have some experience with flexicurity type of agreements.

Moreover, only a few months after the Commission produced its Communication on flexicurity, the European social partners presented a joint analysis of the challenges facing the European labour market (ETUC *et al.* 2007). In this document, it is stated that 'European Social Partners recognise that in today's labour market it is necessary to improve policy measures which address both the flexibility and security dimensions for workers and employers alike. Applied in the right way, the flexicurity approach can create a win-win situation and be equally beneficial for employers and employees' (*ibid.*: 53). This would seem to express an agreement on the importance of flexicurity for labour market reform and a willingness to engage in social dialogue on this issue, even though beyond the general endorsement no specific commitments or agreements were made on flexicurity in the document.

But to what extent do both sides indeed agree on flexicurity and its implications and what are the chances that they will agree on actual labour market reforms that go beyond these very general statements? As demonstrated above, the flexicurity concept provides only limited guidance to policy makers and many different views can be forwarded under the flexicurity flag. A more detailed examination of the position of the two sides on the various elements of the flexicurity debate is therefore presented in Table 12.1, focusing on the views of BUSINESSEUROPE and the ETUC as expressed in their policy documents published in the same period as the joint analysis.

The most striking result of this comparison of the positions of BUSINESSEUROPE and the ETUC is that they seem to disagree on most key aspects of the flexicurity debate. This starts already with their general diagnosis of the problems with the labour markets in the EU. BUSINESSEUROPE claims that Europe's labour markets need more flexibility to allow companies to be competitive, while ETUC claims that companies already have extensive flexibility and that the main problem is excessive flexibility that leads to precariousness. Other examples are: for BUSINESSEUROPE flexicurity is about adaptation to the market while for the ETUC it is also about human, social and sustainable development and better jobs; BUSINESSEUROPE pictures employment protection legislation as hampering job creation while the ETUC sees it as a factor that rather allows for proper adaptation to labour market changes, that prevents unfair dismissals and that acts as an incentive for investment in human resources; BUSINESSEUROPE underlines the need for and advantages of flexible contracts while the ETUC wants them to remain an exception; BUSINESSEUROPE argues for employment friendly unemployment benefit systems that foster a quick re-entry of the unemployed into the labour market, while the ETUC argues for comprehensive and generous welfare systems.

**Table 12.1 Confronting employers' and unions' views on flexicurity**

| *Issue* | *BUSINESSEUROPE* | *ETUC* |
|---|---|---|
| *General diagnosis EU labour market* | Structural reforms are required to increase flexibility on Europe's labour markets to allow companies to be competitive and seize new market opportunities. Workers need new forms of security that promote mobility and enable them to cope with change: employment security rather than job security | Business in Europe is already enjoying high adaptability. The problem is rather the increase of precarious jobs with 'excessive' flexibility. Also, a flexible labour market, even when it is a secure one, does not create more jobs. Macro-economic policies supporting growth and the creation of new jobs are needed. |
| *On flexicurity* | Flexicurity is about facilitating the creation of new jobs as opposed to trying to preserve existing ones, and supporting companies and workers' efforts to adapt to market changes. Flexicurity implies removing the obstacles to creating new jobs while equipping workers to grasp and maximise their chances in the labour market. | Flexicurity is about finding a socially acceptable balance between the needs of adaptable enterprises and the long-term objective of human, social and sustainable development, as well as more and better jobs. This balance, which must lead to a win-win situation, is decided primarily by the social partners themselves, through negotiations. |
| *Employment protection legislation* | Stringent Employment Protection legislation (EPL) hampers the creation and growth of new businesses, the adjustment to shocks and productivity growth. Strict EPL also has a negative impact on the entry of less advantaged into the labour market and increases the average duration of unemployment. Member States should review EPL under standard employment contracts to reduce dismissal costs and remove unnecessary rigidities. | Job protection systems function as an 'early warning' system, giving workers that are fired time to prepare for change and to start looking for a new job or a retraining programme. As a result, the time spent in unemployment is reduced and workers find a new and productive job more easily. Job protection also reduces unfair dismissals. Moreover, it creates incentives for employers to invest in workers through training and help to improve productivity. |

| *Issue* | *BUSINESSEUROPE* | *ETUC* |
|---|---|---|
| *Flexible contracts* | In order to stimulate job creation, it is essential to have access to a variety of contractual arrangements. Part-time, fixed-term, agency work, etc. enable employers to adapt to changes and demand while allowing workers to respond to their personal needs and preferences. Flexible forms of work also constitute a stepping stone for disadvantaged groups to access the labour market. | The principle agreed by social partners in the framework agreement on fixed term contracts, transposed by Directive 1999/70/EC, is that atypical forms of work should remain exceptions. The ETUC's policy is also to integrate 'non-standard' contracts fully into labour law, collective agreements, social security and lifelong learning systems and to improve enforcement of existing national and EU labour law. |
| *Work organisation* | In addition to strengthening external flexibility there is a need to increase internal flexibility, i.e. internal mobility and variations in working patterns and working-time arrangements. | Internal flexibility is an alternative to external flexibility. Aims to advance productivity, innovation and competitiveness and a better combination of work with other activities. Hence, it should be an outcome of collective bargaining and respect labour legislation. |
| *Labour costs* | High levels of employment require that labour costs remain contained. A reduction of non-wage labour costs, notably through lower social security contributions, is key for job creation. | Wages need to be fair and competitiveness should focus on productivity instead of wage competition. |
| *Lifelong learning, training* | Crucial role of lifelong learning for the competitiveness of firms as well as for the long-term employability of individuals. But a right to training has little impact for the workers who are most in need: the less qualified. Legislation is not the right instrument to influence learning behaviours. Personal motivation remains the key to the development of lifelong learning. | An educated work force with updated skills is a flexible one, both in terms of internal as well as external flexibility. However, business invests less and less in the training of its workforce, and this despite the increasing demand for better qualifications. To remedy this business should take its responsibility and every worker should have an annual qualifications development plan and the necessary training. |

| *Issue* | *BUSINESSEUROPE* | *ETUC* |
|---|---|---|
| *Active labour market policies* | Their aim is to spur the unemployed to look for work more actively and/or to improve their employability. | Active labour market policies are crucial to build bridges from one job to another job. In combination with generous benefits, they allow workers to prepare for and search for new suitable and rewarding employment. |
| *Unemployment benefits and social security* | Employment friendly social security systems that do not discourage a quick re-entry of the unemployed into the labour market. | Comprehensive and generous welfare systems that limit loss of income and allow workers to prepare for and search for a new suitable job. |

Clearly, whereas they were positive on flexicurity in the joint analysis in very general terms, the more detailed positions of the two social partners concerning flexicurity and its elements are worlds apart. They, by and large, represent the 'traditional' views of capital and labour, suggesting that the commitment in the joint analysis was rather symbolic.

This interpretation is further supported by the developments in more recent years. Most importantly, in the context of their joint Work Programme 2009–11, the European Social Partners undertook a joint study on 'The implementation of flexicurity and the role of the social partners' (Voss, Dornelas, Wild *et al.* 2011), which was presented at a conference in early 2011. The study, based on a survey among social partners across the EU, confirms that flexicurity is a controversial subject for the social partners and that they diverge strongly on the assessment of flexicurity and its importance for the reform debate in the EU. The study shows that most trade unions (two-thirds) and almost all employers' organisations are of the opinion that flexicurity can provide a win-win situation for workers and enterprises if implemented in a balanced and holistic way. They, however, have very different views on how to interpret the labour market situation in the EU during the early 2010s and on what labour market and welfare reforms were required. Indeed, some 85 per cent of trade unions argue that the flexicurity has not yet proven itself as a win-win approach and that the actual labour market situation does not offer a balance between the needs and interests of workers and enterprises; the respective percentage is substantially lower in the case of employers' organisations: 45 per cent (*ibid.*). As a result, the ETUC concluded that flexicurity has not been implemented in a balanced way, since during the last decade inequalities, social gaps and labour market segmentation have grown and that trade unions have strong doubts as to whether flexicurity has the potential to tackle these challenges.[2] At the same time, the European employers' organisations stressed that from the point of view of employers, flexicurity is the right concept to tackle major challenges in contemporary labour markets.[3] Clearly, the flexicurity discourse has not managed to bring the two sides of European social dialogue closer to each other, even though both have stressed the importance of flexicurity, and consensus or a cross-class alliance on the reform of European labour markets and welfare states seems as far away as ever. And this is not only the case at the European inter-sectoral level but at the level of most sectors as well.

To some extent, a European-level exception is constituted by the temporary work agency sector. Within the context of the flexicurity debate, in February 2007, in the run-up to the Council's adoption of the common principles, the European employers' organisation in this sector (Eurociett) and the respective trade union (Union Network International (UNI)-Europa) produced a Joint Declaration as a contribution to the flexicurity debate (Eurociett and UNI-Europa 2007) within the context of their sectoral social dialogue committee. In this declaration, the two sides outlined the growing importance of the temporary work agency sector in the contemporary European economy; underlined the importance of reaching a fair balance between the protection of agency workers and enhancing the positive role that agency work may play in the European labour market; and rejected to compete to the detriment of workers' rights and working conditions. Very much in the spirit of the flexicurity discourse, they paint a role for temporary work agencies in creating pathways between unemployment and employment, facilitating the transition between education and work, smoothing transitions in the labour market, promoting conversion between different types of work contracts, and improving life–work balance by providing flexible working time arrangements. It also sets out a series of regulatory and operational principles that should ensure such a positive role of the sector, as well as a set of positive and negative examples.

At the same time, the declaration is not simply a manifestation of the support for the flexicurity approach. No specific endorsement is given to flexicurity and the term is only mentioned when reference is made to the respective debate started by the Commission. In fact, UNI-Europa saw the declaration as a step towards the strengthening of sectoral social dialogue and the improvement of the position of workers in the sector; it did not consider it a statement of support to the Commission's flexicurity proposals or an acceptance of flexicurity as the solution to labour market problems (Bekker 2012). On the contrary, in the period 2007–11, through leaflets, press statements, conference interventions and other means, Eurociett has repeatedly expressed its belief in the flexicurity approach and its view that temporary work agencies are pivotal flexicurity actors, providing flexibility and security for both workers and businesses (see the Eurociett website www.eurociett.eu). However, following the diverging levels of acceptance of the concept of flexicurity as such, no further initiatives on flexicurity have been included in the work programmes of the sector's Sectoral Social Dialogue Committee since the joint declaration. Indeed, although in the declaration and several other activities of the social partners in the sector can be argued to be in line with the spirit of the Commission's flexicurity initiative, the social partners have not jointly embraced the concept as such.

Indeed, at the European level, flexicurity has not managed to create consensus between trade unions and employers' organisations, and it has not become a key issue in European social dialogue. Flexicurity appeals more to the European employers than to the European trade unions, suggesting that the way the concept is used in the European debate is more in line with employers' ideas and interests than those of workers.

## National-level industrial relations and flexicurity

As discussed, flexicurity originally emerged in the mid-1990s as a label for national level reforms based on agreements between national employers, unions and the state in the Netherlands and also in Denmark, which subsequently became the 'archetypical' flexicurity example. Social dialogue and consensus between unions and employers on the regulation of the labour market and the welfare state have been underlined as key to the success and persistence of the Danish model (Madsen 2006). Hence, although at the European level flexicurity has not become an impulse for social dialogue, has it been more successful in creating consensus and promoting dialogue at the national level?

In general terms this does not seem to be the case. The earlier cited comparative study by Voss *et al.* (2011) already demonstrated that across the EU national unions and employers often have very different views on the extent to which flexibility and security are balanced and what labour market reforms are required. This is confirmed by another comparative study done a few years earlier (Pedersini 2008). This study shows that, even though unions and employers in the EU member states may at a very general level support the idea of flexicurity, 'when it comes to assessing specific measures, the positions of the social partners seem to reproduce traditional patterns and approaches, as employers are essentially interested in flexibility, while trade unions highlight the need for, and the commitment to, security' (*ibid.*: 10). Indeed, the interpretation of what flexicurity is or should be about often differs dramatically between the two sides of industrial relations, and instead of fostering consensus, in a number of countries it has rather become a divisive concept. This is the case first and foremost because 'A number of trade unions consider that the debate on flexicurity, as well as the interpretation of the concept and the connected policies supported by the EU, focus an overwhelming amount of attention on the flexibility aspect, while largely neglecting the issue of security' (*ibid.*: 10).

Within this overall picture it is instructive to consider a few national cases. Germany is a typical case that fits the general points made above. The debate on labour market reform has been quite polarised since the Harz reforms of the early 2000s (Voss 2011). Trade unions underline their preferences for flexibility within the company or organisation, supported by high levels of job security, whereas employers' organisations argue for high levels of internal and external flexibility and see this both as a responsibility of, and an opportunity for, individual employees

(Pedersini 2008). Within this context, reaching a consensus on flexicurity-inspired reforms has been out of the question. Instead, employers focus on flexibilisation as a competitive requirement while trade unions rather stress the need for *gute Arbeit* (good jobs) that offer substantial security and good working conditions to employees.

But also in the 'heartland' of the flexicurity, i.e. the Netherlands and Denmark, consensus seems to be under strain. In the late 2000s in the Netherlands, labour market reforms had increasingly been opposed by the trade unions, among others because the number of flexible jobs, in particularly fixed-term contracts and self-employment without employees, was rapidly increasing and anxiety about the quality and security of jobs was rising (Muffels, Wilthagen and Dekker 2011). Also, the evaluation of the impact of the flexicurity reforms of the late 1990s raises concerns. One of the key elements of these reforms, which seemed to fit very well with the Dutch *polder* model, was that the law left considerable space to collective agreements to influence the levels of flexibility and security of non-standard contracts. Research however shows that this space is almost entirely used to make jobs more flexible and hardly to increase levels of security (Houwing 2010). This is the case, among others, because at the sectoral level, where collective agreements are negotiated and hence the space provided by the law is filled in, trade unions often do not have the same strength as they have at the inter-sectoral level (*ibid.*) One of the outcomes of these developments is that Dutch trade unions more and more reject the notion of flexicurity and that consensus is replaced by polemics. In addition, for many years, there has been a debate on the reform of dismissal protection in the Netherlands. But reforms have been limited to those included in the flexicurity reforms of the late 1990s, resulting in greater flexibility concerning fixed-term contracts, affecting some 15 per cent of the labour market. Where standard contracts are concerned, quite traditionally and lacking any new understanding or new compromise on labour market regulation, employers advocate for increased flexibility while unions reject any reduction of dismissal protection, which has proven to be an 'immovable object' (Houwing, Keune, Pochet *et al.* 2011).

In Denmark, the historically developed constellation of low dismissal protection, high unemployment benefits and extensive active labour market policies has traditionally been supported by trade unions and employers, who also have an active role in the implementation of policies (Madsen 2006). Indeed, in several instances in the past the two sides successfully rallied together against reform attempts from the side of the government. Peculiar in comparison with most other EU countries is that the Danish unions are outspoken supporters of flexicurity (see for example, CO Industri 2006).

Since the early 2000s, however, when a right-wing government came into office, the system has been subject to reforms. These include a stronger emphasis on work first measures, a reduction of the period during which unemployment benefits can be received combined with a declining replacement rate of these benefits, and a gradual exclusion of the social partners of public policy (Jørgensen

2010, Jørgensen 2011). Also, consensus between workers and employers seems to be fading. Employers have been calling for a reduction in the entitlement period for unemployment and a gradual reduction of the benefit itself; while unions are calling for a raise of unemployment benefits which, they argue, have a replacement rate too low for many workers (Mailand 2009). More in general, unions are concerned about the erosion of some of the main components of the Danish flexicurity model (Voss *et al.* 2011).

Still, this does not mean the Danish model is collapsing (Jørgensen 2011). Also, although differences are becoming more pronounced, it would be a mistake to argue that Danish social partnership is over. Indeed, in the 2010 collective agreement for the manufacturing sector the issue of the declining replacement rate of unemployment benefits was addressed. It was agreed that employees with a minimum of three years of seniority are entitled to severance pay as a supplement to the unemployment benefit for one or two months (depending on the length of employment), to reach an 85 per cent replacement rate. Hence, negotiated solutions are continued to be found, even though there may be less consensus, and the two sides of industrial relations by and large seem to continue to support the Danish flexicurity model.

However, we do not see many other countries where social partners are in agreement on a national flexicurity model or working on institutionalising such a model. An exception may be Bulgaria where the government has initiated national-level dialogue on the development of a Bulgarian flexicurity pathway which has led to some agreements, in spite of the fact that employers and unions have quite opposed views on labour market and welfare reforms (Tomev 2009, Republic of Bulgaria 2011). Naturally, in many other countries social dialogue and collective agreements address issues concerning flexibility or security, but they did so as well before flexicurity entered the European debate. The added value of the flexicurity approach should be that it inspires broad agreements that cover and interconnect measures dealing with a broad range of labour market and welfare issues. Hardly anywhere does this seem to be the case.

At the same time, this does not mean that the flexicurity discourse does not influence national dialogue and policies. As a result of the insistence of the European Commission and the central place of flexicurity in the European Employment Strategy, the issue is one way or the other on the agenda across the EU and referred to in policy documents. Also, more and more labour market and social policies are being discussed in terms of their impact on different types of flexibility and security. In addition, in several countries new concepts guiding labour market and welfare reforms have been developed that are akin to flexicurity. One example is the Finnish concept of change security, introduced in 2005, with the aim to 'accelerate the reemployment of workers who lose their jobs for production or financial reasons by tightening cooperation between employers, workers and the labour administration in such cases' (Ministry of Finance 2008: 90). It entitles workers that are going to be dismissed to an employment leave of five to twenty days paid by the employer during the notice period without a reduction in earnings; an individual employment plan and participation in active labour market policies provided by the employment offices; and an increased unemployment benefit for the period of the employment plan, with a maximum of 185 days in total (Duell, Grubb and Singh 2009). Change security obliges employers to negotiate a plan of action with employee representatives when redundancies are planned. It was an objective of the Finnish trade unions who managed to get it included in the 2005–07 national incomes policy agreement (Jokivuori 2009). Both the Confederation of Finnish Industries (EK) and the Central Organisation of Finnish Trade Unions (SAK) have positively evaluated the experiences with this new approach (*ibid.*).

Another example is France where *flexicurité à la française* emerged as a 'domesticated' or 'Frenchified' version of flexicurity, even though most French actors refrain from using the specific term flexicurity or *flexicurité* (Barbier, Colomb and Madsen 2009). This is exemplified by the agreement on *la modernisation du marché du travail et la sécurisation des parcours professionnels* (the modernisation of the labour market and security of employment) of January 2008. This agreement, proposed by the government, was signed by the major employers' organisations and the major trade unions, with the important exception of the Confédération générale du travail (General Confederation of Labour). It aimed at a comprehensive reform of the labour market and scheduled complementary collective negotiations in three fields: planned management of employment and skills, unemployment insurance and career development assessment (Freyssinet 2009). However, following the onset of the crisis, just after the January 2008 agreement was signed, circumstances changed so dramatically that it proved hard to reach comprehensive settlements on these three issues in the subsequent years, as often most of the unions were not in conformity with the proposals of the government and employers (*ibid.*). At the same time, it can be argued that the flexicurity push coming from the European level and the debate about the Danish model that took place in France in the second half of the 2000s were instrumental in revamping social dialogue on labour market and social issues, even though this did not result in a new comprehensive agreement (Barbier *et al.* 2009).

## Conclusion

Since the mid-2000s, when it was adopted by the European Commission, flexicurity has become a core concept in the European debate about labour market and welfare reform. In very general terms it has received support from both trade unions and employers' organisations. However, in practice this support has proven to be an empty shell: flexicurity has failed to become a central issue in social dialogue at the European or national level and has hardly inspired consensus or agreements on comprehensive labour market and welfare reforms. Unions and employers strongly disagree on how to translate the general flexicurity idea into actual policy and in their assessment of the extent to which actual labour markets and welfare states offer a proper balance between flexibility and security. Indeed, flexicurity has not managed to build a bridge between unions and employers and to overcome differences of interest between capital and labour.

Two major factors can be put forward to explain why flexicurity has not been able to foster consensus. One concerns the ambiguous nature of the concept as such. This makes it an inclusive concept that can appeal to a wide variety of interests. At the same time, however, the concept is widely open for interpretation and gives little guidance on how flexibility and security should be combined in practice or how to judge if a balance between the two exists. This allows unions and employers to subscribe to widely diverging versions of flexicurity, each in line with their own ideas and interests. These differences of interest cannot be overcome by forwarding a concept that in the eyes of its proponents is a win-win concept that caters to the needs of all.

The other concerns the use of the concept in the political debate. It has become part of the 'battle of ideas' in Europe in which different actors try to shape hegemonic interpretations about what are the most acute labour market and social problems and how they should be solved (Serrano Pascual 2009). The dominant player in the flexicurity debate, the European Commission, has been promoting a version of flexicurity that emphasises the need for market-based reforms, increased labour market flexibility and activation; however it has little more to offer in terms of security for workers than assistance in the adaptation of skills to the requirements of employers that should lead to increased employability or 'employment security' (*ibid.*; Keune and Jepsen 2007). It comes as no surprise then, that flexicurity appeals more to employers than to trade unions. The latter increasingly consider flexicurity a covert flexibilisation strategy that is detrimental to workers' interests.

Finally, not only has flexicurity failed to strengthen social dialogue in Europe, it also seems unlikely that it will strengthen the social identity of the EU and in this way will increase the legitimacy of the economic integration process. It may rather reduce this legitimacy because of its perceived emphasis on the interests of capital to the disadvantage to labour.

## Notes

1 These include job security, employment security, income security, combination security, external numerical flexibility, internal numerical flexibility, functional flexibility and wage flexibility.

2 See the conference notes on EU Synthesis Conference 'Social Partners and Flexicurity in Contemporary Labour Markets', Brussels, 31 March–1 April 2011,www.resource-centre.etuc.org/linked_files/documents/Flexicurity%20Final%20Conference_Notes_FINAL%20CLEAN.pdf, accessed 1 April 2012.

3 See note 1.

**References**

Barbier, J., Colomb, F. and Madsen, P. (2009), *Flexicurity – an Open Method of Coordination, at the National Level ?*, CARMA Research Paper 3, Aalborg: CARMA.

Bekker, S. (2012), 'Flexicurity: explaining the development of a European concept', Unpublished Ph.D. thesis, University of Tilburg.

Burroni, L. and Keune, M. (2011), 'Flexicurity: A Conceptual Critique', *European Journal of Industrial Relations* 17(1), 75–91.

BUSINESSEUROPE (2007), Commission communication 'towards common principles of flexicurity', BUSINESSEUROPE Position Paper, www.businesseurope.eu/DocShareNoFrame/docs/2/ONJAKENCJDHGAHIFOCIFGIBKPDB39DW1269LTE4Q/UNICE/docs/DLS/2007–01553-E.pdf, accessed 10 April 2009.

CEC (2007), *Communication from the Commission to the Council, the European Parliament, the European Economic and Social Committee and the Committee of the Regions 'Towards Common Principles of Flexicurity: More and Better Jobs Through Flexibility and Security'*, COM (2007) 359 of 27 June 2007, http://ec.europa.eu/employment_social/news/2007/jun/flexicurity_en.pdf/.

CEC (2010), *Communication from the Commission. Europe 2020, A Strategy for Smart, Sustainable and Inclusive Growth,* http://eur-lex.europa.eu/LexUriServ/LexUriServ.do?uri=COM:2010:2020:FIN:EN:PDF, accessed 1 April 2012.

CO Industri (2006), *Flexicurity – A Danish Trade Union View*, www.lo.dk/English%20version/~/media/LO/English/Congress2007/Flexicurity%20%20%20a%20Danish%20trade%20union%20view.ashx, accessed 1 April 2012.

Crouch, C. (2008), *The Governance of Labour Market Uncertainty: Towards a New Research Agenda*, Discussion Paper 2008–08, Amsterdam: Hugo Sinzheimer Instituut.

Davies, P. and Freedland, M. (1993), *Labour Legislation and Public Policy: A Contemporary History*, Oxford: Oxford University Press.

Duell, N., Grubb, D. and Singh, S. (2009), *Activation Policies in Finland*, OECD Social, Employment and Migration working papers no. 98, Paris: OECD.

Esping-Andersen, G. (1990), *The Three Worlds of Welfare Capitalism*, Princeton, NJ: Princeton University Press.

ETUC (2007a), *The Flexicurity Debate and the Challenges for the Trade Union Movement*, www.etuc.org/IMG/pdf/Depliant_Flexicurity_EN.pdf, accessed 1 April 2012.

ETUC (2007b), *Collective Bargaining Information Bulletin 2007/4: The European Strategy For Flexicurity: How the OECD Indicator on Employment Protection Legislation will Undermine Social Europe and Transitional Security*, www.etuc.org/IMG/pdf_EPLOECD.pdf, accessed 1 April 2012.

ETUC, BUSINESSEUROPE, UEAPME and CEEP (2007), *Key Challenges Facing European Labour Markets: A Joint Analysis of European Social Partners*, www.businesseurope.eu/content/default.asp?PageID=568&DocID=19533, accessed 1 April 2012.

Eurociett and UNI-Europa (2007), *Eurociett/Uni-Europa Joint Declaration within the Framework of the "Flexicurity Debate" as Launched and Defined by the EU Commission*, www.eurociett.eu/fileadmin/templates/eurociett/docs/Eurociett_Uni-Europa_joint-declaration_on_Flexicurity_28–02–07.pdf, accessed 1 April 2012.

Freyssinet, J. (2009), *Tripartite Responses to the Economic Crisis in the Principal Western European Countries*, Dialogue Working Paper no. 12, ILO.

Houwing, H. (2010), 'A Dutch Approach to Flexicurity? Negotiated Change in the Organisation of Temporary Work', unpublished Ph.D. thesis, University of Amsterdam.

Houwing, H., Keune, M. Pochet, P. and Vandaele, K. (2011), 'Comparing Flexicurity Arrangements in Belgium and the Netherlands', in Barry, M. and Wilkinson, A. (eds), *Research Handbook of Comparative Employment Relations*, London: Edward Elgar.

Hudson, J. and Kühner, S. (2009), 'Towards Productive Welfare? A Comparative Analysis of 23 OECD Countries', *Journal of European Social Policy* 19(1), 34–46.

Jessop, B. (2002), *The Future of the Capitalist State*, Cambridge: Polity Press.

Jokivuori, P. (2009), *Finland: Flexicurity and Industrial Relations*, EiroOnline, www.eurofound.europa.eu/eiro/studies/tn0803038s/fi0803039q.htm, accessed 1 April 2012.

Jørgensen, C. (2010), *Innovative Concession Agreement in Manufacturing Sector*, EIRO, www.eurofound.europa.eu/eiro/2010/03/articles/dk1003011i.htm, accessed 1 April 2012.

Jørgensen, H. (2011), *Danish 'Flexicurity' in Crisis – Or Just Stress-tested by the Crisis?*, Friedrich Ebert Stiftung.

Keune, M. (2012), 'The Social Dimension of European Integration', in Burroni, L., Keune, M. and Meardi, G. (eds), *Economy and Society in Europe: a Relationship in Crisis*, Cheltenham: Edward Elgar.

Keune, M. and M. Jepsen (2007), 'Not Balanced and Hardly New: The European Commission's Quest for Flexicurity', pp. 189–214 in Jørgensen, H. and Madsen, P.K. (eds), *Flexicurity and Beyond*, Copenhagen: DJØF Publishing.

Madsen, P.K. (2006), 'How Can it Possibly Fly? The Paradox of a Dynamic Labour Market in a Scandinavian Welfare State', in Campbell, J., Hall, J. and Pedersen, O. (eds), *National Identity and the Varieties of Capitalism: The Danish Experience*, Montreal: McGill-Queen's University Press.

Mailand, M. (2009), *Denmark: Flexicurity and Industrial Relations*, EIRO, www.eurofound.europa.eu/eiro/studies/tn0803038s/dk0803039q.htm, accessed 1 April 2012.

Ministry of Finance (2008), *The Lisbon Strategy for Growth and Jobs 2008–2010: The Finnish National Reform Programme*, Helsinki: Ministry of Finance.

Muffels, R.J.A., Wilthagen, A.C.J.M. and Dekker, R. (2011), 'Flexibiliteit en werkzekerheid: Diversiteit en dynamiek op de Nederlandse arbeidsmarkt', pp. 25–49 in Sol, E. and Nysten, C. (eds), *Wat is de zekerheid in flex en zeker?* Amsterdam: Flex Work Research Centre.

Pedersini, R. (2008), *Flexicurity and Industrial Relations*, Dublin: Eurofound.

Republic of Bulgaria (2011), 'National Reform Programme (2011–2015)', in *Implementation of 'Europe 2020' Strategy*, Sofia.

Rogowski, R. (2008), 'Governance of the European Social Model: The Case of Flexicurity', *Intereconomics* 43(2), 82–91.

Sabel, Ch. and Zeitlin, J. (eds) (2010), *Experimentalist Governance in the European Union. Towards a New Architecture*, Oxford: Oxford University Press.

Scharpf, F. (2002), 'The European Social Model: Coping with the Challenges of Diversity', *Journal of Common Market Studies* 40(4), 645–70.

Serrano Pascual, A. (2009), 'The Battle of Ideas in the European Field: The Combat to Defeat Unemployment and the Struggle to Give ie a Name', *Transfer* 15(1),

53–70.

Tomev, L. (2009), *Social Partners Discuss National Flexicurity Pathway*, EiroOnline, www.eurofound.europa.eu/eiro/2009/04/articles/bg0904049i.htm, accessed 1 April 2012.

Vielle, P. and Bonvin, J.M. (2008), 'Putting Security at the Heart of the European Social Pact – Proposals to Make Flexicurity More Balanced', *Transfer* 14(3), 419–33.

Voss, E. (2011), *Joint Study of the European Social Partners 'The Implementation of Flexicurity and the Role of the Social Partners*, National fiche, Germany, www.hpl.fi/eu/fi/liitteet/Germany_Fiche_w.pdf, accessed 1 October 2011.

Voss, E., Dornelas, A., Wild, A. and Kwiatkiewicz, A. (2011), *European Social Dialogue 2009 – 2011: Social Partners and Flexicurity in Contemporary Labour Markets. Synthesis Report*, http://resourcecentre.etuc.org/linked_files/documents/IP2%20-%20Sinthesys%20Report%20-%20Social%20Partners%20and%20Flexicurity%20in%20Contemporary%20Labour%20Markets.pdf, accessed 1 April 2012.

Weiss, M. (2010), 'European Labour Law in Transition from 1985 to 2010', *The International Journal of Comparative Labour Law and Industrial Relations* 26(3), 1–16.

Wilthagen, T. (2005), 'Striking a balance? Flexibility and Security in European Labour Markets', pp. 253–67 in Bredgaard, T. and Larsen, F. (eds), *Employment Policy from Different Angles*, Copenhagen: DJØF Publishing.

Wilthagen, T. and Tros, F. (2004), 'The Concept of "Flexicurity": A New Approach to Regulating Employment and Labour Markets', *Transfer* 10(2), 166–86.

Zeitlin, J. (2005), 'The Open Method of Coordination in Action. Theoretical Promise, Empirical Realities, Reform Strategies', in Zeitlin, J., Pochet, P. and Magnusson, L. (eds), *The Open Method of Coordination in Action: the European Employment and Social Inclusion Strategies*, Brussels: Peter Lang.

ROLAND ERNE

# 13

# European industrial relations after the crisis: a postscript

Since the revitalisation of the European integration process by the Delors Commission, European institutions have been encouraging social dialogue and the emergence of a European system of industrial relations. Certainly, the proponents of a social Europe have recurrently deplored the discrepancies between the development of the EU's stern market-making regulations and the relative weakness of its social policies and labour law directives. Nevertheless, the asymmetric nature of the European integration process did not weaken the more or less implicit functionalist consensus among European integration and industrial relations scholars that the tensions created by the EU's market-marking initiatives will also prompt market-correcting rules, institutions, and processes.

The chapters in Part I and II of this book that discuss recent developments show indeed that industrial relations at European cross-sectoral, sectoral, and company level are evolving, despite obstacles and difficulties. The lack of political will from the Barroso Commission to promote improved labour standards has not prevented European social partners from developing various initiatives at different levels. At the same time, the contributions of Peter Turnbull, Nick Parsons and Maarten Keune in Part III demonstrate how the Commission's current liberalisation agenda is undermining the social consensus that was at the heart of the European integration process. Social dialogue remains an important feature in many European countries, especially in Scandinavia and in the German manufacturing sector. But the global financial meltdown in 2008 and the subsequent European debt crisis undeniably further accentuated the European authorities' preferences for unilateral market-based solutions.

Janine Goetschy concluded her contribution in this volume by stating that the European debt crisis could lead to a major breakthrough in European economic governance with huge consequences for the EU altogether. The crisis forcefully demonstrated that those who already argued in the 1990s that the European Monetary Union also needed to include a political union were correct (Pochet

1999, Martin and Ross 2004). After the crisis even neo-liberal opponents of a political union had to concede that the belief in a spontaneous convergence of the real economies within a Eurozone without stringent government structures was naive. However, the political solutions that have been implemented by European leaders amid the crisis are hardly comforting for supporters of an integrated, social and democratic Europe. Instead of laissez-faire, financial elites are advocating authoritarian solutions to the crisis that are completely in tune with their winner-take-all attitudes of the pre-crisis boom and bubble years. Accordingly, European economic governance is taking a direction which entails profound social and democratic consequences including 'the risk of social explosion and a disintegration of cohesion' (Degryse and Pochet 2011: 4).

## The political consequences of the crisis

The responses of the EU authorities to the crisis are changing how trade unions see the EU's role as a facilitator of a European system of industrial relations. These changes are particularly visible at the periphery of the Eurozone. The Europhile Irish Congress of Trade Unions, for example, has adopted a surprisingly belligerent tone in its dealing with the EU/ECB/IMF Troika considering the important role it played in the Yes-campaign for the Lisbon Treaty in 2009 (ICTU 2011). After the No-vote of the Irish people in the first Lisbon referendum in 2008, the Vice-President of the European Commission quoted the 1916 Declaration of the Irish Republic in an address to the Irish Parliament in order to highlight the traditional pro-European stance of the Irish people: 'The Irish are known as committed Europeans: even your proclamation in 1916 referred to "gallant allies in Europe"' (Wallström 2008). After the imposition of the harsh austerity measures by the European Commission/ECB/IMF Troika, however, David Begg, the moderate general secretary of Irish Congress of Trade Unions (ICTU), spoke of help 'from our gallant allies in Europe' in quite different terms: 'Well our gallant allies in Europe have arrived 95 years too late and uninvited and instead of guns to help the revolution they have brought economic weapons of mass destruction' (Wall 2010). When the ITUC leader, who belonged to the most adamant supporters of social partnership and the EU integration process within the European Trade Union Confederation (ETUC), feels compelled to revert to the radical rhetoric of the Irish war of independence in response to the Troika's interventions in Ireland, then the prospects for European integration and social dialogue must be quite grim indeed.[1] In this climate, it is not surprising that the Irish government did not enthusiastically support the so-called 'fiscal compact', that is the new international treaty proposed in December 2011 by the heads of all EU Member States except Britain (European Council 2011). But whereas the Irish government already supported a stricter surveillance of national fiscal and economic policies when it endorsed the six new EU laws contained in the so-called 'six-pack on economic governance' in October 2011 (see the next section), the Irish and European economic and political elite have every reason to be worried about the distinct possibility of a new European referendum in Ireland (Barrett 2011).

Against the hopes of many Keynesian economists, the global financial crisis did not lead to a policy shift away from the corporate pro-business paradigms that have dominated economic policy-making since the late 1970s. Certainly, when the speculative bubbles burst in 2008 and governments were forced to ride to the rescue of failing banks, the free market ideology became a hindrance. But when the debt the state was accumulating to bail out private financial institutions predictably resulted in a budget crisis, the crisis was used as 'justification for deep cuts to social programmes, and for a renewed push to privatise what is left of the public sector' (Klein 2008). The intellectual victories of heterodox economists over free-marketeers in September 2008 did not prevent 'the great American robbery' (Stiglitz 2010: 109) and the other bank bailouts that followed suit across the world. Moreover, predictions that the subsequent austerity measures will only prolong the crisis and therefore cause unnecessary sufferings have been ignored (Krugman 2010). Paradoxically, the financial crisis showed that even the imminent failure of a corporation can become an effective political tool for business interests (Erne 2011a). In this context, governments are not only implementing further privatisations of public services and welfare cuts, but also outright wage cuts, working time extensions, retirement age increases, and substantial labour law changes. Although neo-liberal theory had been discredited by the global financial crisis in 2008, neo-liberalism did not die a normal death (Crouch 2011). On the contrary, the political project that aims 'to re-establish the conditions for capital accumulation and to restore the power of economic elites' (Harvey 2005: 19) is more present than ever.

The austerity measures that have been imposed across Europe in response to the crisis are without precedent. Wages have been cut in the public sector (for instance by 5 per cent in Spain, 15 per cent in Greece,[2] up to 20 per cent in Ireland, and 30 per cent in Romania) setting corresponding precedents for the private sector. Public services, pensions and social benefits have been reduced across the EU and retirement ages have been raised. In addition, many governments further liberalised their countries' labour markets (namely Greece, Spain, Italy, Romania, Hungary, Portugal and Ireland), for instance, by easing protection against unjustified dismissals, by hollowing out multi-employer collective wage bargaining, or by truncating the fundamental right to strike (Pedrina 2011).

These policies are the result of a coordinated European liberalisation agenda which is meticulously pursued by the Directorate General for Economic and Financial Affairs (DG EcoFin) of the European Commission, the European Central Bank, and the International Monetary Fund. Ever since the Commission/ECB/IMF Troika provided joint financial assistance to Latvia, Hungary and Romania in 2008 and 2009, the Troika systematically included severe austerity and liberalisation obligations in its 'rescue' packages for struggling EU countries. Yet, it would be incorrect to assume that these European economic governance prescriptions only apply to the European periphery.

## The 'six-pack' on European economic governance

After the final approval of the 'six-pack' of five regulations and one directive on 'economic governance' on 4 October 2011 by the Council of the European Union (2011), the EU Member States will not only be notionally obliged to respect the EU guidelines for the economic policies of the Member States and the EU. According to these six new EU laws that came into force after their publication in the EU's *Official Journal* on 23 November 2011,[3] Eurozone countries that do not comply with the revised EU Stability and Growth Pact or find themselves in a so-called macroeconomic excessive imbalance position, can be sanctioned by a yearly fine equalling 0.2 per cent or 0.1 per cent of GDP respectively. These fines effectively strengthen the Commission's authority over national economic policy-making, especially as they will be applied automatically unless the Council is able to veto them by a qualified majority within a period of ten days. According to this new 'reversed qualified majority' procedure, Member States can be punished by an alliance of the European Commission with a minority of states. Hence, the time in which European economic policy guidelines could be dismissed as 'soft law' seems to be coming to an end, regardless of the fate of the new European 'fiscal compact' which has been agreed in principle by the heads of all EU Member States except Britain at the European Council meeting in December 2011. Ironically, the adoption of the six pack's new European economic governance rules was brought about in part because the British Conservatives endorsed this transfer of power to Brussels in the European Parliament, partly because the six-pack laws passed through the EU legislative process largely unnoticed by national media, and partly because the fines will only apply to Eurozone countries.[4]

The 'six-pack' is based on Article 121.6 TFEU according to which EU Member States' fiscal and macroeconomic policies shall become subject to 'multilateral surveillance procedures'. As stated in the introduction, a European coordination of national economic policies may be a reasonable proposition. Wage moderation has held sway in all Eurozone countries during the past decade, as wage increases did remain below the distribution-neutral margin of inflation plus productivity increases almost everywhere. Nevertheless, in some countries – such as Germany – wages had been restrained much more severely than elsewhere (Erne 2010). This contributed substantially to the growing economic imbalances within the Eurozone, as self-critically acknowledged by the Germany trade union economists, Klaus Busch and Dierk Hirschel (2011).

Incidentally, the European Metalworkers' Federation (EMF) and the European Trade Union Confederation (ETUC) adopted wage bargaining coordination benchmarks for their national affiliates as far back as 1999 and 2000 respectively in order to avoid the adoption of disruptive beggar-thy-neighbour wage policies. Yet, the ETUC/EMF bargaining guidelines failed to achieve their goals, in part because of their non-binding and technocratic character (Erne 2010). In turn, the idea of strengthening the EU's economic policy competences in all areas including wage policy has also been supported in principle by social democrats, trade unionists and Euro-Keynesian economists (Delors, Fernandes and Mermet 2011, Busch and Hirschel 2011, Collignon 2010).

On the opposite side of the political spectrum, the recent recession also seems to have triggered learning processes, as employers, central bankers, British conservatives, and German liberals alike now seem to accept the hitherto unthinkable suggestion of a *gouvernement économique européen*. Until very recently employers and business-oriented policy makers emphatically dismissed any idea of coordinated economic governance at an EU level, especially in the area of wage policy (Leonard, Erne, Marginson *et al.* 2007). Business groups believed that any coordination attempt would only be in the interest of labour, because market competition within the Eurozone would – according to textbook neoliberal economics – automatically lead to the desired downward convergence of wage rates and wage-setting structures across the Eurozone. But when existing markets in the Eurozone caused economic imbalances rather than convergence, business interests had no problem with replacing the invisible hands of the market with calls for authoritative EU structures in order to tackle Europe's economic and structural problems. In contrast to its Euro-Keynesian supporters, however, the emerging *gouvernement économique européen* should not be conceived as a democratic government in the classical sense, but rather as a regulatory agency that is monitoring and enforcing defined economic policy rules.

## European economic governance and democracy

Supporters of so-called regulatory policy-making argued long ago that leaving economic policy to agencies that are effectively insulated from domestic popular pressures and interest associations, such as independent central banks, would enhance the quality of policy outputs (Hayek 1997). The disregard by leading EU and ECB officials for democratic procedures is indeed striking. On 3 August 2011, for instance, Mario Draghi and Jean-Claude Trichet (2011) urged the Italian Government to immediately implement a long list of 'business friendly' measures by a single executive order (*decreto legge*). The list not only included calls for outright wage cuts, a hollowing out of Italy's multi-employer collective bargaining structures, the end of the Italian labour law provisions that protect employees against 'unjust dismissals', the dissolution of Italy's provinces, the implementation of 'business friendly' performance indicators in Italy's public services (including the judiciary), and so forth, but also 'the full liberalisation of local public services ... through large scale privatisations', ignoring the fact that 95.5 per cent of Italian voters had rejected the privatisation of local water services in a valid national referendum less than eight weeks earlier.

Noticeably these leading European central bankers believe that democratic decisions that they deem to be wrong ought to be overruled. Indeed, Jean Claude Trichet is actively propagating a new institutional framework within which European authorities – namely the Council on the basis of a proposal by the

Commission, in liaison with the ECB – can take decisions that are directly applicable to any national 'economy' of their choice (Trichet 2011). Hence, theories and concepts of public law do change under the impact of political events, as Carl Schmitt (1985), the leading intellectual of the German *Führerstaat*, had argued during an earlier systemic crisis. Even in Switzerland, which is frequently portrayed as the world's most direct democracy, the UBS bank bailout had been adopted through an emergency ordinance which effectively shielded the deal from being a subject of parliamentary and popular scrutiny (Erne 2012). As Crouch (2009) warily predicted, there has been a decline of democracy in economic policy-making in the wake of the global crisis. The implementation of European multilateral surveillance procedures by means of the 'six pack' on European economic governance is no exception. This raises a crucial question: Who defines the content of the European guidelines in the area of economic governance?

Economic policy choices directly impact on the life chances of all workers and citizens. For this reason, one would expect the corresponding European policy guidelines to be shaped by European citizens via their directly elected legislators or – in case of wages and working conditions – by the representative organisations of capital and labour. Yet, neither the European Parliament, nor national parliaments, nor social partners can formulate the broad economic policy guidelines for the Member States and the Union. Article 121.2 TFEU merely states that 'the Council shall inform the European Parliament of its recommendation'.

Nevertheless, it would be wrong to blame the Treaty alone for this democratic deficit. Incidentally, the European Parliament's right-wing majority failed to push for co-decision rights in this area, although the European Parliament would have had the power to veto the adoption of the 'six-pack' according to Article 121.6 TFEU. Instead, the European Parliament empowered the European Commission to design and operate multilateral surveillance procedures largely undisturbed of democratic influences. Although the 'six pack' is establishing serious sanctions against noncompliant Member States, the six new EU laws on economic governance fail to define clearly several key terms. What constitutes, for example, an 'economic imbalance' in the Eurozone? What exactly harms the 'proper functioning of the economy of a Member State'? Article 2 of the 'Regulation (EU) No 1176/2011 of the European Parliament and of the Council of 16 November 2011 on the prevention and correction of macroeconomic imbalances' does not answer these questions at all:

> For the purposes of this Regulation:
> a) 'imbalances' means any trend giving rise to macroeconomic developments which are adversely affecting, or have the potential adversely to affect, the proper functioning of the economy of a Member State or of economic and monetary union, or of the Union as a whole;
> b) 'excessive imbalances' mean severe imbalances, including imbalances that jeopardise or risk jeopardising the proper functioning of economic and monetary union.

These legal definitions are so all-encompassing that the Commission is able to bend the meaning of the regulation's concepts as it pleases. In addition, the regulation also counterfactually implies that there are 'proper' and 'improper' rather than, say, neo-liberal business-friendly or Euro-Keynesian labour-friendly economic policies. The technocratic assumption that there are only 'good' or 'bad' policies is also at variance with the anti-totalitarian core principles of democracy and social dialogue. Whereas the regulation assumes that there is a general truth that enlightened elites are capable to identify, the principles of liberal democracy and social dialogue acknowledge that what may be good for one person may be bad for another. Therefore, democracy and social dialogue are above all conflict resolution mechanisms that are at odds with a totalitarian free market utopia that assumes that there is only a single truth in economic policy-making (Supiot 2012).

No wonder Jürgen Habermas, who is arguably one of the most outspoken supporters of a democratic European Union, is very worried about a situation in which EU experts rather than 'parliaments (and trade unions where applicable)' (Habermas 2011: 65, my translation) – are determining the socio-economic priorities for years to come. Yet, one question remains unanswered. Why did the right-wing absolute majority of the European Parliament MEPs – across all Member States from Germany and Finland to Ireland and Greece (see www.votewatch.eu) – nevertheless approve the 'six-pack'? Maybe the centre-right reduced the scope for democratic politics in economic policy-making, because of its confidence that the adopted authoritarian and technocratic procedures will produce the desired policy outcomes. It is indeed noteworthy that similar majorities have delegated legislative powers to executives in the past, notably during the profound economic and social crisis of the 1930s.

## European economic governance and wages policy

Article 4 of the Regulation No 1176/2011 on the prevention and correction of macroeconomic imbalances also obliges the Commission to design a scoreboard of quantitative economic and structural indicators to evaluate the economic policies of EU Member States. In so doing, the Commission is entitled to include any indicator which it deems necessary and is free to set whenever appropriate the lower and upper limits of any measure included in the scoreboard. In addition, the Commission will guide national fiscal and economic policy-making through a broad spectrum of additional instruments set out in this Regulation and the five other EU laws that are part of the six-pack, which range from country-specific in-depth reviews, corrective action plans, and surveillance visits. Regulation no. 1176/2011 on the prevention and correction of macroeconomic imbalances also contains a list of indicators that ought to be included in the scoreboard. This includes measures belonging to policy areas that are explicitly excluded from the competencies of the European Union, such as wages policy. Certainly, the ETUC successfully lobbied the European Parliament to add a paragraph to ensure that the Commission's corrective action plans for incompliant Member States issued under this Regulation shall respect the bargaining autonomy of the social partners:

> The application of this Regulation shall fully observe Article 152 TFEU, and the recommendations issued under this Regulation shall respect national practices and institutions for wage formation. This Regulation takes into account Article 28 of the Charter of Fundamental Rights of the European Union, and accordingly does not affect the right to negotiate, conclude or enforce collective agreements or to take collective action in accordance with national law and practices (Article 1.3 of the Regulation No 1176/2011 on the prevention and correction of macroeconomic imbalances).

In turn, however, the Commission and the ECB have demonstrated – most notably in their dealings with struggling Eurozone countries – how the tension between their demands for increased wage flexibility on the one side, and the bargaining autonomy of trade unions – as enshrined in national constitutions and industrial relations acts – on the other can be solved:

> In most Member States, wages are formed in a collective bargaining process without formal involvement of governments. Nevertheless, policy-makers can affect wage setting processes via a number of ways, including the provision of information or wage rules, changes to wage-indexation rules and the signalling role played by public sector wages. In addition, reforms of labour markets should also contribute to make wage setting processes more efficient. (European Commission 2010: 15)

If one reviews the 'memorandums of understanding' in the area of wage negotiations that the EU/ECB/IMF Troika is imposing across Europe, there cannot be any doubt about what is actually meant by making wage-setting processes more efficient. In the Irish case, for instance, the Troika's 'memorandum of understanding' contains very clear commitments in this regard, namely a 'review of sector specific minimum wage agreements, with a view to their elimination' (IMF 2010: 27). Hence, trade unions should lose their capacity to set binding sector-wide wage norms, as incidentally already advocated by leading bankers at a French and German businesses roundtable on the European Monetary Union in 1997 (Erne 2010: 54).

## Conclusion

Although the adoption of the six-pack has significantly reinforced the EU authority over national economic policies, the EU Treaties are still limiting the ability of EU institutions to determine the content of national economic policies, especially in the area of industrial relations. European economic governance still heavily relies on 'soft' enforcement mechanisms, such as peer pressure and the naming and shaming of those countries that do not comply with the EU's deregulation and liberalisation agenda. Nevertheless, Klaus Dräger's assessment of the economic policy responses across Europe has shown that the so-called 'soft-law' mechanisms of European economic governance proved to be much more effective than many scholars of industrial relations and EU integration had initially thought:

> By skilfully playing this game of 'labelling' national budgets and economic policies, the EU authorities successfully put 'market discipline' on their side in order to push through austerity, further liberalisation and privatisation. We have witnessed this already in the cases of Greece, Ireland, Portugal, whose governments first attempted to settle their sovereign debt problems on their own. But when their ratings were going down and the risk premiums to re-finance debt went through the roof, they finally sucked up to the Commission's and Council orchestrated campaign that they must submit themselves to an EU-ECB-IMF led rescue operation. The same is true for the launching of the series of austerity packages of Spain in 2010/2011 and the packages of the Italian government in 2011. (Dräger 2011)

It is widely accepted that the European economic and financial crisis has been caused primarily by reckless lending practices tolerated by the ECB, and by the huge bank bailouts approved by the Commission to protect the banking system against 'systemic' capital market risks. But whereas support for banks and their bondholders, worth hundreds of billions of Euro, is apparently compatible with the internal market – in spite of Article 107 TFEU that forbids state aid – EU economic policy makers increasingly target Member States for their allegedly rigid labour laws and industrial relations practices. Unsurprisingly, however, no Member State has been criticised for failing to provide Dutch or Danish levels of unemployment benefits to protect workers against labour market risks, despite the EU's official 'flexicurity' discourse (Erne 2012). In today's Europe, trade unions are struggling to cope with the drastic results of the crisis for their members. They have differed in their approaches, with some militant trade unions organising numerous general strikes, while others more or less reluctantly went along with unprecedented attacks on their members' wages and working conditions (Erne 2011b). These are early days, but one thing is clear. The time now seems set for one of increasing conflict, paradoxically also because conflicts of interest have no place in the technocratic frame of reference that governs European economic governance.

## Notes

1 It is noteworthy that David Begg deliberately chose these words in his concluding speech at the national ICTU rally of approximately 100.000 demonstrating trade unionists before the General Post Office in Dublin that used to be the headquarters of the armed Irish 1916 Easter Rising.

2 Incidentally, at the time of writing the Greek Parliament discussed a series of new austerity measures requested by the Troika, including new wage cuts in public utility companies (35 per cent of the 2009 wage level).

3 *Official Journal of the European Union*, L 306, 23 November 2011, 1–52.

4 One of the six reports by means of which the European Parliament endorsed the 'six-pack' was drafted by the British Conservative Party MEP and former JP Morgan banker Vicky Ford: *Report on the proposal for a Council directive on requirements for budgetary frameworks of the Member States* (COM(2010) 0523–C7-0397/2010–2010/0277(NLE)). Committee on Economic and Monetary Affairs.

## References

Barrett, G. (2011), 'Securing treaty change will be a hard sell', *Irish Times*, 19 December, www.irishtimes.com/newspaper/opinion/2011/1219/1224309257084.html, accessed 2 April 2012.

Busch, H. and Hirschel, D. (2011), 'Europe at the crossroads. Ways out of the crisis', Friedrich Ebert Stiftung. International Policy Analysis Paper, http://library.fes.de/pdf-files/id/ipa/08066.pdf, accessed 2 April 2012.

Collignon, S. (2010), 'Democratic requirements for a European Economic Government' Friedrich Ebert Stiftung. International Policy Analysis Paper, http://library.fes.de/pdf-files/id/ipa/07710.pdf, accessed 2 April 2012.

Council of the European Union (2011), 'Council confirms agreement on economic governance', 4 October, www.consilium.europa.eu/uedocs/cms_data/docs/pressdata/en/ecofin/124882.pdf, accessed 2 April 2012.

Crouch, C. (2009), 'Privatised Keynesianism: An Unacknowledged Policy Regime', *British Journal of Politics & International Relations* 11(3), 382–99.

Crouch, C. (2011), *The Strange Non-Death of Neo-liberalism*, Cambridge: Polity.

Degryse, C. and Pochet, P. (2011), 'Monetary union, economic coordination and democratic legitimacy', *ETUI Policy Brief*, Issue 5, www.etui.org/Publications2/Policy-Briefs/European-Social-Policy/Monetary-Union-economic-coordination-and-democratic-legitimacy, accessed 2 April 2012.

Delors, J., Fernandes, S. and Mermet, E. (2011), 'The European semester: only a first step', Notre Europe Policy Brief, no. 22, February, www.notre-europe.eu/uploads/tx_publication/bref22-EN.pdf, accessed 2 April 2012.

Dräger, K. (2011), 'Sado-monetarism rules ok?! EU economic governance and its consequences', Paper presented at the 17th Euro Memo Group workshop on alternative economic policy in Europe, 16–18 September, Vienna, www2.euromemorandum.eu/uploads/background_paper_draeger_sado_monetarism_rules_ok_eu_economic_governance_and_its_consequences.pdf, accessed 2 April 2012.

Draghi, M. and Trichet, J.-C. (2011), 'Letter to the Prime Minister of Italy', 5 August, www.corriere.it/economia/11_settembre_29/trichet_draghi_inglese_304a5f1e-ea59-11e0-ae06-4da866778017.shtml, accessed 2 April 2012.

Erne, R. (2010), *European Unions: Labour's Quest for a Transnational Democracy*, revised edn, Ithaca, NY: Cornell University Press.

Erne, R. (2011a), 'Interest Associations', pp. 259–74 in Caramani, D. (ed), *Comparative Politics*, 2nd edn, Oxford: Oxford University Press.

Erne, R. (2011b), 'Flexicurity – useful oxymoron or genuine class compromise?', *Social Europe Journal*, 20 July, www.social-europe.eu/2011/07/flexicurity-useful-oxymoron-or-genuine-class-compromise/, accessed 2 April 2012.

Erne, R. (2012), 'European Unions After the Crisis', in Burroni, L., Keune, M. and Meardi, G. (eds), *Economy and Society in Europe: a Relationship in Crisis*, Cheltenham: Edward Elgar, www.ucd.ie/t4cms/WP%2011-1%20Roland%20Erne.pdf, accessed 2 April 2012.

European Commission (2010), 'Surveillance of Intra-Euro-Area competitiveness and imbalances', *European Economy* 1, http://ec.europa.eu/economy_finance/publications/european_economy/2010/pdf/ee-2010-1_en.pdf, accessed 2 April 2012.

European Council (2011), 'Statement by the Euro Area Heads of State or Government',

Brussels, 9 December, http://consilium.europa.eu/uedocs/cms_data/docs/pressdata/en/ec/126658.pdf, accessed 2 April 2012.

Habermas, J. (2011), 'Die Konstruktionsfehler der Währungsunion', *Blätter für deutsche und internationale Politik* 56(5), 64–6.

Harvey, D. (2005), *A Brief History of Neoliberalism*, Oxford: Oxford University Press.

Hayek, F.A. (1997 [1944]), *The Road to Serfdom*, London: Routledge.

ICTU (2011), 'Don't let the troika diktat snuff out flicker of hope', *The Union Post*, September, 3, www.ictu.ie/download/pdf/union_post_september_2011.pdf, accessed 2 April 2012.

IMF (2010), 'Ireland: Request for an Extended Arrangement – Staff Report; Staff Supplement; Staff Statement; and Press Release on the Executive Board Discussion', IMF Country Report no. 10/366, December.

Klein, N. (2008), 'Banking crisis: Expert views: After a week of turmoil, has the world changed?', *Guardian*, 20 September.

Krugman, P. (2010), 'The pain caucus', *The New York Times*, May 31.

Leonard, E., Erne, R., Marginson, P. and Smismans, S. (2007), *New Structures, Forms and Processes of Governance in European Industrial Relations*, Luxembourg: Office for the Official Publications of the European Communities, www.eurofound.europa.eu/pubdocs/2006/94/en/1/ef0694en.pdf, accessed 2 April 2012.

Martin, A. and Ross, G. (eds) (2004), *Euros and Europeans: Monetary Integration and the European Model of Society*, Cambridge: Cambridge University Press,

Pedrina, V. (2011), 'Schuldenkrise & europäische Gewerkschaften', *Sozialismus*, 38 (7–8), www.sozialismus.de/archiv/sozialismus/2011/heft_nr_7_8_juli_2011/detail/artikel/schuldenkrise-europaeische-gewerkschaften/, accessed 2 April 2012.

Pochet, P. (ed.) (1999), *Monetary Union and Collective Bargaining in Europe*, Brussels: Peter Lang.

Schmitt, C. ([1922] 1985), *Political Theology: Four Chapters on the Concept of Sovereignty*, Cambridge, MA: MIT Press.

Stiglitz, J. (2010), *Freefall: Free Markets and the Sinking of the Global Economy*, London: Allen Lane.

Supiot, A. (2012), *The Spirit of Philadelphia*, London: Verso.

Trichet, J.C. (2011), 'Speech on receiving the Karlspreis 2011in Aachen', 2 June, www.ecb.int/press/key/date/2011/html/sp110602.en.html, accessed 2 April 2012.

Trichet, J.C. and Draghi, M. (2011), 'Letter to the Prime Minister of Italy', 5 August, www.corriere.it/economia/11_settembre_29/trichet_draghi_inglese_304a5f1e-ea59-11e0-ae06-4da866778017.shtml, accessed 2 April 2012.

Wall, M. (2010), 'Ictu questions bailout terms', *Irish Times*, 27 November, www.irishtimes.com/newspaper/breaking/2010/1127/breaking19.html, accessed 2 April 2012.

Wallström, M. (2008), 'Ireland's Future in the European Union. Opening remarks at the Oireachtas Sub-Committee in Ireland', 13 October, http://europa.eu/rapid/pressReleasesAction.do?reference=SPEECH/08/618&format=PDF&aged=1&language=EN&guiLanguage=en, accessed 2 April 2012.

# Index